THE EXIT STRATEGY HANDBOOK

THE COMPLETE GUIDE TO PREPARING YOUR BUSINESS FOR SALE

JACOB OROSZ

President and Founder of Morgan & Westfield
Host of *M&A Talk*, The #1 Podcast on Mergers & Acquisitions

For general information about our products and services,
please visit Morgan & Westfield at www.morganandwestfield.com.

Books by

JACOB OROSZ

The Art of the Exit
The Complete Guide to Selling a Business

A Beginner's Guide to Business Valuation
Lessons Learned from 20 Years in the Trenches

The Exit Strategy Handbook
A Complete Guide to
Preparing Your Business for Sale

Closing the Deal
The Definitive Guide to
Negotiating the Sale of Your Business

Acquired
The Art of Selling a Business with
$10 Million to $100 Million in Revenue

Acknowledgments

The purpose of this book is to educate entrepreneurs on the entire process of planning their exits and selling their business. This book is a team effort, and without the significant contributions from several amazing people, this book would never have come into existence.

I dedicate this book to the entrepreneurs who demonstrate the imagination, focused preparation, hard work, and courage necessary to create and grow the businesses that drive our economic engine. You are a precious resource that should be recognized and rewarded.

I am grateful to all of the people who generously gave their time and provided me with information for this book, including small- and medium-sized business owners, lawyers, accountants, investment bankers, partners at private equity groups, industry analysts, and others with specific knowledge of the issues I address.

I am also thankful for the many guests I have had the pleasure of interviewing on my *M&A Talk* podcast. Your insights have proven invaluable in rounding out my knowledge of this complicated topic. M&A is a complex multidisciplinary topic. No one expert can do it all. Hearing a diversity of viewpoints from a variety of experts has increased my appreciation for the complexity and subtle nuances of this field.

I am particularly grateful for the help of our team of four editors, Pamela Eastland, Bob Bogda, Graham P. Johnson, and Barbara Wright, who have patiently stood by my side throughout the entire process and who have taken what was initially a mess of ideas and turned it into a cohesive story. Thank you for your attention to detail, persistence, and ability to tie up loose ends to make this a finished product.

A special thank you for the help of my father, Emery Orosz, who has carefully reviewed this book. On a side note, thank you for providing me with the discipline I needed as a child and the patience to allow me to mature and blossom into a successful professional. I love you and could never thank you enough for standing by me every step of the way.

Jacob Orosz

About the Author

Jacob Orosz is President of Morgan & Westfield, author of numerous articles and books, including *The Art of the Exit, A Beginner's Guide to Business Valuation, The Exit Strategy Handbook, Closing the Deal, Acquired,* and host of the *M&A Talk* podcast series. He has over 20 years of experience facilitating mergers, acquisitions, sales, and other business transfers with transaction values up to $75 million. Jacob has successfully participated in or managed the sale of over 300 privately held companies representing both buyers and sellers.

Jacob has represented clients in North America, Central America, South America, Europe, and Asia. He founded Morgan & Westfield in 2008 and is actively involved in both Main Street and middle-market transactions, assisting domestic and international clients with business sales, mergers, acquisitions, valuations, and exit planning. Jacob focuses on sell-side services and is the leader in many middle-market transactions.

About Morgan & Westfield

Morgan & Westfield is a leading M&A firm specializing in business sales, mergers, acquisitions, and valuations for privately owned businesses. Morgan & Westfield's transaction focus is on companies that produce between $1 million and $10 million in earnings before interest, taxes, depreciation, and amortization (EBITDA), as well as companies with annual revenues from $5 million to $100 million. Morgan & Westfield has completed hundreds of transactions on behalf of clients in over a hundred industries and represented business owners and buyers in North America, Central America, South America, Europe, and Asia. Regardless of sector, size, and location, Morgan & Westfield's tailored approach has been defined, developed, and refined over the course of hundreds of successful and unsuccessful transactions – after all, learning from failures is a powerful and respected teacher.

Acronyms

Here are the acronyms you will encounter as you read this book:

- **ABA:** American Bar Association
- **AP:** Accounts payable
- **AR:** Accounts receivable
- **B2B:** Business-to-business
- **B2C:** Business-to-consumer
- **CAC:** Customer acquisition cost
- **CapEx:** Capital expenditures
- **CIM:** Confidential information memorandum
- **COGS:** Cost of goods sold
- **CPA:** Certified public accountant
- **CRM:** Customer relationship management database system
- **DBA:** Doing business as
- **DCF:** Discounted cash flow
- **DCR:** Debt coverage ratio
- **EBITDA:** Earnings before interest, taxes, depreciation, and amortization
- **ESOP:** Employee stock ownership plan
- **FBNS:** Fictitious business name statement
- **FDD:** Franchise disclosure document
- **FIFO:** First in, first out
- **FMV:** Fair market value
- **GAAP:** Generally accepted accounting principles
- **IP:** Intellectual property

- **IRR:** Internal rate of return
- **KPI:** Key performance indicators
- **LIFO:** Last in, first out
- **LTM:** Last twelve months
- **LTV:** Lifetime value
- **LOI:** Letter of intent
- **MVP:** Minimum viable products
- **NDA:** Non-disclosure agreement
- **NWC:** Net working capital
- **P&L:** Profit and loss statement
- **PE:** Private equity
- **PEG:** Private equity group
- **Q of E:** Quality of earnings
- **R&W:** Representations and warranties
- **ROI:** Return on investment
- **RVD:** Return on value drivers
- **SBA:** Small Business Administration
- **SDE:** Seller's discretionary earnings
- **SEC:** Securities and Exchange Commission
- **TTM:** Trailing twelve months
- **UCC:** Uniform Commercial Code
- **USP:** Unique selling point
- **VC:** Venture capitalists
- **YTD:** Year-to-date

For a full definition, check out the Glossary in the Resources section at the end of this book.

ADDITIONAL RESOURCES

More Resources on Selling a Business

You can download a spreadsheet of all the potential action steps you can take to prepare your business for sale that are outlined in this book in the Resources section of our website at morganandwestfield.com/resources. While there, you can find more information about buying, selling, valuing a business, or dozens of other topics related to mergers and acquisitions:

- **Ask the Expert:** Links to common M&A questions and answers. Ask any question related to buying, selling, or valuing a business.

- **Downloads:** Links to forms and other useful resources for selling your business.

- **Books:** A complete list of my books on selling, valuing, or buying a business, and all other topics related to M&A.

- **Glossary:** A glossary of terms used throughout this book. Don't be confused or intimidated by any terms or abbreviations in the M&A world – you'll find answers here.

- **M&A Encyclopedia:** The most exhaustive encyclopedia in the industry with over 800 pages of insight on every step of the process of selling, buying, or valuing a business.

- **M&A Talk:** The #1 podcast on mergers and acquisitions, produced by Morgan & Westfield and hosted by Jacob Orosz. At *M&A Talk*, we bring you exclusive interviews with a wide variety of experts in mergers and acquisitions, private equity, investment banking, business valuations, law, finance, and all topics related to M&A, buying, selling, and valuing businesses.

- **M&A University:** Complete courses related to buying, selling, or valuing a business. Courses are led by industry experts with decades of industry experience and are designed to give you in-depth knowledge regarding every aspect of the process of preparing your business for sale, valuing it, and closing your deal.

The Art & Science of Selling a Business Course

Have you ever wished you could get into the head of the party on the other side of the negotiating table? Here's your chance. Join us in this nine-hour audio course as we take a deep dive into the sales process to discuss the perspective of both the buyer and the seller with Jim Evanger, a serial entrepreneur and operating partner for several middle-market private equity firms. Jim has founded, started, operated, and sold multiple middle-market businesses and assisted in acquiring dozens of companies as both a corporate buyer and private equity partner, giving him deep experience on both sides of the table.

The Art & Science of Selling a Business contains priceless advice for entrepreneurs of middle-market businesses with revenues up to $100 million. This course wasn't built on theory – it is grounded in practical advice that's been field-tested in the real world. Listen as Jim shares the lessons he's learned on both sides of the table from over 20 years of experience as both a seller and an acquirer. He's already made the mistakes, so you don't have to. You'll learn how to avoid the most expensive errors business owners commonly make that can harm the value of your business or even derail your sales process entirely.

Additional Books

- ***The Art of the Exit:*** The Complete Guide to Selling Your Business: This is the definitive guide to planning your exit, broken down into 10 simple steps from preparing your business for sale to orchestrating the closing. Selling a $500 million company requires an entirely different process than selling a small to mid-sized business. This handbook contains essential tips for owners of both Main Street and lower middle-market businesses valued at $500,000 to $10 million. The Art of the Exit is loaded with proven strategies on the art and science of selling a small to mid-sized business.

- ***A Beginner's Guide to Business Valuation – Lessons Learned from 20 Years in the Trenches***: This book walks you step-by-step through valuing a business with $1 million to $50 million in revenue. You'll learn the fundamental factors that determine the value of any small to mid-sized business and simple methods for maximizing value when it comes time to sell. This practical guide is based on what I've gleaned from 20 years in the trenches selling businesses. It's written for the layman, specifically meant to address the real-world methods buyers use to value businesses.

- ***Closing the Deal – The Definitive Guide to Negotiating the Sale of Your Company:*** This book teaches you the art and science of negotiating the sale of your business. You'll learn the fundamentals of every step of the process, from the letter of intent to the closing. This essential field manual offers you an effective blueprint to maximize your negotiating leverage and foolproof strategies to optimize your deal structure and after-tax proceeds. *Closing the Deal* is for owners of businesses valued from $1 million to $50 million and contains proven tactics for avoiding the most common pitfalls in negotiating the sale of your company.

- ***Acquired – The Art of Selling a Business with $10 Million to $100 Million in Revenue:***
  For a business to sell for what it's really worth – or even more – you need to properly prepare. But too many entrepreneurs put off planning the sale of their business until the last moment. *Acquired* will help you prepare your middle-market business for sale and walk you through the sales process, dodging the pitfalls along the way. With a significant amount of your wealth tied up in your business, planning your exit is one of the most critical initiatives you'll undertake. Don't go it alone.

Other Resources

- If you're interested in selling your company, please visit morganandwestfield.com to schedule a free consultation.

- If you'd like the author of this book, Jacob Orosz, to perform an independent assessment of your business before you begin the sales process, please visit morganandwestfield.com/sellers/step-1/.

A Few Important Notes

The Audience for This Book

I wrote this book not only for sellers, but for anyone involved in the M&A process, such as buyers, attorneys, accountants, and business appraisers. For the sake of clarity, I address sellers directly throughout the book, but I wrote this book with all of you in mind.

A Note on Asking Price

Mid-sized businesses, or those generating more than $2 million to $3 million per year in EBITDA, generally go to market without an asking price. But, to help readability, throughout this book I refer to asking prices without mentioning each time that businesses in the middle market almost always go to market without an asking price. When I mention the asking price in the context of a mid-sized business, you can consider this synonymous with the value of the business.

A Note on Exceptions

I've based the advice and guidelines in this book on what you can expect to encounter 95% of the time or at the middle of the bell curve. When selling or valuing your business, you shouldn't count on exceptions – you should target the middle of the bell curve and base your strategy on what works the majority of the time. Doing so will increase your odds of success and significantly lower your risk of not meeting your expectations. Encountering an exception that works to your advantage is always a nice bonus, but you shouldn't count on it, or you will likely be disappointed.

There are exceptions to every rule. For example, a company earning $18 billion a year is unlikely to acquire a company that generates only $3 million per year. But I've interviewed the head of M&A for an $18 billion company on my podcast, *M&A Talk*, who did just that. You can listen to the episode titled *The Acquisition Process with Brian McCabe* at morganandwestfield.com/resources.

Most seller notes are for three to seven years, but I concluded a transaction in which the seller note was one year and another transaction in which the note was 10 years. There are always exceptions to every rule, but to make this book readable and keep my advice sensible, I have avoided listing every imaginable exception throughout these pages.

Instead, the goal of this book is meant to illustrate 95% of the bell curve you're most likely to encounter. The M&A world is highly idiosyncratic, so there are deviations from every rule in the industry. I have noted when an exception is more likely to occur or when an exception can have disastrous consequences. Otherwise, the aim of this book is what you can expect to happen in the overwhelming majority of the situations you'll encounter when selling and valuing your company.

> When selling your business, you shouldn't count on exceptions – you should target the middle of the bell curve and base your strategy on what works the majority of the time.

A Note on Size

I refer to small and mid-sized businesses throughout this book. I also refer to the Main Street and the middle markets. What's the difference?

There are no clear-cut protocols, but I will offer a few simple guidelines.

Perhaps the simplest guideline relates to what type of buyer is most likely to purchase your business. If the probability of selling your company to an individual is high, you should consider it a small business. However, if the odds are higher for selling your company to a corporate buyer, such as a competitor or private equity group, regard it as a mid-sized or middle-market business.

How do you know who is most likely to buy your business? There are two general benchmarks:

1. **Industry:** So-called Main Street businesses that are generally not scalable and are likely to remain small are most apt to be sold to individuals. They include small retailers, small service-based businesses, and other companies in industries primarily dominated by small businesses and mom-and-pop shops.

2. **Size:** The larger your business's revenue and profitability, the more likely you'll be able to sell it to a corporate buyer. Generally, once your profitability exceeds $1 million per year, your business begins to appeal to more corporate than individual buyers.

Hence the reason for this book.

Let's get started.

TABLE OF CONTENTS

INTRODUCTION

*"My interest is in the future because I am going
to spend the rest of my life there."*

– Charles F. Kettering, American Inventor

If you're looking to sell a business that brings in $1 million to $50 million in revenue, you've come to the right place. Ditto if you're seeking to determine how much your business is worth – and the steps you can take to make it worth even more.

This book isn't theoretical. The advice I'm about to share with you is based on over 20 years of experience as an M&A advisor in the trenches selling businesses. I've dealt with thousands of buyers, from strategic acquirers to corporate purchasers to private equity firms to wealthy individuals. The lessons I've learned are rooted in actual transactions made in the real world – both successful and unsuccessful – not in the abstract world of college textbooks.

Preparing your business for sale and maximizing its value can't be boiled down to a few simple metrics. Rather, there are scores of elements that can affect the value of your business. In the chapters that follow, I'll walk you through these factors along with specific actions you can take to turn them to your advantage.

I've seen many deals die that could have been prevented. Why? It's simple – lack of preparation. By properly preparing your business for sale, you'll dramatically increase your odds of success.

- The value of your business will increase.

- The chances of a successful sale will escalate.

- The sale process as a whole will accelerate.

- Your negotiating posture will be stronger.

- Your business operations and profitability will improve.

Preparing your business for sale allows you to be ready to sell your business at any time. Why is that important? Because the best offers are often unsolicited. Following the advice outlined in this book will help ensure you maximize the value of your company regardless of when the sale takes place. You should always be ready to sell. You must be prepared if you wake up Monday morning and discover an email from a competitor with a note regarding a "potential strategic relationship." (Rule 1: If you get that email, don't book that long-awaited vacation cruise just yet.) By taking the steps outlined in this book, your company is likely to be camera-ready.

The fact is that most entrepreneurs don't know what buyers are looking for or even the type of buyer most likely to buy their business. And even if they do, few know what steps they should take to prepare their company for sale.

That's where this book comes in. There are hundreds of ways to make your business more appealing to the right buyer. My goal is to arm you with steps you can take every day to increase the value of your company and dramatically expand its marketability. I'll then help you prioritize these actions in a way that will have the most impact on your unique business.

That's the purpose here – to demystify the process and help you unlock real value in your business and dramatically increase your odds of success. It's my 20 years of experience boiled down into this concise guide. I wrote this book not only for sellers but also for anyone involved in the M&A process, such as buyers, attorneys, accountants, and business appraisers. For the sake of clarity, I address sellers directly throughout the book, but I wrote this book with all of you in mind.

Let's get started.

PART ONE

Overview

CHAPTER 1

Background Information

"The future is purchased by the present."

– Dr. Samuel Johnson, English Essayist

Introduction

Before you begin the process of preparing your company for sale, it's helpful to understand two things – what makes a business salable and how long it can take to sell your business.

When it comes to increasing the salability of your business, it's advantageous to review case studies of deals gone bad with both individual and corporate buyers. By reviewing stories of business owners who were unsuccessful in selling their business, you can learn some of the reasons your business may not sell and what you can do to prevent this from happening. In this chapter, I've gathered a collection of deals and case studies that didn't make it to the finish line, extracting a lesson from each so that future entrepreneurs don't make these same mistakes.

It's also important to understand how long it may take to sell your business so you can begin the process with realistic expectations. Not only is understanding how long the process may take important, it's also critical to learn the factors that can affect the time frame so you can reduce the time it takes to sell your business. Why is this important? It's simple – time kills deals.

A point I make time and again is that speed is necessary to maximize your price. By preparing your business for sale, you'll help ensure the process unfolds as smoothly and as quickly as possible, which not only helps maximize the price you receive but also reduces the number of things that can go wrong during the process.

Why Deals Die

Why don't some businesses sell, and what can you do to ensure a successful sale and maximize the price of your company?

Most transactions die during one of the following stages of the sale process:

- **Marketing:** These transactions never get off the ground because the seller and their M&A advisor or investment banker can't get the traction necessary to generate meaningful discussions with buyers.

- **Offer:** The seller has generated interest from a buyer, but then they lose interest after taking a closer look at the business.

- **Due Diligence:** The buyer makes an offer, but the transaction dies during due diligence for various reasons.

- **Closing:** The buyer successfully concludes due diligence, but then the deal dies sometime before the closing.

In the following section, we'll examine and analyze real-world case studies from businesses that ultimately didn't sell. Reviewing these examples gives you insight into the salability of your own business, what can potentially go wrong, and steps you can take to help ensure your company sells for top dollar when you decide to put it on the market. Here we go ...

What follows are some actual scenarios of sales that never materialized and why they failed to do so:

- **Risky:** One business was considered too risky for buyers due to a recent entry of venture-backed competitors into the industry. No buyer was willing to make an offer due to the increased competitive nature of the industry.

- **High Customer Concentration:** One customer generated over 40% of the revenue for a business, and no buyer was willing to take the risk inherent with such a high level of customer concentration.

- **Inaccurate Financials:** A buyer made an offer on this business and then discovered multiple inaccuracies in the financial statements during due diligence. The buyer attempted to clarify the inaccuracies with the seller's accountant, but the accountant couldn't assuage the buyer's fears in a timely fashion, so the buyer walked as a result.

- **Competition:** A technology business generated significant buyer interest. During the process, an announcement was made that a major competitor received a large capital injection from a venture capital group. Once the news reached the buyers, they became apprehensive and downgraded their valuation of the business, which the seller was unwilling to accept.

- **Personality Conflicts:** An offer was made and accepted. Due diligence began smoothly, but personality conflicts between the buyer and seller developed and spiraled out of control. The parties became deadlocked on several issues, and both refused to budge. The problems mounted to the point where the transaction reached a stalemate, and it died a slow death.

- **Rural Location:** The business was located in a small, rural market in Indiana, and there wasn't a large enough buyer base in the town to generate sufficient buyer activity. The business couldn't be relocated, and the area wasn't attractive enough to entice outsiders. No companies would consider acquiring the business due to the difficulty of finding a talented manager in the area to run it post-acquisition.

- **Niche Business With Limited Buyer Pool:** The business was in a niche segment of the construction industry and required a specialty contractor's license that few individuals or companies in the area possessed.

- **Business Easy to Replicate:** A service business was considered easy to replicate by most buyers. Despite a high level of profitability, no buyers felt an investment in the business was justified due to the ostensibly low cost of replicating it.

- **High Growth:** One business was growing at a rate of 30% per year. Buyers were only willing to buy the business based on the historical earnings, but the owner wanted to be paid based on the next 12 months' projected earnings and wasn't willing to consider an earnout.

- **Unattractive Industry:** An industry was considered unattractive by many buyers due to the emergency nature of the business and accompanying odd work schedule. Marketing activities generated few results despite multiple iterations of the marketing strategy.

- **High Revenue, Low Profitability:** A business had high revenue but was breakeven. Online marketing efforts yielded poor results because buyers dismissed the business due to its lack of profitability.

- **Landlord Raised Rent:** This large retail business was successful, so an opportunistic landlord attempted to raise the rent by 30% for the new buyer. The buyer balked and walked away.

- **Revenue Declined:** For one business, revenue declined by 10% between the time a letter of intent was accepted and the time due diligence was completed. The recent decline in revenue implanted fear in the buyer, and they walked as a result.

- **Unattractive Franchise:** Our marketing efforts yielded several interested buyers for a multi-unit franchise, but as each buyer dug into the details of the business model, they walked. Several of these interested buyers told us they considered the turnover in the franchise to be excessive, which must be disclosed in Item 20 of the Franchisor Disclosure

Document. They talked to several franchisees in the system and discovered that new ownership at the franchisor was considered unfavorable, so the transaction died.

- **Minority Partners:** We put a business on the market, successfully generated several buyers, accepted an offer, and began the due diligence process. The owner then contacted us with the news that their minority partner was demanding a 200% premium for their minority share of the business. The owner refused to give in to the demands of the minority partner, and the buyer subsequently walked.

- **Industry:** Recent changes in the consumer goods industry related to consumer preferences were expected to negatively impact the sector. A buyer made an offer on a business in the consumer goods industry, and the seller accepted the offer. However, as the buyer performed due diligence, it became evident that the impact of the changes in the industry was uncertain and difficult to predict. As a result, the buyer retracted the offer.

- **Lack of Preparation:** A construction-related business for sale seemed like a promising investment for a buyer in the industry, and in fact, an offer was eventually made from a competitor. During due diligence, the buyer uncovered numerous defects in the business that could have been prevented with proper preparation. Some of these defects included inaccurate financials, a lack of proper insurance (cash flow was overstated due to inadequate insurance coverage), no tax planning (the business was a C Corporation and subject to double taxation in an asset purchase), lack of approval from a minority partner, and a lack of employment agreements or retention plan with key employees.

- **Third-Party Delays:** A seller of a service-based firm in the Midwest accepted an offer, and the buyer began due diligence. During due diligence, the buyer noticed several inconsistencies in the financial statements. The seller forwarded the questions to their CPA, but two months later, the questions remained unanswered, and the CPA was generally unresponsive. The buyer walked as a result of the delays.

- **Lack of Bank Financing:** A potential buyer of a specialty manufacturing business made an offer and conducted due diligence, which proved to be successful. However, the buyer was unable to obtain financing and didn't have an adequate down payment for the seller to consider financing the sale.

- **Owner Not Willing to Finance:** A buyer made an offer on a middle-market business in the healthcare industry. The offer included a 50% cash down payment, but the seller was unwilling to finance more than 20% of the purchase price, and the offer wasn't accepted.

- **Asking Price Too High:** An appraisal for a technology company valued the business at approximately $6.5 million. The owner believed his company was worth $8 million to $10.5 million. The seller attempted to market the business at $10 million but generated little response. The revenue in the business subsequently declined, which reversed the positive trend in the business, and the owner dropped his price to $8 million. The original valuation was downgraded to $5 million due to the recent decline in revenue, but the owner chose not to drop the price, and as a result, very little buyer activity was generated.

- **Dependent on Owner:** A professional services firm received significant buyer interest in a short period of time. But as most buyers dug deeper, they discovered the owner was inextricably tied to the business and determined that a transition would be too difficult, costly, and risky. Most of the clients were close friends of the owner, and the name of the firm was tied to the owner's name, though the owner wouldn't allow a buyer to use the company name moving forward. As a result, no buyer was willing to make an offer despite the high cash flow and attractive price of the business.

- **Family Involved in Business:** Multiple family members were involved in a business in the service sector. A marketing campaign generated several interested buyers, but every buyer that dug deeper into the mechanics of the business discovered risk associated with having several family members involved who were instrumental to the operations. The family members' compensation was below the market rate, and no family members were willing to stay past the initial transition period. As a result, buyers considered it too risky to replace the owner and the spouse, as well as two additional family members involved in the business.

- **Key Employee Dependency:** In another transaction, a valuation was performed on a business in the online education space. An offer was received, and the buyer began performing due diligence. During due diligence, the buyer discovered that two employees were instrumental to the operations of the business. The seller allowed the buyer to talk to the employees to ensure they would be retained, but the employees demanded a salary increase that was far beyond what the buyer considered reasonable. The buyer walked as a result.

- **Employees Fail to Cooperate:** An offer was received on a commercial landscaping business. Once the employees received news of the offer through the grapevine, they felt slighted and were determined to derail the transaction. Despite the seller's attempts to pacify the employees, their resentment couldn't be contained. Once the buyer received news of the lack of cooperation from the management team, they rescinded their offer.

- **Tax Returns Not Reconciled to Financials:** An offer was accepted on a roofing company, and due diligence uncovered disparities that couldn't be reconciled between the financial statements and federal income tax returns. The differences couldn't be explained by the seller's accountant, and the buyer downgraded their offer, which the seller was unwilling to accept. Upon the advice of the buyer's CPA, the buyer walked.

As you can see from these examples, there are a variety of factors that can cause a business to not sell. But, every single one of these business owners could have dramatically improved their odds of success if they had invested time in preparing their business for sale well in advance.

Many of these problems could have been dramatically mitigated or entirely prevented through proper preparation.

While some problems cannot be completely overcome, buyers often consider the totality of the circumstances. The less risk the buyer perceives, the less likely they are to walk away from a deal. For example, if a business has high customer concentration, but the customers are secured by a long-term contract, a buyer may view this scenario as less risky. Or, if a management team is in place that has a relationship with key customers while the current owner has no personal relationships with key customers, the buyer may also feel comfortable. Even the most severe issues threatening to kill a deal can be mitigated through preparation.

Keep in mind, too, that many of the factors above can occur simultaneously. For example:

- The business can be located in a rural area.

- The business can be in a niche field with a limited buyer pool.

- The business may not be pre-approved for bank financing.

- The seller may not be willing to finance a portion of the sale price.

The more risk factors that are present in your business, the harder it will be to sell, the more nervous buyers will become, and the less they will pay for it. But many of these problems can be successfully prevented if you give yourself ample time to prepare your business for sale. Even if a problem can't be completely eliminated, it may still be possible to mitigate the effects of the problem, so you reduce the buyer's *perception* of risk. The result of preparing your business for sale is that you will dramatically tilt the odds of success in your favor. That's the purpose of this book.

> The more risk factors that are present in your business, the harder your business will be to sell and the less buyers will pay for your business.

If you're serious about selling your business and would like to maximize its value, I recommend you prepare for the sale as early as possible. As you read this book and identify and mitigate as many risk factors in your business as possible – well before you put your business on the market – you will be able to:

- Explore the ideal exit options for your business that help you maximize the price you receive.

- Evaluate the salability of your business.

- Establish a range of potential values for your business from low to high.

- Create a plan to help you maximize the value of your business.

- Identify risk factors in your business.

- Identify potential deal killers in your business.

There's a lot that can go wrong in a sale. It pays to invest time maximizing the worth of what is likely your most valuable asset.

Statistics on How Long It Takes To Sell

The truth is that the longer it takes to sell your business, the more that can potentially go wrong. The smoothest sales happen quickly and uneventfully. The good news is that most of the factors that increase the value of your business also reduce the time it will take to sell it.

So, how long will it take to sell your business once you've decided to put it on the market? For all transactions since 2000, the average time on the market is 200 days, or about 7.3 months. But the average time to sell a business has increased over the years, from 6 months in the early 2000s to 10 months in recent years. Selling a business has become more difficult and takes longer than it did 10 years ago.

Why?

I attribute this to four factors:

1. **Internet:** The internet has provided buyers of all goods and services with more options, and they have become more selective as a result. When I started in the business in 2000, I used newspapers to sell businesses. These days, I don't know anyone in the industry who advertises a business for sale in a newspaper. In the "old days," businesses were easier to sell and often changed hands more quickly, likely due to a lack of qualified alternatives and businesses for sale. In the new age, the internet has opened up a range of alternatives for buyers, and they have become much more selective. The time frame to sell a business has increased as a byproduct of this change.

2. **Information:** The internet has also provided a wealth of information on buying or selling a business. As a result, today's buyer is more educated, able to consider more options, and is more selective in the businesses they decide to purchase.

3. **More Businesses for Sale:** In recent years, the number of businesses for sale has steadily increased, and access to these businesses has improved due to the internet. This rise has resulted in a larger number of choices for buyers, which has exerted downward pressure on the price of less desirable businesses and lengthened the time frame it takes to sell a business.

4. **More Options:** Today's would-be entrepreneurs have more options available to them than in years past. Job mobility has allowed many to work remotely or freelance, and many potential buyers have instead opted to take a job "for free" as opposed to buying

a business. This has significantly impacted the value of smaller businesses, and these businesses are much more difficult to sell than in past years as a result.

But don't be discouraged. While selling a business takes longer than it did two decades ago, it's still possible to sell your business in a reasonable period of time and for the maximum value.

> The longer it takes to sell your business, the more that can potentially go wrong. The smoothest sales happen quickly and uneventfully.

Sources of Data and Their Accuracy

There are a few useful sources of statistics on how long it takes to sell a business:

- **BIZCOMPS:** This is a database of transactions for businesses that have been sold in the United States, including the length of time the business was on the market. BIZCOMPS contains over 13,000 transactions dating back to 1996.

- **Business Brokerage Press:** This publication produces an annual survey of its members, who primarily consist of full-time business brokers. The survey is mainly aimed at business brokers and M&A advisors in the Main Street and lower middle market who sell businesses priced up to $20 million. The survey consists of several dozen questions, of which one is, "How many months is the average period between beginning the process and the closing?" Recent results from surveys have ranged from 6 to 12 months, with the time period slowly increasing over the years.

- **IBA Market Database:** Another helpful transactional database that contains more middle-market deals, the IBA Market Database, includes over 37,000 transactions. While the database does provide useful information on comparable transactions, it doesn't provide details on how long a business takes to sell.

- **DealStats:** DealStats (formerly Pratt's Stats) is a state-of-the-art platform that boasts the most complete financials on acquired companies in both the private and public sectors.

While this data can be useful, it's far from perfect. The data should be used as a rough guide only and supplemented with a dose of common sense and professional advice.

You can view complete statistics on how long it takes to sell a business at our Morgan & Westfield website morganandwestfield.com/knowledge and search for the article titled *How Long Does it Take To Sell a Business.*

Variables That Affect How Long It Takes To Sell a Business

The Selling Price

Based on my experience, smaller businesses sold more quickly in the past, but that trend is reversing. My experience is that businesses become much easier to sell once EBITDA (earnings before interest, taxes, depreciation, and amortization) exceeds $1 million per year. The more profitable a business is, the more desirable it is viewed by buyers and the faster it will sell. Larger businesses are easier to sell due to stronger demand from corporate buyers. Almost all larger businesses are purchased by financial or corporate buyers, and the demand for quality businesses in the lower-middle market is always high. In addition, the more reasonable the initial asking price, the faster the business should sell. But businesses valued in excess of $5 million to $10 million often go to market without a stated selling price.

The Region

Businesses for sale in desirable, high-population growth areas tend to sell faster due to demand from more buyers in the local market. For instance, it's easier to sell a business in California (211 days) than it is to sell a business in Iowa (252 days), but this depends on who the ultimate buyer of your business may be. Individuals are more selective about where a business is located than corporate buyers. Many individuals looking to buy a business will consider relocating. In fact, a substantial portion of businesses that change hands in the Southwest and Southeast are sold to individuals moving to the area. If your business is located in a highly desirable region, the fact that people are willing to relocate opens up the number of potential buyers, which effectively speeds up the selling process. Having more buyers means that your business will be easier to sell and will often sell faster.

Financing and Down Payment

The more financing you're willing to offer, the faster your business should sell. But, again, this depends on who the ultimate buyer of your business may be. Wealthy individuals generally put less down than private equity investors and other corporate buyers. If you sell to an individual, expect to finance a significant portion of the purchase price if the buyer can't obtain third-party financing. Offering reasonable seller financing terms should result in a faster sale unless a buyer can obtain a Small Business Administration (SBA) loan (which are limited to $5 million) or unless they are a corporate or financial entity.

The Industry

A correlation exists between industry type and the number of days a business is on the market. Manufacturing and technology businesses tend to attract more buyers and therefore sell faster than many retail and service-based businesses. If your business is in an attractive industry, such as technology or manufacturing, it likely will sell sooner than if it's in a low-growth or unattractive industry.

Attractiveness

The more positive attributes your business possesses, the more attractive your business will be perceived by buyers. Here are some traits that can help spur a sale:

- Increasing financial trends, such as increased revenues or margins

- Desirable industry

- Strong industry growth or stability

- Scalable business model

- Business is difficult to replicate

- High barriers to entry

- Weak competition

- Strong competitive differentiation

- Strong brand awareness

- Strong history

- Strong customer loyalty or repeat business

- Minimal customer concentration

- Strong customer contracts

- Recurring revenue

- Strong management team

- Strong infrastructure

- Valuable intellectual property

- Favorable lease terms

- Desirable location

- Ability to relocate the business

- Minimal dependency on the owner or key employees

- Long employee tenure

- Limited industry regulations and licensing requirements, although this can be a positive barrier to entry if the buyer already possesses these requirements

Your Marketing Strategy

Aggressively marketing your business for sale through the appropriate channels will also help sell your business faster. Find the best M&A advisor or investment banker possible and give them everything they need to help you market your business.

> Most of the factors that increase the value of your business also reduce the time it will take to sell your business.

A Timeline for Selling a Business

Here are the steps involved in selling a business and the time frames involved for each:

- **Prepare the Business for Sale (1-2 Months):** Preparing your business for sale includes normalizing your financial statements, valuing your business, and creating an offering memorandum, teaser profile, and other key documents. Preparation is often a controlled and predictable step and usually takes one to two months.

- **Marketing the Business and Negotiating a Letter of Intent (1-12+ Months):** This step involves confidentially marketing your business for sale and meeting with buyers. It can take 1 to 12 months to locate a buyer, and generally 1 or 2 months to negotiate an offer once you identify them. This period is often frustrating for the seller because they may feel as if nothing is happening. But it's important that you keep your focus on your business and maintain consistent revenue while it's being marketed.

- **Due Diligence and Closing (2-3 Months):** Conducting due diligence usually takes four to eight weeks, although it can sometimes take longer depending on who the buyer is and how organized you are. Due diligence can be held up for many reasons, such as delays in obtaining bank financing, or as the result of inaccurate financial information. Negotiating and closing the transaction usually takes from one to two months once due diligence has been completed. In some cases, it can take several months to close the transaction due to third-party delays from attorneys, accountants, franchisors, banks, or license-transfer approvals. These guidelines are rough estimates only, and you should be fully prepared for the transaction to take significantly longer.

Conclusion

When it comes to selling your business, understanding what can go wrong is useful to ensure your sale unfolds as smoothly and as quickly as possible. The above stories illustrate what can potentially go wrong. Unfortunately, what can go wrong can't be reduced to a simple set of 8 or 10 factors. Rather, the truth is more complex. In this book, I'll thoroughly explain what can potentially go wrong and the specific actions you can take to dramatically improve not only the odds of success but also the value of your company.

Regarding how long it may take to sell your business, remember that an average is just an average. The actual time can vary from one day to more than three years. In most cases, you should plan that the sale process will take about a year, not including the transition period. In some cases, the transition period may only take 30 days, while in other cases, it may take a year or longer. This means that you must factor how long it will take to sell your business into your overall time frame.

Many business owners must spend a minimum of six months preparing their business for sale before they can begin the sale process. Most of the quick clean-up work can be handled within this time frame, but more serious changes, such as building your management team or restructuring your products or services, can take much longer. If you're unsure, I recommend you begin the planning process at least three years before you desire to fully exit your business.

After you have read this book, you should have a much more accurate understanding of what actions you need to take before you begin the process, and you will be able to more accurately predict the timing.

How can you prepare your business for sale, maximize its value, and speed up the process? That's the subject of the rest of this book.

CHAPTER 2

Introduction to Value Drivers

"Any difficult task seems easier if you break it down into manageable steps."

– Unknown

Introduction

In a recent survey, Consumer Reports found that a "modern and updated kitchen" still rules when it comes to ideal features among home buyers. And just as there are any number of other actions you can take to increase the value of a house – finishing a basement and painting high-traffic areas come to mind – there are many steps you can take to enhance the value of your business.

Understanding which value drivers and risk factors to focus on is critical to maximizing your company's value before you sell.

What is a value driver? A value driver is any action you can take that may potentially improve the value of your business. So, how can you determine which value drivers to prioritize without becoming overwhelmed by all the possibilities?

The Return on Value Driver's (RVD) Model is a proprietary tool I developed that helps identify which aspects of your business to improve that will have the greatest impact on its value. The goal of the RVD Model is to help you increase the value of your business with the least amount of effort by helping you prioritize all the potential actions you can take.

In this section, we'll go through a step-by-step process for deciding which aspects of your business to focus on first – actions that will pay you the highest dividends for the least amount of effort. The result will be a high return on investment (ROI) on the time you take to prepare your business for sale.

The RVD Model helps you prioritize which value drivers to focus on first based on the following criteria:

1. **Return:** What is the potential impact, or return, on the business's value from implementing the value driver?

2. **Risk:** What is the risk associated with implementing the potential value driver?

3. **Time:** How much time will the value driver take to implement?

4. **Investment:** What financial investment is required to implement the value driver?

Exploring the range of potential value drivers you can execute is the first step in increasing the value of your business.

> Understanding and improving the value drivers and risk factors is critical to maximizing your company's value before you sell.

Steps to Completing the RVD Model

The RVD Model will help you determine the action steps that'll have the most significant impact on the value of your business in the shortest time and that represent the lowest risks to implement.

- **Step 1 - Compile your value drivers:** The first step is to read through this book and make a list of potential actions you can take to improve the value of your business and prepare it for sale.

- **Step 2 - Rate each value driver on these four criteria – return, risk, time, and investment:** The second step involves rating each potential value driver based on the four factors of return, risk, time, and investment. The rating shouldn't be considered definitive. Instead, the purpose of the rating is to allow you to loosely prioritize the potential actions you can take. This helps you focus first on the highest impact actions that represent the lowest in risk and that require the least amount of time and energy to implement.

- **Step 3 - Prioritize the value drivers based on the overall rating:** The third step involves prioritizing the value drivers based on their overall rating. Improving the value of your business shouldn't be done in a haphazard fashion. Rather, it's best to prioritize the potential actions you can take, and then strategically execute a few value drivers at a time in a systematic fashion. Most business owners take a hodge-podge approach to value maximization instead of a strategic, intelligent, and rigorous one. The objective of the RVD Model is to provide you with a structured framework you can use to increase the value of your business. In addition, the RVD Model helps prioritize possible actions you can take based on potential returns, the risk involved in achieving those returns, and the associated cost in terms of time and money.

Sample RVD Model

Below is a sample chart of potential value drivers for the hypothetical middle-market technology company, "Acme Software." My analysis includes commentary about why and how I rated each value driver, and a rating based on the four key criteria – return, risk, time, and investment.

Note: I rated the criteria from 1 to 10, with 10 being the most favorable and 1 being the least favorable. For example, a 10 rating for risk means the action is considered low risk, and a 2.0 rating for risk represents a greater risk. A 9.0 rating for investment indicates that a low investment is required, and a 2.0 rating denotes a significant investment is necessary. The weighting below will vary significantly from company to company. For example, in a business with underperforming metrics, the potential return on improving a particular value driver may be as high as a 9 or 10, but in a company with favorable metrics, this represents a possible return as low as 2 or 3.

Return on Value Drivers: Acme Software					
Value Driver	**Return** *(Potential Return)*	**Risk**	**Time** *(Time Required)*	**Investment** *(Investment Required)*	**Overall Rating**
Increase Pricing	10	7	10	10	**9.25**
Document Comparable Transactions	7	10	10	10	**9.25**
Reduce Staff-Related Risk	9	8	5	9	**7.75**
Reduce Concentrations of Risk	7	9	6	5	**6.75**
Increase Revenue and EBITDA	10	7	4	4	**6.25**
Code Audit	7	7	6	5	**6.25**
Strengthen IP	5	9	7	4	**6.25**
Sales and Marketing	8	7	5	4	**6.00**
Increase Cost to Replicate	10	6	3	4	**5.75**
Increase Recurring Revenue	10	6	2	5	**5.75**
Strengthen Customer Base	7	4	6	4	**5.25**

Improve Documentation, Infrastructure and Scalability	7	8	3	4	**5.50**

Commentary on the Sample Model

Here are my comments on Acme Software's RVD Model. Factors are ordered by priority based on the chart above:

- **Increase Pricing (Rating 9.25):** The potential returns from increasing pricing are high for Acme because 100% of any price increase will fall straight to the bottom line, less any sales commissions. If Acme increases prices by 20%, EBITDA could potentially double. Revenue was $10 million, and a 20% price hike could raise EBITDA by $2 million or double EBITDA to $4 million from $2 million. The company considers such an action to be low risk because it requires little time and money to implement and is reversible. As a result, Acme focuses on this value driver first due to its potential for high returns and the low amount of time and investment required to implement it.

- **Document Comparable Transactions (Rating 9.25):** Acme is aware of several transactions that occurred within their industry that received multiples from 7 to 8, but they have no documentation to back up the multiples their competitors received. Acme believes they could obtain more information regarding the transactions through several well-connected individuals in their industry, as well as through their investment bankers and professional advisors. While the potential return from this value driver is less than that of increasing pricing, little in the way of time and money is required to obtain this information. As a result, Acme will begin executing this value driver immediately after they increase pricing.

- **Reduce Staff-Related Risk (Rating 7.75):** Acme has several key employees who lack employment, confidentiality, and non-solicitation agreements. They understand this represents a significant risk to a potential acquirer and realize this could be cleared up with minimal cost in a matter of several weeks. Acme will ask its attorney to prepare employment agreements for key staff that includes a non-solicitation clause and a retention bonus to ensure the employees would be retained in the event of a sale. The retention bonus serves as a form of consideration, which is required for contracts and improves the enforceability of the non-solicitation agreement.

- **Reduce Concentrations of Risk (Rating 6.75):** Acme also has key employee, customer concentration, and product concentration risks. While these risks can't be immediately assuaged, plans could be put in place to mitigate these risks over time. Key employee concentration can be mitigated by more evenly spreading duties across the management team. Customer concentration risk can be mitigated by asking key customers to sign long-term contracts. Finally, product concentration risk can be eased by developing strategies to invest more in marketing their entire product line, as opposed to just a few products.

- **Increase Revenue and EBITDA (Rating 6.25):** While the potential impact of increasing revenue and EBITDA is significant, doing so requires a considerable amount of time and investment. Acme realizes that the primary method for increasing revenue, and therefore EBITDA, is to hire a more experienced sales manager and invest in building the sales infrastructure so the sales team could scale up their impact on the business. This requires a significant investment in time and money, as well as a moderate level of risk. But Acme can mitigate the risk by hiring a third-party expert to help interview and screen potential sales managers.

- **Code Audit (Rating 6.25):** Acme's owners have some background in development, but they aren't entirely sure the software is clean and well documented. They realize a buyer might retain a third party to conduct a code audit during due diligence, and they believe it would be a wise investment to hire an independent firm to conduct a code audit before beginning the sale process. The audit is expected to cost about $20,000, but they feel the investment is justified given the potential impact on improving the certainty of closing once a buyer is located.

- **Strengthen IP (Rating 6.25):** Acme's name is well respected and known in the industry, and they feel they can obtain a trademark, which would add value to the company. They also lack invention-assignment agreements for their developers, which represents an increased risk to the buyer. They plan to hire an intellectual property (IP) attorney at an estimated cost of $25,000 to perform a trademark search, file for a trademark, and prepare invention-assignment agreements for key staff. The process is expected to take four to six months. While doing this isn't expected to significantly impact their valuation, it does mitigate risk for the buyer and, therefore, could reduce the due diligence risk for Acme and improve the certainty of close.

- **Sales and Marketing (Rating 6.00):** Acme lacks sales and marketing documentation and infrastructure, and they realize this might take a significant amount of time and money to build. Since the potential impact isn't as substantial as value drivers higher on the list – such as increasing pricing and reducing staff-related risk – they assign this value driver lower priority given the amount of time and money required to execute it. Acme assembles a team to document the sales and marketing processes, expecting this to take about three months.

- **Increase Cost to Replicate (Rating 5.75):** Acme believes a few competitors could replicate the functionality of their software, but they feel they can implement several defensive strategic actions that could make replicating their software more difficult. Acme plans to implement these strategies over a period of three months.

- **Increase Recurring Revenue (Rating 5.75):** Acme's enterprise customers' agreements are renewable annually, and many customers stall during the renewal process. Acme believes they could create an incentive to motivate customers to sign an automatically renewable contract. Still, this transition process would take at least a year, as they think it would be best for customers to sign the new contract upon the expiration of each annual contract. Acme begins implementing this process simultaneously while documenting their sales and marketing processes since they realize that transitioning to automatically renewable contracts will take a significant amount of time.

- **Strengthen Customer Base (Rating 5.25):** Acme lacks agreements with the majority of its customers and realizes this represents a significant risk to potential buyers. So, the company creates several pricing models with various contract terms and tests those models over a period of 10 weeks. Acme's goal is to create a pricing model that incentivizes customers to sign long-term agreements.

- **Improve Documentation, Infrastructure and Scalability (Rating 5.50):** Acme lacks the documentation and infrastructure that could help it scale quickly, but they realize that improving the documentation and infrastructure would require an enormous investment of time and money – perhaps up to nine months or longer. They also realize that this work would distract their employees from other projects. As a result, they decide this is their lowest priority value driver and plan on executing it as their last priority.

Tips for Completing the RVD Model

Following are several tips for completing the RVD Model and implementing your value drivers:

- **Prioritize Your Value Drivers:** Priorities will vary significantly from company to company. For example, in a company with underperforming metrics, the potential return on improving metrics may be given a high rating of 9 or 10, but in a company that already has favorable metrics, there may be a much lower potential return, with a rating of 2 or 3. Note that for Acme, there is considerable subjectivity regarding the individual criteria of return, risk, time, and investment, and the overall rating for each value driver. But there is a clear distinction between the highest-priority value drivers and the lowest-priority value drivers – based on the overall rating. Priorities aren't absolute, but should be considered relative to one another. The individual ratings aren't important – what is important is the overall ranking or priority of the value drivers relative to one another. For example, it's clear from reviewing Acme's RVD Model that increasing pricing should be prioritized over improving documentation. Because completing the RVD Model is simple and requires little time, Acme could perform this analysis in a few hours with the assistance of an M&A advisor or investment banker, and could begin executing the top value driver within a matter of days. There is no need for extensive planning and procrastination – the RVD Model encourages lean planning and action, emphasizing results.

- **Obtain Multiple Opinions:** Consider giving a copy of a blank RVD Model to your C-level executives and M&A advisor to complete independently. By asking them to complete it blindly, you counteract the bandwagon effect, which is the psychological phenomenon in which people do or say something mostly because other people are doing or saying it. Or consider showing your value drivers model to your professional advisors, such as your accountant and attorney, for their input. Don't show a copy of your completed model to those who are completing it for the first time. Asking others to complete the model blind without seeing your completed model first will unveil important assumptions your advisors may have regarding some of the value drivers. For example, a CEO may have a different perspective than the CFO, CMO, or CTO.

- **Reconcile Different Opinions:** Once you have obtained multiple opinions, combine the results into one spreadsheet and discuss the reasons for any differences with your team and advisors. By carefully weighing everyone's opinion, the model flushes out differing opinions and helps prioritize those actions that everyone believes could have the greatest impact, and that could be executed for the least cost, time, and risk. In other words, openly debating the model will result in a wiser course of action based on input from multiple perspectives.

- **Assemble a Deal Team:** It's helpful to assemble a deal team to initially discuss the value drivers and formulate your strategy. The more help you have to execute the value drivers, the more progress you will make. This may also be a wise time to consider implementing a retention plan for your key executives. A retention bonus will help align incentives and motivate your key staff to improve the value drivers, especially if the amount of their retention bonus is tied to the purchase price.

- **Break Value Drivers Into Specific Action Items:** Consider breaking the value drivers down by specific actions, such as creating a retention bonus for key employees, as opposed to themes or categories, such as staff. Ratings, and therefore priorities, may be significantly different for specific actions as opposed to categories of actions, and it may therefore make sense to rank the model by specific actions as opposed to categories.

> Priorities aren't absolute but should be considered relative to one another. The individual ratings aren't important – what is important is the overall ranking or priority of the value drivers relative to one another.

Conclusion

Identifying your value drivers is an important element for increasing the value of your business and preparing it for sale. Systematically improving your value drivers will push you into the upper limits of valuation for your company. As you read through this book and identify your value drivers, write them down. Once you have collected all the potential value drivers, prioritize them based on their potential return and the risk, time, and investment required to achieve them. Doing this will allow you to maximize your time when preparing your business for sale.

To download a free version of the RVD Model and a spreadsheet with a list of all actions mentioned in this book, or learn more about buying, selling, valuing a business, or dozens of other topics related to mergers and acquisitions, visit the Resources section of the Morgan & Westfield website at morganandwestfield.com/resources.

PART TWO

Decision to
Sell & Exit Options

CHAPTER 3

Deciding to Sell

"The price of anything is the amount of life you exchange for it."

– Henry David Thoreau, American Author and Philosopher

Introduction

Planning your exit starts with the decision to sell. While making up your mind to sell may be simple for some, it may be gut-wrenching for others. Why do most business owners decide to sell their business? What are the most common reasons? Is your motivation for selling unique, or does it fall into one of several standard categories, such as burnout or retirement? Does your reason for selling even matter?

Your motivation will help determine how best to prepare your business for sale. The process of preparing your business and selling it should be based on your specific circumstances and reason for selling.

For professionals who regularly buy and sell businesses, the decision to sell a business is far less emotional than for an independent owner. For corporations, the determination to sell is as straightforward as deciding what to have for lunch that day. The decision usually starts with management and then goes to the board for approval. The board then hires an investment banker to handle the sale.

For independently owned businesses, the decision to sell can be gut-wrenching. Selling a business may bring about major life changes for the entrepreneur. For a small family-owned business, planning for the sale and thoroughly exploring your motivations are key to ensuring a smooth transition.

Deciding to sell your business and committing to the process are critical. It's therefore wise to fully explore your reason for selling before you begin to prepare your business for sale. Your motives will figure into the specific improvements you should make, and also determine the extent to which you may want to be involved in your business after the closing.

For example, if you're burned out, you're unlikely to have the drive and patience to commit to longer-term goals such as building a management team, so you may choose to focus on short-term objectives that have a more immediate impact. Or, you may wish to retire but retain an ongoing part-time role in your business after the closing. If you've simply "had enough," it's unlikely you'll want to play a continued role in your business. Likewise, if you want to diversify your wealth, you have a different range of exit options you may consider than if you're already diversified. If you want to sell because you have a more promising opportunity on the horizon, the process of preparing your business for sale will differ from if you're going through a divorce.

In the section that follows, I explore the most common reasons business owners decide to sell their companies and offer concrete advice for preparing for your transition based on your specific circumstances. I also walk you through the rigorous process of deciding to sell your business and offer a framework to help you decide if and when you should sell.

> The process of preparing your business for sale and selling it should be based on your specific circumstances and reason for selling.

Why Owners Sell

Business owners decide to exit their business for a variety of reasons. The exact reason for deciding to sell your business can impact both how you prepare your business and the sales process itself. In this section, I'll walk you through some of the most common reasons owners sell their business and what implication your situation can have on the sales process.

A Better Opportunity

Some owners may be seeking more profitable or more attractive opportunities. This is often the case for small business owners who struggle on a daily basis and may have friends who are thriving in another industry. At the same time, some businesses may be a poor fit based on an owner's skill sets or passions.

If seeking a better opportunity for your personal circumstances is the reason for selling, there's nothing wrong with pointing this out to a buyer. In this case, focus on quick improvements you can make so you can move on to other opportunities as quickly as possible.

Bankruptcy or Financial Pressures

Few sellers admit to having financial issues because doing so is tantamount to admitting failure. But financial troubles may not be the root cause behind their lack of success – instead, the root cause may have to do with management issues, fierce competition, or an inability to obtain financing.

Other owners sell because their business is unprofitable. Despite their best efforts, they simply haven't been able to turn things around. Unfortunately, unprofitable businesses are difficult to sell except to those within that industry, especially if there are little to no assets or proprietary technology in the business.

When a seller tells a buyer they want to sell to pursue another opportunity, the real reason is often that the seller believes the business has limited potential. When Ray Kroc purchased McDonald's in 1955, the buyers thought they were pulling a fast one on him. Kroc proved that opportunity is in the eye of the beholder and went on to turn the business into the behemoth that it is today.

When analyzing an unprofitable business, a buyer will attempt to determine if the root cause can be fixed. Often, the problem can be resolved with a new owner or management team. Other times, the problem may stem from competition or another issue in the industry that can't easily be mitigated. Regardless, it's important for a business owner who is selling due to financing pressures to prepare a growth plan for the buyer to demonstrate the future potential of the business.

Boredom

One of the most prevalent reasons for selling a business is boredom or lack of interest. This is common in small businesses and isn't usually a cause for concern for most buyers. Certain industries, such as retail, are more prone to this because they may not present enough challenge to the owner, and the daily grind and monotony may quickly bore talented entrepreneurs. Many entrepreneurs lose interest in industries in which they can't express their creativity.

This may also be common with franchises where you must follow a specific formula, as opposed to innovating and creating a business model from scratch. Boredom and burnout are often masked as "other business interests" by the seller because many owners believe they should hide the fact that they're bored or tired from the buyer. But boredom isn't a deal-breaker, and there's no need to hide this fact from the buyer.

Other owners enjoy building a business, but not running it. They enjoy the thrill of the startup phase and are looking for the next exciting idea to chase. This type of business owner often has a drawer full of ideas they wish to start on. This shouldn't be a warning sign for a buyer because everyone is wired differently. Many successful entrepreneurs thrive at starting businesses, but when it comes to the daily grind, not so much. While these types of owners may find the everyday monotony of running a company tedious and uninspiring, the business may be exactly what a buyer is looking for. By selling, this type of owner can use the capital from the sale to jumpstart their next idea. Entrepreneurs in this category should focus on building substantial value before considering an exit. And they should be honest with the buyer – there's nothing to be ashamed of about losing your passion in an industry. It happens to the best of entrepreneurs.

If you're in this situation, focus on making quick fixes and get out as soon as possible if your business is no longer growing.

Burnout

"Burnout" is a legitimate reason for selling a business. That being said, many sellers believe they must keep their lack of passion a secret from the buyer. It's common for entrepreneurs to become tired after working 50 to 60 hours every week in their business with no vacations for decades. In these cases, they likely haven't built processes and a management team that allows them to escape the business and rejuvenate on a regular basis.

For these businesses, it's important that the owner elicit help to build infrastructure, allowing them to capitalize on their strengths and delegate anything else that doesn't fall within their wheelhouse. Often, the business can be restructured, and talent can be hired to allow the owner to focus solely on what they enjoy and do best. While the learning curve to building infrastructure is steep, those who successfully do so find the journey is worth the effort.

Alternatively, try taking a vacation or a break to see if your burnout is due to a lack of recovery or if you've lost interest in your business. If you're burned out and decide to sell, it's important to point out to the buyer the opportunities you haven't been able to capitalize on due to your lack of motivation. You can also point out to the buyer that you haven't built the proper systems in your business to allow it to run smoothly, and your business would likely operate much more efficiently if systems were put in place.

> The exact reason for deciding to sell your business can impact both how you prepare your business for sale and the sales process.

Inability to Manage Growth

Less common is an owner selling due to an inability to manage growth. Sometimes, a talented sales or marketing-oriented entrepreneur may drive revenue to the point where they have a difficult time internally financing their own growth. This is common in businesses with a long cash flow cycle in which growth requires an increase in working capital, such as businesses with a long sales cycle or that offer significant terms.

These owners often must seek outside capital, and debt financing may be hard to obtain. Talented entrepreneurs who can drive sales but can't fund growth internally or seek outside financing may believe that another industry will be a better fit for them.

Entrepreneurs in this situation might find that growth equity from a private equity firm is a promising alternative. In this situation, the private equity firm will purchase a stake in your business and help you build up and scale your business, and position it for a much larger exit in three to five years. Private equity firms are experts at scaling companies, and can offer you advice and other resources that will help you institutionalize and scale your business.

Competition

If competition is increasing in your industry, you should focus on quick fixes and go to market as soon as possible while you still have a valuable business to sell. Sometimes, an owner knows in advance that competition may adversely affect their business, but this problem isn't always evident when reviewing a business's financial statements. In many cases, your business can be sold to a competitor who is fighting for market share.

Death or Disability

Death is a traumatic event for all affected parties. Without proper planning, an untimely death can drastically reduce the value of a business overnight. An exit plan can help prevent the degradation of the value of the business in the event of a death or disability.

Disputes

Arguments among family members or partners are all too common in small businesses. When these problems are irreconcilable, the owners may decide to sell. This type of situation can represent an opportunity for a buyer.

Problems can take the form of friendly disagreements, such as discussions over key strategic decisions, or they may be unfriendly. Regardless, it's critical for any business with partners, including family members and spouses who co-own a business, to create a buy-sell agreement that addresses various types of conflict resolution. Such an agreement should also offer all partners a method for selling their interest or purchasing another partner's interest in the event of a dispute, death, disability, or other crisis.

It's common for partners to disagree on issues in a business. If they come to a standstill, they often have no way out other than selling. There may not be enough cash available to buy out other partners, or they may be unable to agree on a price, and there may not be a buy-sell agreement in place to resolve these problems. If buying out a partner isn't possible, the company must often be put up for sale.

Unfortunately, it's nearly impossible to sell a minority interest in a small business. Often the only way out is to sell the entire business. For small businesses, it's also difficult, although not impossible, to sell a majority interest in the business if one partner remains.

If you're in this situation, find and hire a family business coach who can help you work out your problems in the short term while you prepare your company for sale. Ideally, you will have cooperation from your partner to prepare and sell your company, or you will leave significant value on the table.

Diversification

Some owners of larger, successful businesses may want to take some chips off the table and diversify their holdings. They may be reaching retirement age and could be uncomfortable with such a large portion of their net worth tied up in an illiquid asset – their business. Selling a portion of the company creates liquidity for the owner and allows them to diversify their wealth, thus lowering their risk.

These owners may want to consider a recapitalization, which is different from the sale of an entire company. When structuring a recapitalization, or "recap," for short, a private equity group purchases a portion of the company and retains you as a key manager. You retain a portion of ownership in the business. This allows you to partially cash out while creating the possibility for a second sale in the future. Private equity groups can bring more than just money to the table – they can bring industry and operational experience to help scale your business. This often results in a substantial increase in the value of the business.

Divorce

Divorce is another legitimate reason to sell a company. Selling a business while going through a divorce can be a stressful event. The sale will have to be approved by the trustee. In nearly all cases, it's wise to obtain the consent of both spouses, even if one of the spouses isn't a shareholder. This is particularly true in community property states.

If you're going through a divorce, I recommend hiring a family business coach or counselor to help you work out your problems while you prepare to sell your business. If you can amicably resolve your differences on a temporary basis, the sale process will unfold much more smoothly as a result.

Economic Reasons

Some entrepreneurs, primarily serial entrepreneurs, sell solely for economic reasons. They may attempt to sell at an industry's peak, for example. These owners are experienced and sophisticated, and will deal with all parties in a no-nonsense manner. Typically, they won't sell unless they achieve their financial objectives. If you're selling for purely economic reasons, you'll likely want to take as much time as possible to prepare your company for sale, and be prepared to sell at all times in the event you receive an unsolicited offer.

Health Reasons

Sometimes owners are forced to sell their business due to unexpected health reasons. If the health problems are chronic or acute, the owner should begin preparing for the exit as soon as possible. In the case of acute health problems, it's likely a significant amount of money will be left on the table.

Many owners claim to be selling due to health reasons because they believe that burnout and boredom aren't legitimate reasons to sell. "Health problems" is often the default reason an owner provides if they aren't comfortable disclosing the real reason for a sale.

Your business shouldn't be so dependent on you that it collapses in the event of a health crisis. With proper planning and documentation, your business should be able to survive disasters and run without you. Building your business so it can smoothly operate without you not only increases the value of your business, but also ensures that things run smoothly in the event of a personal catastrophe.

Your spouse, a key employee, or a manager could also get sick. With the proper documentation of your operations, your business should be able to survive disasters, such as the temporary disability of an owner or the loss of a key employee. Dependence on a key employee is risky without having backup plans in place. All entrepreneurs, therefore, should plan for unexpected events, such as a potential health crisis.

Relocation

Many owners desire to relocate either due to a spouse accepting a new job offer or for personal reasons. It's common for business owners in the north to seek a warmer climate in the south. Others may wish to be near their family, such as new grandchildren.

Relocation is a valid reason for selling a business. If you're planning to relocate, decide how much time you're prepared to commit to the process and harvest as much value as you can. You should also consider several long-term trips to your dream destination to make sure the grass really is greener on the other side. If you own your home, you'll also likely need to juggle the sale of your business with the sale of your home, which can be stressful for most entrepreneurs. See if you can find alternative living arrangements in each location to provide you with more flexibility during the sale.

Retirement

Retirement is the most common reason business owners sell their businesses. However, for highly driven type-A personalities, an owner may pull the trigger too early and later regret their decision. It may be difficult for them to let go and stop working. For these entrepreneurs, it's critical to find a new passion to keep them busy after the sale. It's also important to try the retirement lifestyle before you commit to it. I estimate that over half of retirees eventually look for something productive to do after deciding to retire.

A buyer might offer you a continued role in your business, which you may initially turn down. But this may sound more appealing after you tire of re-organizing your garage and lounging around the pool, sipping margaritas with little to keep you busy. Without a passion that can keep their mind occupied, combined with an inability to relax, many former entrepreneurs soon itch for something to do, so be open to the idea of possibly playing a continuing part-time role in your business.

Other business owners who decide to sell may delay pulling the trigger, and their health may begin to fail before they let go. For these owners, it's important to create an exit plan before it's too late and the inevitable happens. The exit plan should include objectives such as building a management team and grooming a successor, but every exit plan is different. The plan should also address what to do in the event of an emergency, such as a sudden health crisis.

If you're thinking about retiring, plan well in advance. Only about 30% of businesses transfer to the second generation, and only 15% make it to the third generation. Discuss the possibility with your family well ahead of the sale. It's never too early to find out that your family isn't interested in taking over.

Most buyers ask the seller to stick around after the sale to ensure a smooth transition. The thinner your management team, the longer the buyer will want you to stay for the transition period. By planning for the sale in advance and building a strong management team, you will reduce the length of time the buyer requests you to hang out after the transaction is complete.

Taxes

The sale of a business can trigger both capital gains and ordinary income taxes. Favorable changes in tax rates often motivate entrepreneurs to sell. If you expect such changes, begin preparing your business for sale as soon as possible.

Unsolicited Offer

Unsolicited offers are common from legitimately interested competitors for mid-sized companies. By always being prepared, you can effectively negotiate with any buyer who approaches you.

Combinations of Factors

The reasons for a business sale may not be mutually exclusive – many reasons may contribute.

> *For example, an owner may be experiencing minor health problems and require a back operation that requires a three-to-six-month rest period. They may also be burned out and feel they could benefit from a multi-month respite from the business. It might also be nice to finally get rid of that 20% minority partner who does nothing but cause trouble.*

Any one of these issues in isolation may not provide enough motivation for the owner to sell. But, all three in combination might tip the scales.

Here's the rundown of each of the factors I've mentioned and my advice on your exit strategy.

Advice Based on Your Reason for Selling	
Reason	**Advice**
A Better Opportunity	Make quick improvements before selling.
Financial Pressures	Prepare a growth plan to demonstrate opportunity to the buyer. Emphasize the external reasons for your pressures.
Boredom	Focus on building value before exiting.
Burnout	Be honest with the buyer regarding your burnout. Attempt to restructure the business to focus on your strengths before you consider selling.
Inability to Manage Growth	Consider growth equity from a PE firm.
Competition	Focus on quick fixes and go to market as quickly as possible. Consider selling to a competitor fighting for market share.

Death or Disability	Hire an interim CEO to prepare and sell the company.
Disputes	Hire a family counselor to help temporarily resolve problems while you prepare your company for sale. Create a buy-sell agreement that has a mechanism for resolving disputes and offers all partners exit options.
Diversification	Consider a recap from a PE firm.
Divorce	Hire a family business counselor to help work out problems.
Economic	Communicate your earnest desire to sell your business. Avoid coming across as abrasive or only concerned about the economic aspects of the transaction.
Health Problems	Prepare for the exit as soon as possible to avoid leaving money on the table.
Relocation	Plan your exit well in advance so you don't leave money on the table.
Retirement	Find a new passion to keep you busy. Create an exit plan in case your health fails before you can exit.
Taxes	Begin preparing as soon as possible if you expect tax changes.
Unsolicited Offer	Always be prepared in case you receive an unsolicited offer.

The Big Decision

Making the decision to sell your business can be a difficult one. The following are several suggestions for ensuring you exit your business successfully once you make your decision.

Plan for the Sale in Advance

Your business is likely one of your most valuable assets and an important element of your life. Its value may be tied to 70% or more of your net worth. Unlike selling a house, selling a business is something you'll probably do only once in your lifetime. And selling a home is child's play compared to selling a business, even for sophisticated businesspeople. You only get one chance, so you don't want to screw it up.

Most business owners are so busy with the day-to-day minutiae of running a company that they neglect to plan in advance for the sale of their business. With so much of their net worth tied to the value of the business, failing to plan can put them at a disadvantage.

Less than 30% of small businesses on the market eventually sell, and less than a fifth of small business owners actively plan their exits. Most of the reasons for failure can be prevented by preparing for the sale months or even years in advance. Once you've decided to sell, it's critical to be proactive about the sale process. Decide exactly why you want to sell your business and what your objectives are, then invest the appropriate amount of time to maximize the chances of a successful sale.

Clarify Your Reason for the Sale

Lying to a buyer about your reason for selling your business can kill a deal. Buyers are naturally suspicious of your true motives and will question you multiple times to be sure you aren't running from a problem child. It's difficult and unnecessary to hide your true reason for selling from a buyer. Instead, tell the buyer the truth but put yourself in a strong position, so you don't compromise your negotiating posture.

By clarifying your reason for selling, you will:

- Be more prepared.

- Negotiate more effectively.

- Maintain a cool head.

- Make intelligent decisions during one of the most stressful transactions of your life.

- Not have to worry about hiding the truth from the buyer.

You may be having partner issues, going through a divorce, preparing for retirement without a successor in the family, or experiencing health issues. You may also be successful, but suffer from burnout or boredom. Whatever the case, be honest with yourself, your advisors, and the buyer.

Planning the sale of your business begins with discovering your true motivations and goals before crystallizing your reasons for selling. The reasons people sell businesses are varied. Whatever the motivation, it's critical that you're honest with all parties involved.

> Unlike selling a house, selling a business is something you'll probably do only once in your lifetime. You only get one chance, so you don't want to screw it up.

Be Intellectually and Emotionally Prepared

Accept that you're emotionally attached to your business. You'll need to be both intellectually and emotionally prepared to effectively manage the sale. Taking an active role in the sale of your business and maintaining a cool head will help ensure the process goes as smoothly as possible.

Sometimes buyers make remarks designed to get you to snap as part of their negotiating strategy. By being prepared for this eventuality, buyers will see you as a savvy businessperson, and they will be more likely to respect you throughout the negotiation process. Preparing answers to potentially offensive questions such as, "If your business is so great, why are you selling it?" will allow you to remain calm and collected during these stressful times. The moment you lose your cool, buyers will lose trust and be suspicious of everything you say or do.

Honesty Is the Best Policy

Be honest with yourself and your advisors about the real reason you're considering selling your business. Buyers probe for facts throughout the sale process, so being upfront simplifies the procedure and increases the chances of a successful sale. If your reason for selling doesn't fit your facts, expect buyers to probe deeper, and eventually uncover the true reason.

Rehearse your story with your family members or advisors. If a buyer has previously made an offer on a business and the seller was dishonest, expect them to be suspicious of everything you say. Be prepared for buyers to be cautious – have your documents in order, and be ready to back up your reason for selling with facts and paperwork.

Be Proactive When Deciding To Sell

Planning to sell is all about building a business people want to buy. By planning well in advance and then proactively managing the sale process, you can ensure you will sell your business for the highest price possible. Don't skip this step. Your business is one of your most valuable assets. By preparing to sell early on, you will enhance your odds of a smooth sale at a favorable price when the time comes.

Part of that preparation is crystallizing your reasons and motivations. Do you want to get out altogether, or do you want to stay involved part-time? What do you want to do after you sell? If you're unprepared with your responses, most buyers will develop their own ideas about why you're selling.

Planning to sell is all about building a business people want to buy.

Create an Exit Plan as Early as Possible

Regardless of your situation, begin planning your exit as soon as possible. Your plan should contain a succession plan for ensuring continuity in the event of an acute issue, such as a health problem. The plan can also ensure you have options for exiting your business in the event of retirement, burnout, boredom, or relocation. Any exit plan should also address building a management team for high-growth businesses, or a means of generating funds to finance growth. And, I always recommend that a separate buy-sell agreement be put in place if there is more than one owner, even if the owners are family members.

There are many reasons you might be ready to sell your business, and these reasons can have a significant impact on how the sale proceeds. Understanding the true reason behind the sale can help you navigate the process more successfully.

A Framework for Deciding To Sell

If you've already decided to sell your business, you can skip this part of the chapter. If you're still on the fence, let's continue.

The decision to sell your company is challenging. You've invested years or decades painstakingly building your business and made countless sacrifices along the way. It's an emotional decision that shouldn't be taken lightly.

And when considering such an important decision, there are four important factors to take into account:

1. Your goals, including personal, financial, and business

2. Internal factors, such as emotions

3. External factors, including timing and competition

4. Your business's value and exit options

You can't decide whether to sell your business by going through a simple checklist. Instead, the determination should be made deliberately, taking all factors into consideration, and then balancing emotion and intuition with facts and logic.

While this framework is useful, the four factors mentioned aren't all-encompassing. Rather, these considerations are meant to be jumping-off points to further explore when contemplating the sale of your business. Every entrepreneur's situation is different, and many will need to consider additional factors not addressed here. Regardless, start by considering these four factors and see where your journey takes you.

> You can't decide whether to sell your business by going through a simple checklist.

Factor 1: Your Goals

Bear in mind the words of the Italian Friar, Saint Francis of Assisi, who said "You are that which you are seeking."

Start the process by clarifying your goals – understanding what you want is the first step toward getting it. Only once you understand your long-term goals can you examine how selling your business will move you closer to them.

Many factors must be considered when deciding to sell your business, and considering all of them at once can be overwhelming. Starting with your goals simplifies the decision-making process. The risk in selling your business before examining your goals is making a decision that doesn't align with them. As a result, you may find yourself backing out of the sale or later living with regret.

Would selling help you achieve your long-term goals?

To gain a better focus on your goals, ask yourself these questions:

- What are my long-term goals?

- Would selling my business help me achieve my long-term goals?

- What am I trying to accomplish?

- How does the sale of my business help me achieve my goals?

Align your long-term objectives with the sale of your company. If your business is preventing you from achieving your goals, you should sell it. If selling your business is critical to achieving your goals, spend additional time planning your exit to ensure the sale helps accomplish them.

Is your goal to sell your company to become financially independent? If so, get your business valued and develop a plan for increasing that value. Then track your results to ensure you meet your objectives. Prepare a personal financial and tax plan to make certain your exit will meet your financial goals.

Is your goal to sell your business so you can start another business or switch industries? If so, consider your lost opportunity cost and the cost of remaining in the business. What are you losing now by not pursuing your next business or opportunity in another industry, or a different goal or dream? Ideas are infinite, but time is finite. You have a limited number of ideas you can pursue in your lifetime.

Again, the decision to sell your business should always begin with a thorough and careful review of your long-term goals. If your goals are unclear, then the decision to sell your business will be based on a rocky foundation. It will be harder for you to commit to the sale without a definite goal, and this uncertainty will minimize the overall value you extract from the transaction.

Do you need to sell to achieve your financial goals?

If you must sell your business to achieve your financial goals, consult with a financial planner to ensure you can meet your financial objectives upon a sale, and meet with a CPA to consider the tax implications of the sale.

For most owners, the sale of their business helps achieve a personal long-term objective. They depend on the sale to help them accomplish their financial goals. But it's important to separate your financial goals from your non-financial goals to establish a clear outline of what you want.

It's not always necessary to start your planning process with numbers – after all, money is always a means to an end and not an end to itself. Remember, as business author David Baughier once said, "Once you have enough money, it's not about the money." Instead, ask yourself what stands behind the numbers. First, clarify your long-term goals, and then assign numbers to the goal, if possible.

Ask yourself these key questions to clarify your financial and non-financial goals:

- What are my financial goals?

- How do these fit into my long-term plans?

- What is more important – my financial goals or other goals I may have set?

- What am I going to do with the money?

- Is my goal to take money off the table and diversify my risk?

What other goals can you achieve if you sell your business?

When making the decision to sell your business, consider the lost opportunity cost. Pursuing opportunities is a mutually exclusive decision if you believe in focus. Chasing after more than one objective at a time dilutes your focus and lowers your chance of overall success. There is a significant lost opportunity cost to holding onto a business where you have lost your passion, especially if its value erodes. What other opportunities are you passionate about that you could be pursuing?

If remaining in your business is costing you $500,000 per year due to the value you place on lost opportunities, holding onto your business for an additional three years will cost you $1,500,000. If your company is worth $5 million, it may make more sense to sell your business now for $4 million and experience a $1 million short-term loss, rather than lose $500,000 per year in lost opportunities.

While the decision to sell your business can't always be reduced to numbers, it can be helpful to look at a sale from multiple angles, including both quantitative and qualitative perspectives.

In addition to lost opportunity costs, you need to consider the current state of your industry. Not all industries are created equal, and careful consideration must be given as to when to jump from one ship to another.

Many entrepreneurs make the mistake of thinking that the grass is always greener on the other side – that other industries offer more potential than the one they are currently in. If you believe your industry is in decline, consider consulting with other entrepreneurs who have experience in multiple industries or ask the opinion of a professional who deals in multiple industries. An M&A advisor, for example, likely has experience in various industries and may have perspectives that you lack.

If your other goals are primarily non-financial in nature, your decision can be especially difficult, and you must carefully weigh your options. What is owning your business precluding you from doing? What is that experience worth to you?

Only you can decide. Life is short, but you should take your time when making this important decision.

Factor 2: Internal Factors

As the French poet Charles Baudelaire said, "Everything considered, work is less boring than amusing oneself."

Here are several important questions you should consider that relate to your internal state of affairs:

- Am I happy?

- Am I really happy?

- Is my business making me unhappy?

- Would selling my business make me happier?

Entrepreneurship is a struggle. No entrepreneur is happy 100% of the time. Look at yourself and your business objectively, and determine if a change might make you happier. At the same time, though, beware of trading one set of problems for another.

Would selling your business make you happier?

If you're facing challenges in your company, ask yourself if the root of your problems is a lack of management skills or if the obstacles are caused by external factors beyond your control, such as increased competition in your industry. If your issues are the result of a lack of management skills, trading one business for another isn't guaranteed to solve your problems.

On the other hand, some industries are not known for creating happy entrepreneurs. These include businesses that may have less-than-ideal customers, such as liquor stores, payday loan shops, and collection agencies. Stressors can also include long hours in restaurants, home health care, and retail, demanding clients in professional services, or low margins in personal services. If the general environment of your industry is an unhappy one and you value your well-being, consider making a change.

Would you keep your business if it made you happier? Would you keep your business if you could revamp your schedule and spend 80% of your time on high-value activities you enjoy and less time on minor details? If so, restructure your business to focus on what you love to do and take advantage of your strengths. If you've lost passion for your industry and have a strong gut feeling you need to make a change, it's time to develop a definite plan to exit your business.

Would selling your business cure your burnout or boredom?

Look in the mirror and ask yourself these questions:

- Am I burned out?

- Have I taken a vacation recently?

- What other options have I considered or attempted to cure my burnout?

Burnout is normal in all endeavors, and all entrepreneurs should make time for regular relaxation to de-stress. Professional athletes periodize their training. CEOs take regular time off to recharge. You should do the same to both prevent and treat burnout.

Fatigue is normal if you aren't regularly taking time off to rejuvenate. Just because you're burned out doesn't necessarily mean you should sell your business. First, determine the cause of your burnout and evaluate if selling your business will be a cure, or if other measures are more appropriate for rekindling your passion.

If your burnout is due to problems with your employees, then it's time to either upgrade your management skills or upgrade your team itself. Trading your business for one in another industry won't help if people-management issues are at the root of your burnout.

If you haven't taken a vacation in a long time, other methods are available for relieving burnout. Ideas could include stress-management techniques, or restructuring your business to minimize activities you aren't good at or that cause you stress. First, set out to relieve your burnout. If you find you still lack passion for your industry, are bored, and in need of a change, and if you've attempted to address your burnout and boredom one too many times without effect, then perhaps it's time for a change.

How will you spend your time after you sell your business?

The question to ask yourself is not, "What will I do with my money when I sell my business?" The real question is, "What will I do with my time when I sell my business?"

The matter of what to do with the rest of your life is a difficult topic for entrepreneurs to face. Most business owners are so busy that they don't have time to confront the deeper issues in life. They are so occupied playing whack-a-mole in their business that they don't have the energy to face life's existential questions.

After selling your business, it might be the first chance in decades you've had the freedom to decide how to spend your time. Will you fritter away your days buying toys, or do you plan to pursue something more meaningful? How you spend your days should be based on your values. Your values are the foundation on which you make decisions. Having a clear and documented set of values makes the process of deciding how to allocate your time easier.

After all, as American author Michael LeBoeuf once said, "Waste your money, and you're only out of money, but waste your time, and you've lost part of your life."

Selling your business will leave you with time. If you don't have another passion, you'll be left with a void, lacking your business to fill that empty time. If this void isn't filled, your being may lack meaning. Sitting around the pool sipping margaritas on a giant, inflatable pink flamingo can become unfulfilling after a while, especially for driven entrepreneurs. Of course, some may never tire of this. Examine your own values and goals so you don't build yourself a void after a successful sale. Don't dodge the real question by drowning yourself in material pleasures.

Are you committed to the sales process?

Are you truly committed to the process of selling your business, or have you made this decision on a whim?

Move forward with your plans only if you're fully committed. But be aware that doubts will remain no matter how committed you are. Be deliberate in making your decision, so you can deal with doubts as they arise. Talk with trusted friends who have successfully sold their businesses. Journal. Read. Explore your decision from all angles.

Remember that, as American management consultant Peter Druker once said, "Unless commitment is made, there are only promises and hopes, but no plans."

Selling a business is a process, not an event. The process of preparing a business for sale and successfully exiting takes several years for many entrepreneurs. Shortcutting the procedure can leave money on the table and turn into a big waste of time if you begin the sale then change your mind later. Only you can answer if you thoughtfully and purposefully made this decision or if an impulse is driving you. If you're still on the fence, take more time to explore the decision thoroughly before making a final determination.

> No entrepreneur is happy 100% of the time. Look at yourself and your business objectively and determine if a change might make you happier. At the same time, though, beware of trading one set of problems for another.

Factor 3: External Factors

These wise words come from Warren Buffett, "We've done better by avoiding dragons than by slaying them."

Once you've considered your internal factors, it is time to take a broader look at the external factors that will affect your decision. Industry conditions and competition will play a large part in how smooth and ultimately successful the sales process is for you.

Is the timing right to sell your business?

Timing the sale of a business is difficult, but it can be done. The ideal time to sell is when your business and industry are about to peak. Consult with veterans in your industry to obtain their opinion regarding the current market cycle. Consider both industry cycles and macroeconomic cycles. But remember that, as with most important decisions, the timing will never be perfect.

Align the timing of your goals with the timing of the sale of your business, industry trends, and market activity, if possible. Otherwise, avoid selling in a severe economic or industry downturn. Your revenue should be stable and, preferably, growing by the rate of inflation or more when you put your business on the market. If it's not, have an expert analyze your business to determine if it makes sense to stabilize your company's revenue before putting it up for sale.

How should competition in the industry affect your decision?

You can bet that the "Oracle of Omaha," Warren Buffett, has asked himself these questions more than once regarding his investments:

- Is the competition becoming stronger in my industry?

- Are new venture-backed entrants threatening my market share?

- Do I have enough capital to fight a competitive industry war?

- Are indirect competitors threatening to permanently change the structure of my industry, such as in the cases of Uber vs. the taxi industry, Airbnb vs. the hotel industry, and online news vs. traditional news?

If competition is increasing and becoming more fierce by the day, but you lack the passion and capital to compete, exit as quickly as possible if you can. The value of your business will decline proportionally to a decline in your revenue and cash flow. Face the inevitable conclusion and sell while you have something to sell. Unfortunately, too many entrepreneurs hang on for too long, only to have nothing valuable left to sell.

Don't make this common mistake.

The ideal time to sell is when your business and industry are about to peak.

Factor 4: Value and Options

John D. Rockefeller, American business magnate, had this advice to offer: "Don't be afraid to give up the good to go for the great."

Knowing what questions to ask yourself is half the battle, like these:

- Have I had my business appraised recently?

- Am I aware of current multiples in my industry?

- Have multiples remained steady within my industry, or have there been significant variations over time?

- Do I know what changes I need to make to unleash the value of my business?

- Do I know what my business would be worth if I made these changes?

Consider these questions and many more as you begin to explore your exit options.

What is your business worth?

Your business is likely one of your most valuable assets, and may comprise the majority of your net worth. Intelligent financial planning is difficult without having an accurate idea of the value of your most valuable asset – your business.

It's a wise investment to pay a professional to value your business, and have an idea of the steps you can take to increase its value. It's best if you and your business are prepared at all times for the unexpected buyer, and that you regularly take action to increase the value. The buyers most likely to pay the highest price are those who approach you directly, unsolicited. So be ready for them.

Consider diversifying your risk if your net worth is highly concentrated in your business. There are many options for diversifying your risks, such as a recapitalization or an outright sale. An appraisal of your business is the most prudent place to start and can help you make this decision.

Knowing what your business is worth also enables you to determine a bottom-line price if a competitor approaches you. Without such planning, you may be caught off guard and end up selling your business for far less than what it's worth.

What are your exit options?

Ask yourself these questions that go to the heart of the choices you will face:

- What are my options for exiting my business?

- Should I consider selling or gifting my business to family members?

- Is my management team, or someone on the inside, a potential fit?

- Is a sale to a competitor most practical?

- Is a private equity group likely to buy my business?

Most entrepreneurs lack the experience to determine the exit options that are most suitable for their business and industry – options that will unlock the most value. That's why you should consider having a third party perform an unbiased assessment of your business.

This assessment should outline your exit options and steps to prepare your business for sale. The risks and opportunities vary depending on who you sell your business to. Different steps will need to be taken, depending on whether you plan to sell your business to an insider, a competitor, or a financial buyer. You should carefully consider these issues before deciding which exit option to pursue.

There are also creative alternatives to a conventional sale. Again, before proceeding, establish your goals. With clearly defined goals, a professional can easily and efficiently lay out the most practical exit options for your business based on your goals, along with tips for reducing the risk associated with each option. In the words of the Oracle of Omaha – "Should you find yourself in a chronically leaking boat, energy devoted to changing vessels is likely to be more productive than energy devoted to patching leaks."

Is the value of your business increasing or decreasing?

Sell while you're able to extract any remaining value. If the value of your business is decreasing, and you lack the drive to turn it around, consider the lost opportunity cost of holding onto your business. If revenue continues to decline, so will the value of your business. Selling a business with consistently declining revenue is difficult, but it can be done. Selling a business with stable or increasing revenue is far easier.

Take an honest look and ask if you can turn your business around. If you're burned out, and competition is increasing, it's time to get out. If the decrease in the value of your business is due to a one-time event or an internal factor, and you have time to cure the problem, then do so.

Is your business ready to be sold?

These aren't always easy questions to answer, which is all the more reason to ask yourself:

- How salable is my business right now?

- Are there deal-killers present in my business that need to be fixed? If so, how long will it take to fix them?

- Is it worth the time and energy to attempt to straighten out these issues, or is it best to sell my business in its current state?

- What is my personal ROI if I fix these issues before selling my business?

- What is my lost opportunity cost in attempting to cure these potential deal-killers?

- Could my time be better used elsewhere?

Ideally, you should invest several years in preparing your business for sale to maximize its value. The more salable your business, the more your business will be worth. There are two ways to improve salability – eliminate deal-killers and optimize your business's value drivers.

> Different steps will need to be taken depending on whether you plan to sell your business to an insider, a competitor, or a financial buyer.

Start by fixing any deal-killers. These could include inaccurate financial statements or undocumented intellectual property. Once these issues are addressed, calculate the ROI on the remaining potential changes and start with the highest ROI tweaks – see my "Return on Value Drivers (RVD) Model" in Chapter Two to help you decide which value drivers to focus on first.

Not every business owner has the time and energy to fully prepare their business for sale. In these cases, changes can continue to be made while the business is on the market. If your business is not fully prepared, you may still be able to sell it, but expect to receive less than full value.

Key Points

And finally, this piece of wisdom from Larry Ellison, American inventor and co-founder of Oracle: "See things in the present, even if they are in the future."

Choosing whether to sell your business will be one of the most important decisions of your life. Use the framework outlined here for making this determination:

- **Goals:** Start by considering your objectives and lost opportunity costs. This is the foundation of your decision.

- **Internal Factors:** Address the emotional or internal factors of a sale – namely, those relating to happiness. This step takes time to do correctly, so don't rush it.

- **External Factors:** Once you've thoroughly explored your emotional objectives, consider the external factors, such as the timing of selling your business and the state of your industry.

- **Value and Options:** Finally, you can commit to the process after considering your goals and both the internal and external factors. Only then should you explore the additional facts related to the decision – such as timing, value, exit options, and salability.

By following this framework, you can make sound decisions on your company's future with the assurance that you've taken the most important factors into consideration.

Deciding What's Next

After being business owners for years, many entrepreneurs are initially relieved to retire or move on to something else. You may have dreams of traveling, spending time with your family, fishing, reading, learning a new hobby, or any other kind of activity you can imagine. And, in theory, this is a great plan. You've worked hard all your life, and now is the time to slow down and relax.

But a year or less after the sale, most entrepreneurs end up looking for something else to do with their time. Many sellers even return with a desire to play a role in their former business. For some business owners, their emotional needs are just as important as their financial needs. Keep this in mind during the process. You can hear what some of our previous clients have to say by checking out Client Stories on our website at morganandwestfield.com/sellers. Like them, you may experience periods of last-minute anxiety. Addressing your emotional needs helps ensure a smoother sale.

As we discuss the details of finalizing the sale, I have had several clients ask, "Now what?" Then, when the sale is complete and they're officially "retired," they go off to do all the glorious things they imagined. The hitch is that most won't spend the rest of their lives traveling or playing with the grandkids.

Most entrepreneurs are go-getters. They need something to do with their time, be it a hobby, a new job, a role in a charitable organization, or something that will give them a sense of purpose in their life. Once their business is sold, some entrepreneurs find that what they once thought would be their dream of retirement turns out to be the very thing they resent. A year or less into retirement, many of our clients even come back asking to play a role in their old business.

Another issue is that some entrepreneurs become so stressed during the closing – because they realize they will have nothing to do once the business sells – that they often delay the sale, or even back out entirely. This is because of the anxiety they get at the thought of doing "nothing" after a lifetime of work.

Luckily, there are ways to calm your nerves when selling your business. You need to realize that what happens after you sell your business needs to be planned just as much as the sale itself. You wouldn't sell your house without knowing where you would be moving next. The same principle applies here – why would you sell your business without having a detailed plan about what you will do next? Answering "I'll be retired" isn't enough. Instead, you should direct your energy toward a new passion.

If you're preparing to sell your business and aren't sure what you'll do next or you plan to just retire, I challenge you to spend some time answering this question – "What do I want to accomplish over the next 5, 10, or 15 years?"

Writing down your short-term goals, such as traveling or visiting family, as well as your long-term goals, such as learning a new language or starting a not-for-profit undertaking, will help you feel less overwhelmed as you get closer to selling your business. You can even gather information now about the different things you would like to accomplish once your business is sold. The more detailed your plan after your business sells, the better. You'll find that a little preparation now will save you stress and anxiety about your future as you navigate through the complex process of selling your business.

Your interests may provide enormous ongoing value to the business, such as recruiting, sales, marketing, or establishing key alliances. You may be talented at one or more of these roles and be willing to continue performing these if your other needs are met.

Sellers are sometimes willing to work in these positions if the role is structured to align with their lifestyle goals. Most entrepreneurs who have just sold their business desire flexibility, and if the buyer can offer you this, you may develop a win-win situation in which the buyer retains valuable talent and in which your lifestyle needs are met. Structuring an arrangement like this can also assist in retaining key customers or employees, which can help maximize the value of your business. Key partners feel more comfortable if they observe your ongoing participation in the business, and this can add significant value to the buyer.

Selling a business is an emotional shock to some people. It may have been a part of your life for so long that you feel empty afterward. Be prepared to deal with the loss.

Retirement from your business is not retirement from life. Start to look ahead at new interests and areas you want to pursue. You'll find that a little preparation now will save you stress and anxiety about your future as you navigate the complex process of selling your business.

> For some business owners, their emotional needs are just as important as their financial needs.

Conclusion

Selling your business is one of the most critical decisions you'll ever make. But you're not alone. Every day, thousands of entrepreneurs decide to move on. Take your time making this decision by fully exploring the decision from as many angles as possible. Compare your reason for sale to some of the other common reasons outlined in this chapter. If you're still on the line, use the model I've outlined in this chapter to guide you through the decision-making process. Once you've made your decision, it's time to roll up your sleeves and start preparing for your exit.

CHAPTER 4

Exploring Alternatives to a Sale

"We work to become, not to acquire."

– Elbert Hubbard, American Writer

Introduction

Should you sell your business, or should you double down? Or should you explore other alternatives? If you sell now, you may be leaving money on the table. But if you run your business as usual and maintain the status quo, your competition will eat you for lunch, and you'll have nothing left to sell. At the same time, if you double down, a large payout glimmers in the distance.

You may be at a point in your life when you prefer to diversify your wealth instead of concentrating it. You may feel it's risky if too much of your net worth is concentrated in one illiquid source. If a competitor puts you out of business, you could lose the majority of your net worth.

If you're in a highly competitive industry, you must invest cash back into your business to remain in the game. Instead of taking money out of your business, you must put money back into your business – perhaps the exact opposite of what you want to do at this stage in your life.

As a result, you face a critical decision. Do you sell now and get out while you can, or double down and risk spending your life flipping burgers?

It's a decision that will determine the fate of … the rest of your life. These critical life decisions are often made as a response to an acute event. Or, they may be made in a frame of mind that's sometimes fleeting. As Marcel Proust, a 19th-century French novelist, said, "All our final decisions are made in a state of mind that is not going to last." As a successful entrepreneur, you've learned to temper your optimism with realism. But what should prevail now – your optimism or realism?

Going All In or Cashing Out

The answer to your decision depends on you and the state of your industry. You must look both inward – to yourself – and outward – to your industry – for the answer. In the section that follows, I show you how to look both ways and create a framework to help you decide how to navigate this difficult decision. For this framework, I've separated my advice for each section into three topics: your business, your industry, and your competition. Each of these topics is important to examine internally and externally to best make a decision. So let's begin.

Look Outward – To the State of Your Industry

Knowledge is collecting information; wisdom is simplifying it. First, collect the necessary data, and then step back to simplify the information you've collected.

Step 1: Collect Information

Start by gathering information. But remember to withhold your judgment while doing so. Stick solely to the task at hand – collecting data. Think objectively without the need to weigh the facts or assess their impact. Once you've gathered the necessary information, then it's time to analyze and synthesize it.

Start by asking yourself the following questions about the external variables within your business, industry, and competition:

- **Your Business**
  - Are your revenues stable, declining, or increasing?
  - Are your gross margins stable, declining, or increasing?
  - Is your net profit stable, declining, or increasing?
  - Is your value proposition still competitive?
  - Are you gaining or losing competition?

- **Your Industry**
  - Is your industry fragmented and run by small, independent businesses? Or is it slowly consolidating?
  - Is your industry growing, or is it in decline?

- **Your Competition**
  - Are your competitors stealing your market share? Is your market share slowly eroding?
  - How strong are your competitors?
  - Are there any new competitors in your industry that are backed by institutional money, such as venture capital?
  - Have any competitors introduced a new value proposition that has the potential to change the industry and make your business obsolete?
  - Will you continue to remain competitive if you only innovate incrementally, or are dramatic changes needed to remain competitive?

Knowledge is collecting information; wisdom is simplifying it.

Step 2: Simplify Information

Once you've gathered this information, sit down and analyze it at a high level. Be honest with yourself in assessing the state of your industry – don't let your heart fool your intellect. Synthesize your information and look for the following trends:

- **Your Business:** Is your business growing and staying competitive, or are you in a slow decline?
  - If your business is in decline, ask yourself why. Is it due to a lack of skills in yourself, or is it due to your lack of motivation? Is your competition simply more successful than you? If you lack the skills or motivation to compete and your competition is strong, it might be time to sell.
  - If your business is strong and your value proposition is still relevant, it might be worth doubling down.

- **Your Industry:** Is your industry growing or in decline? Are competitors slowly consolidating?
  - If your industry is in decline or your competitors are consolidating, it's time to sell, especially if you lack the ability or motivation to reinvent your value proposition.
  - If your industry is growing and competition isn't actively growing stronger or consolidating, doubling down might be your best option.

- **Your Competition:** Is competition robust and likely to put you out of business?
  - If your competition is getting stronger by the day and you lack the skills or motivation

to compete, selling might be your best option.

- Lack of direct competition might be a reason to recommit and extract more value from a business.

Look Inward – To Yourself

Once you've examined your business and industry, it's time to look inward. While analyzing your business and industry involves your mind, looking inward to yourself involves your heart. As American essayist Anaïs Nin once said, "We do not see things as they are, we see them as we are."

> While analyzing your business and industry involves your mind, looking to yourself involves your heart.

Give careful thought to each of the following three determinations:

Step 1: Assess Your Skills

Do you have the skills to continue to compete in your industry? If not, are you sufficiently motivated to acquire these skills? Is your competition so strong that you won't be able to acquire the skills fast enough to compete? This last situation is most common in innovative industries that require a high degree of technical knowledge, such as technology sectors. If this is the case, it's time to sell.

In cases where you lack the skills to compete and you're having trouble keeping up with the competition, you have two choices:

- **Double Down:** Carve out a niche for yourself in the industry or raise money to enable yourself to compete.

- **Exit the Race:** Sell your business.

Step 2: Assess Your Motivation

Do you have the energy and motivation to commit to your business? If your industry is highly competitive and the sharks are slowly eating away at your market share, you must have an unusually high degree of motivation to remain competitive. On the other hand, if competition is weak, you'll likely be able to get by with an average amount of energy and motivation.

Are you burned out? If so, why? Are you burned out because you haven't had a break in 10 years, or are you burned out because you hate your industry? As they say, only dead fish swim with the stream. So if you're burned out, and the competition in your industry is getting stronger by the day, you must realistically assess your ability to compete – and swim against the stream.

Step 3: Consider Your Dreams

Do you love your business? Do you *really* love your business? Knowing what you know now, would you get into your business again if you had to start all over? What are your dreams for 5 years, 10 years, or 20 years from now? Are you ready, emotionally and financially, to retire?

The answers to these questions first require that you know yourself. What makes you happy? What makes you excited? What does your ideal day look like? Does your business align with your dreams, or is your heart elsewhere? If your heart is elsewhere, perhaps it's time to exit gracefully. If you aren't sure, then your objective is simple – get to know yourself.

Many entrepreneurs are so busy that they have little time to truly get to know themselves. Introspection requires a significant amount of time and exploration through journaling, talking to others, and reading.

One of the best methods for learning more about yourself is traveling. We travel not to see the world but to see ourselves. Travel helps us see what's possible. As French social philosopher and activist Simone Weil said, "Attachment is the great fabricator of illusions; reality can be obtained only by someone who is detached." Travel is a powerful tonic for detaching us from our illusions and allowing us to gain perspective, so we can more clearly see the reality before us.

The better you know yourself, the easier your decision will be. If you feel you don't know yourself enough to be confident in your decision, take a break to self-reflect before making one of the most critical decisions of your life.

As American actor and comedian Lucille Ball said, "I'd rather regret something I've done than something I wish I had done."

Signs You Should Double Down

Now that you've taken a deep dive into both your industry and yourself, the time is right to weigh the results of your exploration and make a decision. Below are guideposts to help you decide if you should double down or sell.

These are signs you should double down based on your gathered information:

- **Your Business:** You realistically determine that your business can continue to remain competitive. Your business is continuing to grow, and your competitive advantages will continue to remain attractive even with only incremental innovation.

- **Your Industry:** Your industry is growing, and you're optimistic about the prospects for your business. Your industry also isn't quickly consolidating – small, independent operators will continue to be successful in the long run.

- **Your Competition:** Competition in your industry isn't strong, and it's unlikely your competitors will put you out of business anytime in the near future. There haven't been any new entrants backed by institutional funding, such as venture capital or wildly attractive value propositions that have been introduced recently.

Beyond your business, industry, and competition, there are two other important factors behind doubling down in your business – your financials and you.

- **Financial Variables:**
  - **Net Worth:** Your net worth isn't concentrated in your business. Your retirement isn't dependent on the sale of your business.

  - **Reinvestment:** You can afford to reinvest cash back into your business if doing so is required to remain competitive.

- **You:**
  - **Skills:** You have the skills and ability to remain competitive.

  - **Motivation:** You love your business – you have the drive, motivation, and energy to continue.

  - **Dreams:** Doubling down on your business aligns with your dreams.

Signs You Should Sell

Let's re-examine each of these same categories for signs you *should* sell:

- **Your Business:** Your revenue is declining, and your value proposition is slowly eroding. Incremental innovation won't be sufficient to survive. If you don't double down, your business will likely fail.

- **Your Industry:** Your industry is in decline. Or, there is an acquisition frenzy in your industry – and large competitors are quickly gobbling up smaller ones in order to become the dominant players. Acquisitions in your industry can be an ideal time to sell because buyers come out of the woodwork and become aggressive to protect their turf. In many industries, however, there's a limited window of opportunity – critical mass must be established as quickly as possible in a "winner takes all" market. If your business is in such a market, and you lack the capital, skills, or motivation to compete, it's time to sell.

- **Your Competition:** Competition is strong. If you don't compete, you'll be out of business soon. Several new venture-backed competitors have entered the market with enticing value propositions. Good ideas are often being pursued by dozens of competitors simultaneously, frequently without them having knowledge of one another – carefully scan your industry to see if any such competitors are quickly gaining market share. If so, sell before a competitor dominates the market, and your business or product becomes obsolete. Smaller, agile competitors can also quickly out-innovate you. Be on the constant lookout for competition that has the potential to unseat you.

- **Your Financial Situation:**
  - **Net Worth:** If your net worth is concentrated in your business and your retirement depends on the sale of your business, these are both signs you should sell. If you're uncomfortable with how much of your personal wealth is tied up in your business, selling might be a good option.

  - **Reinvestment:** You can't afford to reinvest cash back into your business, and doing so is required for you to remain competitive.

- **You:**
  - **Reason for Sale:** You have other hobbies, passions, or businesses to pursue. Your business isn't your life, and your life isn't your business.

  - **Skills:** You lack the skills or ability for your business to remain competitive.

  - **Motivation:** You're burned out – you don't have the drive, motivation, or energy to compete.

  - **Dreams:** You hate your business, and it doesn't align with your dreams.

Be Flexible if the Industry or Economy Changes

Once you've decided to sell, you may have to adjust your time frame based on market cycles instead of establishing a definitive time frame. For example, if you decide to sell once your business hits $10 million in revenue, you should be prepared to unload it at any time if an acquisition frenzy starts in your industry and multiples quickly rise.

The sale process can take from 6 to 12 months, although it may sometimes take much longer. In most cases, you'll need to assist with the transition for one to two more years. If this is the case in your industry, then it may be necessary to begin the exit process several years before you want to fully exit your business.

> Once you've decided to sell, you may have to adjust your time frame based on market cycles instead of establishing a definitive time frame.

You should also be prepared to change your game plan if you obtain new information about your industry or discover new truths about yourself. Time trieth truth – truths may be slowly revealed to you at the most unexpected of times.

Considering Other Options

Maybe selling isn't the right decision, and neither is doubling down. What other options do you have? There are two primary alternatives to an outright sale – a recapitalization and raising money.

Recapitalization

A recapitalization, or recap for short, is simply a partial sale of your company, generally to a private equity group or corporate venture fund. For example, you may sell 20%, 40%, or 60% of your company. The sale can be either a majority or minority interest. In most cases, you must remain on to operate the company.

A recap allows you to take money off the table now while still keeping some chips in play. In other words, you lock in some gains, which allows you to diversify your financial position while keeping the possibility open for a second exit in the future. It's essentially a double exit – you sell 30% of your company today, for example, then sell the remaining 70% of your company in a few years to another buyer, such as a publicly-traded company or a strategic industry buyer.

Private equity groups and corporate venture firms make these investments only in promising companies where significant opportunity exists. Their objective is to make an investment in a portion of your company today and then sell this portion at a significant gain in three to seven years.

Recaps are most commonly funded by financial buyers, such as private equity firms, in which they purchase a minority position in your business.

Private equity firms have a limited time horizon and are counting on you to grow the firm and achieve the second exit in a three-to-seven-year time frame. Recaps, or minority investments, are also made by corporations, but this is less common than those made by financial buyers. Recaps are best for business owners who want to take some money off the table while simultaneously receiving the support of a sophisticated investor with deep pockets willing to inject growth capital into the business.

> A recap allows you to take money off the table now while still keeping some chips in play.

The advantage is that you can sell now, pad your savings account, and work for the larger company for a few years before retiring or starting your next venture. An additional benefit is that the buyer will likely have deep capabilities and resources from which you can benefit, such as wider distribution channels or the brand name of a larger company.

A recap is ideal if you:

- Have a business with a strong competitive advantage and need the expertise or capital funding of a third party to capitalize on an opportunity in your industry.

- Are willing to stay with the company for one to three years or longer after the closing.

- Want to diversify your wealth and take money off the table now.

Raising Money

Raising money can come either in the form of debt, from banks, or equity, such as from angel and venture capital investors. This section will focus on selling equity as opposed to debt. In most cases, this money will be raised by angels or venture capitalists (VC), and this is suitable only for high-growth opportunities that offer the possibility of a 30% to 40% annual return for the investor. The use of funds also differs from that of a recap in that the funds are used to grow the company. They never make it into the entrepreneur's pocket. As a result, this strategy doesn't lead to diversification for the entrepreneur.

The mechanics of the investment look similar to a recap – you sell a portion of your company in the form of equity to an outside investor. But the types of companies that are suitable for this arrangement are different from those that are suitable for a recap.

Raising money from a VC is a grueling process that can take up to a year, and you may have to give up control of your company along the way. VCs only invest in ultra high-growth opportunities that have the potential of developing into nine-figure businesses, $100 million, and more. Less than 3% of those seeking venture capital obtain an investment, and the majority of VC-backed investments fail.

I've interviewed several entrepreneurs who have raised venture capital and successfully exited their business on my podcast, *M&A Talk*. Several of these entrepreneurs had exits in the hundreds of millions of dollars, but the path was far from easy.

In summary, raising VC money is a risky, high-stakes game reserved for scalable businesses that can produce outsized returns. On the other hand, a recap is best for stable businesses with predictable growth and cash flow. Think of it this way – recaps are for more stable, lower growth, lower risk businesses, whereas venture capital is for risky, high-growth businesses.

French chemist Marie Curie said it well: "Nothing in this life is to be feared. It is only to be understood."

Key Points

The ultimate question – do you sell or double down? Every entrepreneur will face this critical junction in their life. Entrepreneurship is a stressful, high-stakes game, but the rewards are often worth it. Look both inward – to yourself – and outward – to your industry for guidance. Once you thoroughly explore yourself and objectively collect the information you need on your industry, you'll often find that the decision has made itself.

Selling Part of Your Business

Selling a business isn't always an all-or-nothing proposition. Just ask Jack Welch.

General Electric CEO Jack Welch was well-known for divesting businesses as a way of "pruning" the company to give way to the growth of the remaining business units within GE. In his first four years as GE's CEO, he divested over a hundred business units accounting for approximately 20% of GE's assets. Welch eliminated over 100,000 jobs through layoffs, forced retirements, and divestitures. During Welch's 20-year reign, GE's profits grew to $15 billion from $1.5 billion, while the market valuation increased to $400 billion from $14 billion.

While considering the sale of your company, selling only a portion of your business may cross your mind. You may have questions about the process of selling just a division, such as whether it's wise or common.

Many owners have a significant portion of their personal wealth concentrated in their business. Selling a segment or division of your business allows you to generate liquidity while still maintaining control of the remaining portion. It also allows you to focus your talents on a division of your business with the most significant potential, or that you most enjoy, or that offers you the greatest opportunity for work-life balance.

Publicly owned companies, which are usually under intense pressure to meet projected quarterly earnings, commonly sell non-core divisions. And so can you, even if you're no Jack Welch.

Why Businesses Make Divestitures

A divestiture is a strategy of focusing on the core competencies of your company by spinning off non-core divisions. In other words, you can divest divisions that aren't part of your core operations to allow your entire company to focus on what it does best.

Sometimes, poor management decisions lead to a need to divest non-performing business units. Selling a weak division is a straightforward management decision.

Selling non-core divisions could also be a way to raise funds. A divestiture generates cash upon a sale, with that cash being invested in more promising opportunities that can yield higher returns. Also, a company's individual components are sometimes worth more than the company as a whole. Therefore, breaking up the company and selling it in pieces can often yield more than if it were sold in its entirety.

Learn More

On my podcast, *M&A Talk*, I interviewed the head of corporate development in charge of divesting business units at a $5 billion company. Russell Iorio was the former Senior VP of Corporate Development at Leggett & Platt, a $5 billion diversified manufacturer with 15 business units in 18 countries. Russell was in charge of deciding whether to divest the companies' business units. If you would like to learn more about what goes on behind the scenes in deciding to sell a business unit, you can find the podcast in the Resources section of the Morgan & Westfield website at morganandwestfield.com/resources/podcast/.

Deciding To Sell a Division

The truth is, as a business owner, you don't need to sell your entire company should you decide to retire or cash out. With proper strategic planning, you can often sell just a piece of your company, allowing you to generate additional funds for your retirement or provide you with growth capital to invest back into your business.

In deciding whether to sell your whole company or only a portion of it, first examine the overall value of your business and then determine the individual value of each division. Once you've performed this analysis, you may decide that it's prudent to sell your business in pieces to extract the most value.

> Selling a division allows you to focus on a segment of your business with the most significant potential, or that you most enjoy, or that offers you the greatest opportunity for work-life balance.

You have two main options in selling a portion of your business:

- **Selling a Percentage:** Selling a certain percentage of your entire company is usually structured as a percentage of your stock. These business owners may just want to take some cash off the table.

- **Selling a Division:** This structure involves selling a division, unit, or category of your business. Many companies are bought for strategic purposes. A buyer may see tremendous value in one division of your company while seeing little value in your other divisions. If this happens, you may consider a spin-off of one of your divisions.

Selling a Division Is a Strategic Decision

Selling a portion of your business doesn't necessarily mean giving up something – it only means letting go of a "part" to enable the "whole" to thrive. The cost of keeping a non-performing or non-core division could be much higher than the returns that could be generated by selling that division. This strategic decision could free up your time and energy, allowing you to focus on your core operations and potentially increasing its value as well.

A common example we encounter is a business that originally started as a single retail location and gradually evolved into a business with multiple retail outlets and significant online sales. Splitting the business into two divisions – an online division and a brick-and-mortar division – may make the company easier to sell and potentially maximize its value. Many buyers have a strong preference for online-based businesses and a strong aversion to brick-and-mortar businesses, or vice versa. Selling the divisions separately solves this problem.

Splitting your company in two may make it easier to sell, increase its value, and ultimately increase the final selling price.

Value is directly related to risk. The higher the risk, the lower the value – and the lower the risk, the higher the value. By splitting the business into two, you potentially reduce the level of risk for the buyer.

Why? Because few buyers possess the skills and knowledge necessary to be successful in multiple domains, such as in both the brick-and-mortar and online realms. Most buyer's skill sets are concentrated in one domain.

> *If your business consists of two segments, but can only be sold as a whole, the buyer may view one segment of your business as excessively risky if they lack experience in that segment, and the valuation will therefore be lower. If both the online and retail divisions can be sold separately to buyers who have a strong background and experience in each domain, the risk will be lower for each buyer, and you'll potentially receive a higher purchase price as a result of the reduced risk.*

Many companies develop additional product lines as a part of their overall corporate growth strategy. In the process, many business owners create product lines they later regret pursuing. The product line may not fit with the overall operations or may make the business owner lose focus on their core business. In that case, selling the product line can make sense.

Additionally, many buyers search for strategic acquisitions and have specific criteria regarding which businesses they will consider. They may be interested in just one component of your business and may not pursue your business as a whole because your other divisions don't align with their strategy.

> *Popular divestitures include the decision of Hewlett-Packard CEO Meg Whitman to spin off and merge HP's non-core software assets with Micro Focus, a British company. This transaction was valued at about $8.8 billion, significantly less than the $11 billion it spent to acquire the division five years earlier.*

Even small-business owners can benefit from splitting their companies into separate divisions and selling them individually. For instance, some businesses require special licensing, and splitting the business into two divisions may be prudent, as some companies may only be interested in the divisions that don't require special licenses.

Regardless, the decision should first be considered from a strategic standpoint – ask yourself if selling a division will help you accomplish your long-term objectives. Only after you've considered the strategic elements of the decision should you consider the tactical components, or the "how to's," which are addressed next.

Consider the Operational and Legal Implications

The decision to sell a division should first be considered from a strategic standpoint – ask yourself if selling a division will help you accomplish your long-term objectives.

When deciding to sell a division, there are two important considerations – operational and legal. Let's explore them both.

Operational Implications

You must first be sure that your business can be divided in two from an operational standpoint before considering the legal implications. Some divisions are so intertwined that it's impossible to separate them, or doing so could prove too costly. Businesses that are most conducive to being sold as divisions can be easily split in two from an operational standpoint.

When determining if your business can be split up, consider the following questions:

- Do you have a separate website, phone number, and facility for each division?

- Can costs be accurately allocated between divisions?

- Do any employees share duties for each division? If so, which division would they remain with?

Consider the answers to these questions as early as possible to determine how practical it is to separate the divisions from an operational standpoint. In many cases, significant work needs to be done to separate divisions operationally.

Few buyers will be willing to take the risk of creating a separate website, hiring new employees, and completing the dozens of other tasks involved unless you're selling a division that can be integrated easily into another company, such as a product line.

If the division is likely to be run as a stand-alone entity by the buyer, you should run it as a stand-alone business with a separate profit and loss statement for as long as possible before beginning the sale process. Doing this will make the business easier to sell and will simplify the process of separately valuing each division. Running it as a stand-alone entity will also increase the chances of the buyer being able to obtain third-party financing for the transaction. The more integrated the division is run prior to putting it on the market, the more difficult it will be to sell.

Legal Implications

There are two general transaction structures from a legal standpoint when selling a division – an asset sale or a stock sale. Following are your options for structuring the transaction from a legal perspective:

- **One Entity:** If your business is one entity, such as a corporation, LLC, etc., with two segments, your only option is to structure the sale of one of the divisions as an asset sale. In an asset sale, your entity sells the individual assets of the division to the buyer via an asset purchase agreement, and the assets are listed and transferred separately in a bill of sale.

- **Separate Entities:** If each division is a separate entity, the sale can be structured either as an asset sale or a stock sale. For example, if Division A is "Acme Incorporated" and Division B is "Summit Incorporated," you can structure the transaction either as a stock sale via a stock purchase agreement or as an asset sale via an asset purchase agreement. In a stock sale, you sell the shares of the entity that owns the division and its assets. Because the entity owns the assets, there's no need to transfer the assets separately.

- **Selling a Percentage:** You also have the option of selling a percentage of your company, but this defeats the purpose of focusing on your core competency because you'll still own both divisions post-closing.

Regardless, the decision to sell a division should begin with a consideration of your long-term goals. If you wish to focus on your core division, selling a percentage of your entity or stock is likely not for you. If, on the other hand, you want to diversify your risk and are willing to continue operating the business for another three to seven years, a recap may be a more sensible strategy for you.

Valuing a Division

The asking price for a division is determined by the same methods used to value a business as a whole. In essence, you're selling and, therefore, valuing a cash flow stream. To properly value the cash flow stream, you must first measure it. But here's where it gets tricky.

If the two segments are closely interwoven, it may be difficult to calculate the cash flow for each division separately unless the divisions are being run as stand-alone units.

If the businesses aren't being run as stand-alone units, a pro forma must be prepared. But be aware that any errors in the pro forma will be magnified by the multiplier. For example, if you overstate income by $500,000, and your business is valued at a 4.0 multiple, then your business will be overvalued by $2 million ($500,000 x 4.0 = $2 million).

Preparing a pro forma for a division can be tricky due to the difficulty of properly allocating expenses between divisions. While revenue may be easier to allocate than expenses, the impact of any inter-division transactions must also be considered on revenue. When allocating expenses, you must also decide how to allocate fixed expenses. For example, if your facility costs are currently $20,000 per month for both divisions, what would a reasonable rent be for each division separately? The same idea goes for allocating other forms of corporate overhead as well, such as salaries, insurance, professional fees, advertising, marketing, and so forth.

An alternate method, if you can make it work, is to value the business as a whole and then assign weights to each division based on the revenue each division generates. For example, if your company generates $20 million in revenue and is valued at $10 million, and Division A generates $12 million in revenue (60% of total revenue) and Division B generates $8 million in revenue (40% of total revenue), then Division A would be worth $8 million ($10 million x 60%).

While this may seem like a reasonable computation, some buyers may not be willing to accept such a calculation. That's because you're likely to understate the amount of fixed expenses and therefore overstate income or margins, meaning profitability may differ significantly between divisions.

Such a calculation would only be reasonable if the two divisions have similar margins and expenses, such as two similar product lines.

Ideally, the divisions can be valued based on the cash flow that each division generates. But doing so involves numerous assumptions that are prone to error. A back-of-the-envelope method for obtaining a ballpark valuation for each division isn't difficult, but such a ballpark estimate is unlikely to suffice for most buyers. A ballpark estimate should only be used for internal planning purposes.

> The asking price for a division is determined by the same methods used to value a business as a whole. In essence, you're selling a cash flow stream.

Making a Strategic Decision

In some cases, it only makes sense to sell your business as a whole. In other cases, the wisest course of action is to break up your company and sell it in separate pieces. Your decision depends on a number of factors that an experienced M&A advisor or investment banker can help you evaluate. First, examine the overall value of your business, and then the value of each division separately. Next, clarify your long-term objectives. The decision to sell a division or segment of your business is a strategic one and should be based on achieving your long-term goals.

Consider the following questions when deciding if selling your company as a whole or in parts makes better sense:

- Would I be happier if I simplified operations and focused solely on my core business?

- Have I spread myself too thin? If so, would selling a division improve my focus?

- Knowing what I know now, would I start both divisions again?

- Which division produces the most profit for me?

- Which segment of the business is most suited to my skills and strengths?

- How hard would it be to sell each segment separately?

- Is it practical to sell each segment separately?

- What's the potential value of each division?

- What's my number one bottleneck now?

- Do I need growth capital to significantly grow my business? If so, would selling one of the divisions free up capital and energy to focus on my core competence?

- If I sold one of my divisions, could I reinvest the money in the remaining division and significantly boost revenue and income?

Once you consider these questions, as well as the previous operational and legal questions, you can determine the best way to move forward with your decision about selling a portion of your company.

Business owners sell portions of their companies for many reasons. Yes, it can be wise to sell just part of your business. It's a fairly common practice, and it can free up cash for you to use as you see fit.

It may make more sense to sell your business as a whole. It depends on several factors that an M&A advisor can help you evaluate, including how much stake you want to have in the future of the company. Also, having your business valued as a whole and in pieces can help you decide what makes the most financial sense for your business. Either way, an M&A advisor or investment banker should be able to assist you with ensuring that the sale of your business will accomplish your objectives, so don't be afraid to seek professional advice.

Remember that selling a portion of your business doesn't mean giving up something – it only means letting go of a "part" to let the "whole" thrive. After all, the cost of keeping a non-performing or non-core division could be much higher than the returns.

Conclusion

One of the first things you should consider when deciding whether to sell your company is if suitable alternatives exist to an outright sale. Selling your business often isn't an all-or-nothing decision. Rather, several potential options exist. But before you explore those options, you should consider how committed you are to your business.

Exploring your level of commitment requires being emotionally honest with yourself. If you decide that you're truly committed to your business and would like to double down, then do just that. But oftentimes, entrepreneurs lack the capital to fuel the growth of their business. If this is your situation, growth equity from a private equity firm might be a suitable option for you. Or, a recap might make sense if you want to take some chips off the table but remain involved with your company.

Finally, you can examine if it might be sensible to break your company down into pieces and sell them individually. In some cases, doing so can yield a higher value. If you're unsure, consult with an M&A advisor to help you determine the most prudent course of action that will help you maximize not only your price, but also your level of well-being and happiness.

CHAPTER 5

Exit Options and Buyer Types

"There are two levers for moving men – interest and fear."

– Napoleon Bonaparte, French Military Leader and Emperor

Introduction

Once you've decided to sell, your next step is to explore your potential exit options. The value of your business will vary widely depending on the type of buyer as well as their reason for acquiring you. For example:

- **Financial Buyers:** Financial buyers are constrained to valuing a company based on its fair market value (FMV) by paying a multiple of a company's earnings. Their objective is to buy your business for a reasonable price with the idea of selling it at a profit in three to seven years.

- **Strategic Buyers:** Strategic buyers are companies looking to buy businesses in the same or similar industry to capture synergies. Because a strategic buyer is expecting to extract additional synergies from your company – usually in the form of increased sales and enhanced productivity – they're more likely to pay a premium price, but only if they're bidding against other buyers.

Value is subjective and differs from buyer to buyer. The difference between the price a financial buyer and a strategic buyer may be willing to pay can be significant. No two companies will view your business through the same lens – either on an individual or collective basis.

Once you understand who is most likely to buy your company and their reasons for doing so, then you can probe deeper into the other factors that can affect the value of your business.

While your business can have a wide range of possible values, there are a common set of value drivers that most buyers within an industry find important. You should first identify the type of buyer most likely to buy your business and then focus on the value drivers most critical to them. By educating yourself about the different types of buyers in the marketplace, you can identify which type of buyer is most likely to pay the highest price for your business. This knowledge is essential to knowing what your business may be worth and maximizing its value.

With that being said, all exit options can be broadly categorized into three groups:

1. **Involuntary:** Involuntary exits can result from death, disability, or divorce. Your plan should anticipate such occurrences, however unlikely they may seem, and include steps to avoid or mitigate potential adverse effects.

2. **Inside:** Inside exit options include selling to your children, other family members, your employees, or to a co-owner. Inside exits require a professional advisor who has experience dealing with family businesses, as they often involve emotional elements that must be navigated discreetly, gracefully, and without bias. Inside exit options also benefit from tax planning because if the money used to purchase the company is generated from the business, it may be taxed twice. Inside exits also tend to realize a much lower value than outside exits. Due to these complexities, most business owners avoid inside exits and choose outside options. Fortunately, most M&A advisors specialize in outside exit options.

3. **Outside:** Outside exit options include buyers from outside your company or family. There are four outside buyer types – wealthy individuals, financial buyers, strategic buyers, and industry buyers. We'll cover these four buyer types in the remainder of this chapter.

Outside exits tend to realize the most value. This is also the area where business brokers, M&A advisors, and investment bankers specialize. This book is written with this group in mind.

What follows is a discussion of the four different types of buyers and the goals, considerations, and risks associated with each. I also explore the reasons a company may acquire you, which will help you determine which value drivers to focus on when attempting to improve the value of your company.

The value of your business will vary widely depending on who the buyer is and their reason for acquiring you.

Who's likely to be interested in your business? Chances are they'll fit into one of the four buyer types outlined in the remainder of this chapter.

Buyer Type 1: Individual Buyers

Wealthy individuals, rather than companies, make up the primary pool of buyers for small businesses that sell for less than $5 million.

Individual buyers have two primary goals – to maximize both income and personal freedom. Their main concerns are how risky the opportunity is and whether financing can be obtained to purchase it. For these individuals, the process of buying a business can be quite emotional. For this reason, they often stick to less risky investments and prefer to buy companies with proven track records. When selling your business to an individual, I recommend minimizing the perception of risk.

This group of buyers consists of three subsets – ex-corporate executives, previous business owners, and employees. While the objectives for all three subsets are similar, their perception of risk varies.

Individual Buyer Subsets

1. **Previous Business Owners:** Previous entrepreneurs tend to be more comfortable with risk than ex-corporate executives, but they still attempt to minimize risk as much as possible, especially if the business will be their primary source of income.

2. **Ex-Corporate Executives:** Ex-corporate executives tend to be the least comfortable with risk, especially if they have never owned a business. If you're selling your company to an ex-corporate executive, you should do everything possible to minimize the perception of risk.

3. **Employees:** While insiders are often comfortable with risk because they work in the business and understand it, they rarely have enough capital to complete the acquisition. In most cases, employees don't have the financial wherewithal to purchase your business, and it may be best to avoid these conversations due to the inherent risk in a deal not happening. Most employees dream of business ownership and may make exaggerated claims regarding their financial resources in order to complete a transaction. Many believe they can find an investor to put up the money, or think the entire purchase can be financed through a bank. In most cases, these deals don't happen, which has the possibility of damaging your relationship with your employee and killing a deal with a future buyer.

While there are differences between the individual buyer types, they often share similar goals and criteria. Let's examine those here.

Goal 1: Income

Individuals are usually looking to purchase an income stream. They may have recently lost their job or are unhappy in their career, and want to pursue the American Dream of owning their own company. For most individuals, the business they're buying will be their primary source of income. As a result, they can't afford to take significant risks.

Goal 2: Freedom

Money isn't everything. Studies show that people start or buy small businesses primarily to achieve freedom. Surprisingly, the goal of getting rich falls lower on their list of reasons to buy a business. While an individual's primary objective for purchasing a business is income substitution, they often value freedom and the ability to control their own destiny more than getting rich.

Criteria 1: Risk

Individual buyers' emotions can impact a transaction to a great extent. That's because buying a business is a risky proposition that often requires parting with a substantial portion of their net worth. If they've never owned a business, the decision may be even more difficult.

For this reason, individual buyers tend to stick to industries they're comfortable with. Some, on the other hand, may consider purchasing a company in an unfamiliar industry if they can quickly learn the business or if the owner is willing to stay for an extended period to ensure a smooth transition.

Former business owners are more likely to pull the trigger than a buyer who has never owned one because they're familiar with the inherent risks – especially if they've owned a business in the same industry. As a result, they may be more comfortable with tolerating risk than, say, ex-corporate executives.

Criteria 2: Financing

Individual buyers finance the purchase of a business primarily through a combination of their own cash, seller financing, bank financing, or the use of their retirement funds. The ability to finance a business is a major criteria for individuals. If it's unlikely your business will qualify for bank financing, it's critical that you be willing to finance a portion of the purchase price yourself if you wish to sell your business to an individual.

Recommendations

If an individual is your target buyer, I recommend the following:

- Minimize the perception of risk. If you have a proven track record, showcase it.

- Be prepared to finance a portion of the purchase if the buyer can't obtain financing from a bank.

Buyer Type 2: Financial Buyers

Financial buyers consist primarily of private equity firms, or PE firms for short. PE firms value a business based mainly on its numbers without taking into account the impact of any synergies, unless they're completing a tuck-in acquisition for one of their platform companies. PE firms are the largest and most common buyers of mid-sized companies. Most require a minimum

EBITDA of $1 million per year. Like other companies, they must hire a manager to run your business, which reduces its cash flow. They then deduct the cost of hiring this manager when calculating EBITDA.

There are a few thousand private equity firms in the United States. In addition, there are family investment offices and other types of investors that function similarly to private equity firms. Private equity firms raise money from institutional investors and then invest these funds into private companies on behalf of those investors. The fund usually has a lifespan of 10 years, and the firm normally has a holding period of three to seven years for each business in which they invest. PE firms make a profit from distributions they pay themselves out of the company's earnings that come from reducing the amount of debt they used to acquire the company, and from selling the company at a higher price than they originally paid.

> The primary pool of buyers for small businesses that sell for less than $5 million are wealthy individuals, rather than companies.

Goal 1: Internal Rate of Return

Financial buyers are one of the most common buyers of middle-market companies. They are focused on the return on investment, technically called the internal rate of return (IRR), as opposed to any strategic benefits of the acquisition. An exception to this is add-on acquisitions to a platform company, which comprise a minority of the acquisitions made by PE firms.

PE firms are experts at scaling companies through building strategic relationships and strong management teams, as well as developing efficient sales and marketing programs. A seller may be able to scale a company more quickly with the strategic assistance and direction of a private equity firm. The end goal is to re-sell the business in a few years at a higher price. Returns can increase or decrease based on the amount of leverage, or bank financing, that's used.

PE firms usually purchase a company as a stand-alone entity, and the changes they make to the business post-closing are designed to increase its value and attractiveness to future investors.

As a result, financial buyers analyze a company's cash flow on a stand-alone basis without taking into account any benefits of integration. Their main focus is on the capacity for increasing earnings, and the value of their investment over the next three to seven years.

Price is a critical consideration for these buyers because the business is typically run as a stand-alone company post-closing unless the PE firm owns a similar company in their portfolio. PE firms don't usually plan to integrate a newly purchased company with another company, as would be done by strategic buyers. As a result, they're restricted as to the multiples they can pay, and these multiples are fairly easy to predict. The only exception to these rules is if they already have a company in their portfolio that shares some synergistic benefit with your company.

Criteria 1: Return on Investment

PE firms use significant leverage when purchasing a company because leverage increases their internal rate of return. Most PE firms target an IRR of 30% to 40% per year, which means they must generate a return on invested capital of two to four times if they exit the investment in three to five years.

IRR is also heavily dependent on the holding period, or the amount of time the investment is held, which is why a PE firm's holding period is shorter than the holding period for other buyers. Because they use leverage, or bank debt, to acquire your business, your business must generate consistent cash flow to cover the debt service. As a result, they can't pay more for your business than the numbers dictate.

Criteria 2: Retain Your Management Team

PE firms almost always prefer to retain you and your management team. After all, PE firms aren't usually experts in your industry and will need someone to run the company post-closing. If you or your management team don't stay to operate the business, they must bring in a team to operate it. As a result, most PE firms require that the existing management team stay to operate the business after the closing.

Recommendations

Selling to a private equity firm allows you to sell a portion of the company now, thereby diversifying your risk and potentially achieving a second, larger exit in three to seven years when you re-sell your business. Financial buyers incentivize you to stay involved in the company through the retention of equity, normally encouraging you to retain a 20% interest in the business.

> For example, you sell 80% of your shares now, which is usually enough to secure retirement, and you retain 20% of the company post-closing. Your remaining 20% equity conceivably could lead to a larger exit for you than the initial 80% sale.

If a private equity firm is your target buyer, I recommend the following:

- Build a strong management team. Financial buyers typically require the existing management team to continue operating the business after the closing.

- Increase EBITDA because it's the primary metric financial buyers use to value a business.

Learn More

If you'd like to learn more about how private equity firms think and the types of businesses they like to acquire, you can listen to the following *M&A Talk* episodes, in which I interviewed experts involved in private equity:

- *The Basics of Private Equity* with Jeff Hooke

- *M&A Perspective as a Corporate Acquirer and PE Firm* with Joan De la Paz Hellmer

- *Behind the Scenes of Private Equity* with Jim Evanger & Brent Paris

> Private equity firms are the largest and most common buyers of mid-sized companies. Most require a minimum EBITDA of $1 million per year.

Buyer Type 3: Strategic Buyers

Strategic, or synergistic, buyers also acquire small and medium-sized businesses. Strategic acquisitions frequently occur in developing industries, especially those dominated by venture-capital-backed companies or "winner take all" industries, such as technology platforms. Industries in which research and development are critical to the ongoing success of a company are also often a target of strategic buyers.

Google, Salesforce, Microsoft, Apple, PayPal, and many other technology companies are perennial acquirers. Once nascent industries mature, companies make acquisitions to eliminate competition, such as Facebook's acquisition of Instagram and WhatsApp, PayPal's acquisition of Braintree, Google's acquisition of Motorola, and HP's acquisition of Compaq. In these industries, the pace of growth is so fast that companies furiously compete to become the dominant industry leader in a winner-take-all pot.

There are a variety of reasons a company may seek to acquire you. Understanding these motivations will help you maximize the energy you spend to improve the value of your business. The reasons for making an acquisition may be similar from company to company, but the acquisition strategies and the multiples that are paid can vary significantly.

Some companies, such as 3M, acquire hundreds of small companies at early stages and, therefore, at lower valuations. Many other companies wait for significant customer validation before considering an acquisition and end up paying higher premiums.

For strategic buyers, M&A is only one weapon used within corporate development, but the aim of corporate development is universal – to maximize company value. By understanding your competitor's strategy and objectives, you can take concrete steps to augment the value of your company in the eyes of a buyer.

Knowing the reasons behind an acquisition will:

- Help you understand why executing certain value drivers may yield a higher potential return than other value drivers.

- Assist you in prioritizing your action plans.

- Help you develop the most suitable strategy for valuing your company.

The following are general reasons companies make acquisitions:

- **Spur Innovation:** Agile upstarts are more willing to take greater risks. Larger companies acquire smaller companies because smaller companies are more innovative – most cutting-edge services and products are created in small companies and then brought into the mainstream by larger ones. The more innovative your business and competitive advantage are, the more your business is likely worth. Examples include Uber and Lyft unseating much larger competitors in the $69 billion taxi industry, Airbnb making a significant dent in the $570 billion global hotel industry, or Netflix dominating the $200+ billion TV industry.

- **Increase the Odds of Success:** By completing a large number of the right acquisitions, a company can increase its odds of success. Competitors establish corporate investment funds to make either majority or minority stakes in a significant number of start-ups. Most well-established tech companies have large, dedicated teams that are exclusively devoted to making acquisitions. If you're in an industry with heavy acquisition activity, such as tech, your business is likely worth more than an industry with low acquisition activity, such as retail.

- **Reduce the Chance of Failure:** Jeff Bezos once told his employees, "One day, Amazon will fail." To think that the founder and CEO of a nearly $2 trillion company expects to fail highlights the dynamic changes that have taken place in business since the tech revolution began less than a generation ago. Losses are huge when an innovation at a large company fails. By acquiring other companies, large businesses reduce their long-term chances of failure. The more potential your company has to reduce the chance of failure for an acquirer, the more your company may be worth.

- **Generate Higher Returns:** Strategic buyers have infrastructure in place to leverage your company and can, therefore, often generate higher returns than your company currently does. Strategic buyers can grow or scale your business more quickly than an individual and can pay a higher price because the acquisition represents less risk for them.

For example, if you sold a recipe for a new beverage to Coca-Cola, they would reap more benefits than if you sold the recipe to an individual. Why? Coca-Cola could plug this recipe into its manufacturing, sales, and distribution network and generate significantly more revenue than any individual could.

Strategic buyers generate synergies that come in two flavors:

- **Revenue Increases:** While revenue increases offer the buyer more upside potential, they represent more risk than achieving synergies through a reduction in expenses. It's uncertain how customers will respond to a price increase, for example, while a cut in expenses is more certain and goes straight to the bottom line.

- **Expense Decreases:** Synergies resulting from a decrease in expenses are less risky than those resulting from an increase in revenues, but the amount of synergies is limited – after all, there's only so much that can be cut. Buyers are more willing to pay for synergies due to a reduction in expenses, but the amount of synergies may be less than those due to an increase in revenue.

While strategic buyers may pay a higher price because they can generate higher returns, they often pay the same multiple as other buyers if you include the value of the synergies. Let's consider two examples of the same company:

- **Example A:** $1 million EBITDA x 4.0 multiple = $4 million price of business

- **Example B:** $1.5 million EBITDA x 4.0 multiple = $6 million price of business – In this example, the buyer brings $500,000 in synergies to the deal, so EBITDA increased to $1.5 million from $1 million per year. It appears the buyer is paying a higher multiple, but the higher price is a result of increased EBITDA (due to the synergies) while the multiple is the same.

But buyers don't pay for 100% of the synergies they bring to the table. In fact, most strategic buyers attempt to avoid paying anything for synergies. You can only get paid for these synergies through a strong negotiating posture and having multiple buyers bidding on your business. If your negotiating position is strong, a buyer may share a percentage of synergies with you.

For example, if a buyer brings $1 million per year in potential synergies to the deal, the buyer may share 10% to 50% of the value of the synergies with you. Again, the multiple remains the same, but EBITDA increases based on the amount of synergies the buyer brings to the table.

The amount of synergies the buyer shares with you is based on several factors:

- **Negotiating Skills:** Your negotiating skills and posture.

- **Number of Bidders:** The number of buyers who are competing to buy your business.

- **Amount of Risk:** The higher the risk associated with achieving the synergies, the less the buyer will pay. If the risk of achieving the synergies is high, the buyer may only share 10% to 20% of the synergies with you. If the risk is low, a buyer may share 50% or more.

- **Degree of Opportunity:** The higher the opportunity associated with the synergies, the more the buyer will pay. This is why some technology companies are sold for billions of dollars, even if they're unprofitable.

Strategic buyers are often considered the holy grail of buyers and may pay a higher multiple than others if they can't easily replicate what your company has to offer. Strategic buyers have longer holding periods and have no defined exit plan. They usually intend to fully integrate your company with theirs and focus on long-term fit.

Goal 1: Alternative to Organic Growth

Strategic, or synergistic buyers, are often direct or indirect competitors that purchase a company as an alternative to organic growth. They can include competitors, customers, or suppliers and may be looking to enter new markets or acquire proprietary products, technology, or access to customers.

Acquisitions are just one of many corporate development strategies for companies. Well-funded companies establish strategic corporate development plans to supplement their strengths and mitigate their weaknesses. Corporate development plans include many strategies, such as:

- Internal research and development

- New product development

- Partnerships

- Joint ventures

- Licensing

- Strategic alliances

- Mergers and acquisitions

- Divestitures and carve-outs to offload unprofitable business segments

These buyers typically plan to integrate your company with theirs and hold it indefinitely. They may sometimes seek to acquire only your technology, intellectual property, or customer base, and then make plans to close your operations and lay off your staff after the closing. In the case of an "acqui-hire," a competitor purchases your company with the sole objective of acquiring only your staff and ceases operations at closing. Acqui-hires, also known as acquisition hires or talent acquisitions, are common in the technology sector and other sectors in which talent is scarce and in high demand.

It may make more financial sense for a strategic buyer to grow through acquisitions than to grow by creating new products and services or by acquiring new customers. This happens most often in mature industries, such as the cellular and media industries, consumer products, or really any sector in which organic growth has slowed, and the most suitable option for increasing revenues is to "buy growth."

Goal 2: Access to Technology

The primary reason companies make acquisitions is access to new products and technology, especially after they've been proven successful. Companies look to the ultimate decision-maker – the customer, through customer validation – to determine the potential success of a product. With superior distribution networks, a large company can scale a solution out to the masses at a much faster clip than a small start-up with a limited marketing budget and sales team. By widening its product suite, an acquirer can provide a broader range of solutions to its customer base, and will likely lower customer attrition and improve retention. If your company's product suite is valuable to another company, you may be able to achieve a premium price for your business.

Goal 3: Access to Markets

Some companies acquire a business as a fast entryway into a different market segment. Without an acquisition, a company may have a difficult time making the leap from one industry to another. An acquisition can cut short the leap and mitigate the risk associated with doing so.

For example, a software company in the restoration construction space could acquire a software company in the industrial construction sector. One of the objectives of the acquisition would be to gain quick access to the customer base and gain immediate reputation and credibility in the industrial sector. Such a move could allow the software company to roll out its existing suite of solutions to the customer base of the company it purchased in the industrial segment.

Goal 4: Access to Customers

Another major objective for some companies is access to strategic customers without having to do a lot of heavy lifting. Perhaps a company has made countless futile attempts to gain access to blue-chip customers in their industry. An acquisition would be a guaranteed method of gaining those customers if a competitor they purchase has existing relationships with those clients. If your company has a client base that's the envy of a direct or indirect competitor, you may command a premium price.

An example of gaining access to customers is investment banker Morgan Stanley's acquisition of the electronic trading platform, E*TRADE. The acquisition, which involved more than 5.2 million client accounts with over $360 billion of retail client assets, strengthened Morgan Stanley's position across all segments in the wealth-management business.

Goal 5: Roll-Ups and Multiple Expansion

A large, well-capitalized company may go on an acquisition frenzy, acquiring multiple small competitors and rolling them up into one large entity with the goal of consolidation and expanding the multiple of their company. This plan of multiple expansion is important because the larger the EBITDA, the higher the multiple will be when the business is sold. In roll-ups, consolidation is rapid, and premium pricing is temporary. If you don't sell, you'll be left to compete with the consolidated entity, which will have more resources – a larger sales force, stronger brand awareness, and premium pricing. Roll-ups are a great time to sell if this is occurring in your industry.

> *In a roll-up, the buyer starts by acquiring a platform company, which is typically a company generating a minimum of $20 million in annual revenue. They then complete a series of small, tuck-in acquisitions to round out the capabilities of the platform company by adding customers, technology, and other products to their line.*

Criteria 1: Long-Term Fit

These buyers focus on long-term fit with your company, synergies, and the ability to integrate your company with theirs. If your business isn't a good long-term fit with a strategic buyer, it's unlikely they will acquire you.

Criteria 2: Cost to Replicate

All strategic buyers will re-create whatever products or services you have to offer if they can do so at a lower price than what it would cost to acquire your company. These companies also take into consideration the amount of time it may take to recreate your value proposition. If the company must move quickly, it may make more sense to acquire your company due to the lost opportunity cost of building it from scratch.

Criteria 3: ROI Based on Alternatives

M&A is one of many strategies in a company's corporate development plan. A company always compares its potential returns on an acquisition to its other corporate development options. If a company's corporate development options are bleak, they may be willing to pay a higher multiple than the norm in your industry to acquire your business.

Recommendations

When dealing with strategic buyers, I recommend the following:

- Focus on building a company whose value is difficult to replicate. If the buyer can easily replicate what your company has to offer, they're unlikely to buy your company.

- Be realistic in determining if your company is a suitable investment for a strategic buyer. Consider retaining a middle-market M&A advisor to perform an unbiased assessment of your business to determine if a synergistic buyer may be a likely candidate for your business. In my estimate, less than 20% of middle-market companies can be sold to a strategic buyer for a premium price.

- Hire an M&A intermediary to conduct a private auction. Strategic buyers don't offer to pay for strategic value unless they're aware that other buyers are also competing to acquire your company.

Learn More

If you'd like to learn more about how strategic buyers think and the types of businesses they like to acquire, you can listen to the following *M&A Talk* episodes in the Resources section of our website at morganandwestfield.com, in which I interviewed the heads of corporate development for strategic buyers:

- *How a $2 Billion Strategic Buyer Thinks* with Charlie Burckmyer

- *The Acquisition Process* with Brian McCabe

Buyer Type 4: Industry Buyers

Industry buyers tend to acquire direct competitors. If your business is asset-intensive with less-than-favorable margins, or if it's so specialized that only a competitor will be interested in purchasing your business, selling to an industry buyer may be your only suitable option. In some industries, selling to a financial or strategic buyer may not be an option at all.

Industry buyers are often seen as the buyer of last resort because they usually pay the lowest price. These buyers know the industry well and aren't normally willing to pay for goodwill if they can easily replicate what your business has to offer.

Selling to industry buyers carries an additional risk – a potential leak in confidentiality. Approaching direct competitors is risky, and it's inevitable the word will get out. Once word leaks, competitors are likely to use this against you and may attempt to poach your customers or employees. This can further undermine the value of your company and may also kill a deal you're currently negotiating.

Goal 1: Acquire What They Can't Replicate

For industry buyers, the value of your company lies in what the buyer can't easily re-create.

> *For example, if you want $10 million for your business and the buyer could achieve the same level of revenue by investing $3 million into marketing, they will not buy your company if it costs more than $3 million.*

As with strategic buyers, a competitor may be more likely to purchase your business if it's at a steep discount or if they feel they can't easily replicate it. Most small businesses grow organically, not by acquisition. This is true until a business reaches at least $10 million in annual revenue. A competitor will always consider the cost of replicating your business from scratch. If they can do so at a lower cost than the asking price of your business, it's unlikely they will purchase your business.

Criteria 1: Size

Most companies require a minimum EBITDA of $500,000 per year to consider purchasing a business, usually requiring at least $1 million. As a general rule, you should attempt to sell your business to a competitor who is at least five times your size. On the other hand, the competitor shouldn't be *too* big. The acquisition of your company should have a positive financial impact on their company. The company has to weigh its use of time and whether or not the cash flow from your business justifies the purchase. Companies like to maximize the use of their time and capital, and buying larger companies often makes more sense.

If a company buys your business, they will often have to hire a CEO and pay them an annual salary of between $100,000 and $300,000, which needs to be subtracted when calculating EBITDA.

Recommendations

When dealing with industry buyers, I recommend the following:

- Hire a professional to negotiate on your behalf, as these buyers initially offer a low price. They will only increase their bid if they believe there may be competition to purchase your company.

- Build value in your company that can't be easily replicated by a competitor, such as intellectual property or long-term customer contracts.

- Never show any signs of desperation. If you do, this will be used against you throughout the negotiations.

> Industry buyers are often seen as the buyer of last resort because they usually pay the lowest price.

Conclusion

When valuing your business, keep in mind who your most likely buyer will be. Consider if it's most likely your business will be acquired by an individual buyer, strategic buyer, financial buyer, or industry buyer, then value your business accordingly, based on its size and individual advantages. Knowing this information will help you determine the steps you need to take to maximize the value of your business. You'll also be in a better position to determine the best marketing strategy and overall sales approach to sell your company.

Reminder: Throughout the remainder of this book, I characterize buyers into the two following general categories:

- **Individual Buyers:** This only includes individuals.

- **Corporate Buyers:** This includes financial buyers, strategic buyers, and industry buyers.

For example, if I say your business is likely to be sold to a corporate buyer, I mean it may sell to a financial buyer, strategic buyer, or industry buyer.

PART THREE

Valuation

CHAPTER 6

How Business Size Affects Value

"All big businesses start small."

– Unknown

Introduction

The degree to which your business is considered a "Main Street" or middle-market operation will impact how your company is valued. The primary differences between smaller businesses and those in the middle market are who the ultimate buyer will be and their goals for purchasing a particular business. Each group of buyers has different value expectations, and the value of your business can vary tremendously depending on who is most likely to purchase it. Let's explore how the size of your business can impact the ultimate price you receive.

Main Street vs. Middle-Market Businesses

On Main Street, you'll primarily find "mom-and-pop" businesses such as restaurants, coffee shops, landscaping companies, auto and truck service centers, convenience stores, most franchises, and small businesses that offer services. Buyers perceive Main Street businesses as riskier, which is why they sell at lower multiples than middle-market businesses. Your business can be classified as a Main Street business if the buyer is an individual looking for income replacement. On Main Street, the buyer isn't purchasing a business as an investment; rather, they will be actively working in the company full-time, and it will be their primary source of income.

The middle market is made up of manufacturing firms, distribution companies, wholesalers, and large service-based companies. The middle market is further divided into the lower, middle, and upper-middle markets. Buyers perceive middle-market businesses as less risky than small businesses, and these businesses sell at higher multiples than Main Street businesses. Your business is likely to be considered a middle-market or mid-sized business if the buyer is an institution such as a private equity group, competitor, or other business that will employ a management team to run your business.

> The primary differences between smaller businesses and those in the middle market are who the ultimate buyer will be and their goals for purchasing a particular business.

The Impact of Size on Value

Understanding the different markets can help you determine who is most likely to purchase your business, how they're likely to value your business, and what you should focus on first to maximize the value of your business.

Understanding Buyers Main Street Businesses vs. Middle-Market Businesses		
Criteria	**Main Street Business**	**Middle-Market Business**
Buyer Type	Individual	Institution
How the Buyer Will Operate the Business	Owner-Operator	With a Management Team
Objective of Buyer	Income Replacement	Investment

Size matters when it comes to valuing your business. The type of buyer most likely to buy your business will determine how you should value and sell your company as follows:

- **Small:** Small businesses are marketed on business-for-sale websites with a set price to a broad audience of buyers. Additionally, the business may require no specialized skills to operate, so a larger audience of buyers may be qualified to operate the business. The value for a small business is easier to measure and predict than the value for a mid-market business.

- **Mid-Sized:** Mid-market businesses are often sold using a targeted approach, which involves creating a list of potential acquirers and contacting them directly. If you own a mid-sized business, it's possible you may sell your business to a strategic buyer. If so, the value is more difficult to predict, and the best you can do is establish a minimum floor based on fair market value (FMV). The only way you can determine the actual value is to conduct a private auction and sell your company.

Here's an overview of the primary differences and their implications:

- **Industry:**
  - **Main Street:** Most Main Street businesses primarily operate in the retail and service sectors.
  - **Middle Market:** Most middle-market businesses operate in the service, manufacturing, distribution, wholesale, and technology sectors.

- **Metrics:**
  - **Main Street:** Seller's discretionary earnings (SDE) is the most common metric used to value a business in the Main Street market.
  - **Middle Market:** Earnings before interest, taxes, depreciation, and amortization (EBITDA) is the most common metric used to value a business in the middle market.

- **Profit:**
  - **Main Street:** Main Street businesses generate less than $1 million in SDE.
  - **Middle Market:** These have a minimum EBITDA of $1 million per year.

- **Revenue:**
  - **Main Street:** Most Main Street businesses generate less than $5 million per year in annual revenue.
  - **Middle Market:** Middle-market businesses generate a minimum of $5 million per year in annual revenue.

- **History:**
  - **Main Street:** In addition to being smaller, Main Street companies may also be newer, though this isn't always the case.
  - **Middle Market:** Businesses in the middle market tend to have been established for longer periods of time.

- **Staff:**

  - **Main Street:** Main Street businesses tend to have either a small management team or none at all. The owner often plays an instrumental role in the business, and the business is heavily dependent on the owner. The labor force is rarely unionized.

  - **Middle Market:** Middle-market businesses tend to have a strong management team, may have layers of management, and their workforce may be unionized.

- **Competitive Advantage:**

  - **Main Street:** Typically, Main Street businesses have no strong competitive advantage or proprietary technology.

  - **Middle Market:** Businesses in the middle market are more likely to have a competitive advantage or proprietary technology, which is often why they're acquired. They are also more likely to have intellectual property such as patents, trade secrets, or trademarks.

- **Documentation:**

  - **Main Street:** With a Main Street business, there is often little internal documentation. Most knowledge of the business is in the owner's head, and the financials are often compiled, not reviewed or audited.

  - **Middle Market:** Middle-market businesses have more thorough internal documentation, and their financial statements are often audited or reviewed.

- **Ownership:**

  - **Main Street:** Owners of Main Street businesses are often less sophisticated, and the business is usually locally owned.

  - **Middle Market:** Owners of middle-market businesses are often more sophisticated, knowledgeable, and experienced and employ a wider variety of professional advisors. Ownership may also be dispersed among several individuals, and different classes of equity may exist. Mid-sized companies are more difficult to manage, requiring a broader range of management skills and experience. Most owners of mid-sized businesses have learned to obtain results through others and spend more time working *on* their business as opposed to *in* the business.

- **Financing:**

  - **Main Street:** The owners of Main Street businesses have often financed the businesses themselves using personally guaranteed loans, credit cards, or loans from friends.

  - **Middle Market:** Owners of middle-market businesses often have more access to capital at lower interest rates.

- **Type of Buyer:**
  - **Main Street:** Buyers of small businesses tend to be former business owners or corporate executives who are "buying" a job.
  - **Middle Market:** Buyers of middle-market companies tend to be other companies, such as direct or indirect competitors, or investment firms such as private equity groups.

Differences Between Main Street and Middle-Market Businesses		
Criteria	**Main Street Business**	**Middle-Market Business**
Industries	Retail and Service	Manufacturing, Distribution, Wholesale Service, and Tech
Metrics	SDE	EBITDA
Profit	Less than $1 million	$1 million to $10+ million
Revenue	Less than $5 million	$5 million to $100+ million
History	Established a shorter time	Established a longer time
Staff	Dependent on owner	Strong management team
Competitive Advantage	Weak	Strong
Documentation	Weak	Strong
Ownership	Less sophisticated	More sophisticated
Financing	Less access to capital	Greater access to capital
Type of Buyer	Individuals	PE firms and companies

Learn More

Not only can size impact the value of a company, but whether the business is privately or publicly held can also significantly impact the value. There are over a dozen differences between valuing private and public companies that I've identified. To learn more, you can find the article *18 Differences Between Valuing Public and Private Businesses* on our website at morganandwestfield.com.

Here's a cheat sheet outlining some of the key considerations for each category:

Selling and Valuing Main Street vs. Middle-Market Businesses		
Criteria	**Main Street**	**Middle Market**
Methods	Business-for-sale portals	Targeted, direct approach
Price	Set price	Price range
Audience	Wide audience	Narrow range
Requirements	Few specific requirements	Specific experience required

Conclusion

It's important to understand that these are only rough guidelines or benchmarks for determining whether your company is considered a Main Street or middle-market business. Some middle-market businesses may generate no revenue, while some Main Street businesses may generate $10 million to $20 million per year.

Businesses that can be classified as either Main Street or middle market are tricky to value. Why? These types of businesses can be sold to either an individual or a corporate buyer. And the value expectations of these two groups of buyers vary considerably, which results in a wide range of potential values.

Regardless, understanding whether your business is likely to be classified as a Main Street or middle-market business is the first step to knowing who is most likely to purchase your company and determining its value.

CHAPTER 7

Normalizing Your Financials

"Profit is not the purpose of a business, but rather the test of its validity."

– Peter Drucker, American Business Author

Introduction

If you're like most business owners, you've operated your company in a manner designed to minimize taxes. You may have given yourself and your family members as many perks and benefits as possible, kept non-working family members on the payroll, and written off other expenses through your business – all of which contribute to decreased earnings, and, therefore, a lower value for your business. These common practices are designed to keep your taxes as low as possible. All well and good. But when the time comes to value your business, you must "normalize" your financial statements before you can properly value your business.

The process of normalizing or adjusting your financial statements involves making numerous adjustments so that the true earning capacity of your business can be measured.

Common adjustments include the following:

- Your salary and perks

- Family members' salaries and perks

- Expenses or income that's not expected to recur or continue after the sale

- Personal expenses or perks such as auto, insurance, cell phone, child care, medical, and travel

- Depreciation and amortization, which are both non-cash expenses

- Investment or other non-operating expenses or income

- Interest payments on any business loans which the buyer would not assume

- Other one-time or non-recurring expenses

- Non-operating revenue

Removing owner-specific perks, benefits, and expenses is necessary to determine your business's actual earning capacity. Adjusting your financials allows you to compare your business with other businesses using seller's discretionary earnings (SDE) or earnings before interest, tax, depreciation, and amortization (EBITDA).

- **SDE:** The most common metric used by buyers, business brokers, and many other professionals for valuing Main Street businesses valued using SDE at less than $1 million per year.

- **EBITDA:** The most common metric used for valuing middle-market businesses with EBITDA greater than $1 million per year.

Adjusting your financial statements is one of the most important steps in valuing your business because buyers compare potential acquisitions using SDE or EBITDA. By comparing the SDE or EBITDA of one company with another, buyers can easily understand the value of your business based on your business's actual profit, rather than its taxable income. This normalization helps facilitate a more accurate comparison between companies when valuing a business. The first step to valuing your business, therefore, is to adjust your financial statements so you can calculate the SDE or EBITDA for your business. I will walk you through the process of normalizing your financial statements in the remainder of this chapter.

> You must "normalize" your financial statements before you can value your business.

Definitions of Financial Adjustments

Here are descriptions of the different types of adjustments that can be made when calculating SDE or EBITDA.

- **Discretionary Expenses:** Expenses paid for by your business that are a personal benefit to you. To qualify, the expense must personally benefit you, not your business or your employees. These expenses must be paid for by your business and be documented as an expense on your profit and loss statements.

- **Extraordinary Expenses:** Expenses for your business that are exceptional or unusual. Examples include expenses associated with a natural disaster or relocation of your business, as both are exceptional events. An example that *wouldn't* qualify could include an unsuccessful marketing campaign for your business. This wouldn't qualify because every business occasionally launches marketing campaigns that are unsuccessful, and this is a normal part of doing business.

- **Non-Operating Revenue and Expenses:** Extraordinary expenses or revenue unrelated to your business operations, such as interest earned on investments, revenue from the sale of equipment that is no longer used in the business, or proceeds from a one-time insurance settlement.

- **Non-Recurring Revenue and Expenses:** Expenses that are unusual or one-time in nature and aren't expected to recur, such as one-time legal expenses associated with litigation.

List of Sample Adjustments

The following adjustments are generally allowable and **can** be fully adjusted:

- **Accounting:** Any accounting fees that you've incurred that are unrelated to your business or for personal matters.

- **Amortization:** All amortization.

- **Barter Fees:** Any barter-related fees and income.

- **Child Care:** Payments for child care.

- **Continuing Education:** Any continuing education expenses that aren't related to business operations.

- **Cost of Goods:** Expenses for anything purchased for personal use that wasn't used for the business.

- **Depreciation:** All depreciation.

- **Entertainment:** All personal entertainment and related expenses. Dining with clients is a critical way of building relationships. Any expenses related to entertaining clients *shouldn't* be removed just because they were optional. Only entertainment that was 100% personal should be removed.

- **Insurance:** Any insurance expenses related to your personal needs, such as your health insurance, auto insurance, dental insurance, and life insurance.

- **Interest:** All interest expenses.

- **Legal:** Any personal legal fees.

- **Meals:** Any personal meal expenses.

- **Medical:** Any personal medical expenses.

- **One-Time Expenses:** Any investments in new equipment, one-time start-up expenses, build-outs, major repairs, or one-time legal fees, for example.

- **Owner's Salary:** Your W-2 or 1099 income, including any payroll taxes that have been paid by your company. But only salary in the form of W-2 or 1099 income that appears on your profit and loss statements can be added back. Draws and distributions can't be added back because they don't appear as an expense on the profit and loss statements. Note that the owner's salary is added back when calculating SDE, but normalized to market rates when calculating EBITDA.

- **Payroll:** Any payroll taxes for your salary and salaries of non-working family members.

- **Personal Vehicle:** Any automotive expenses, payments, fuel, insurance, and repairs for personal use.

- **Repairs:** Any repairs for your personal home or other personal property.

- **Salary:** Salaries paid to non-working family members.

- **Supplies:** Personal supplies, groceries, and other non-business-related supplies.

- **Taxes:** Personal and corporate income taxes.

- **Telephone:** Personal cell phone-related expenses.

- **Travel:** All expenses related to personal or nonessential travel.

The following expenses can be ***partially*** adjusted:

- **Charitable Contributions:** Business owners often make charitable contributions with the expectation of receiving business in return. For example, an owner of a restaurant might sponsor a local sports team. Doing so generates publicity and exposure for the business, but directly measuring the results is impossible. You can adjust any personal contributions made that aren't related to your business or in which your business didn't receive any exposure, such as a private donation to your church, but you should leave in any charitable contributions that were expected to benefit your business.

- **Continuing Education:** Some educational expenses are considered discretionary and shouldn't be removed just because they were optional. These expenses should be removed only if they were personal in nature and weren't related to your business.

- **Dues and Subscriptions:** Any personal fees, such as country club dues that have no expectation of benefitting your business can be removed.

- **Retirement:** You can remove your 401(k) and IRA contributions for yourself and any family members only, but don't remove any fees related to maintaining retirement plans that benefit your employees.

- **Travel:** You can remove any expenses related to personal or nonessential travel, but leave any travel expenses that are necessary for business.

The following expenses should be ***normalized*** to market rates:

- **Bad Debt:** Any bad debt that's considered excessive, based on your prior years should be normalized to market rates. You can often normalize this, but you shouldn't remove it completely. If you had bad debt in the past in your business, you're likely to have it again. This should be normalized based on your prior years by deducting an even amount each year, or by spreading a large bad debt expense over several years.

- **Payroll:** Salaries for underpaid employees, such as family members working in your business, should be adjusted to market value.

- **Rent:** If you own the property, the rent should be adjusted to current market rental rates. This amount should be based on the cost to rent the property, not the cost of ownership.

- **Unpaid Family Members:** Salaries for working family members should be adjusted based on the cost to replace them in the marketplace. Salaries for any non-working family members should be fully added back.

The following expenses should ***not*** be adjusted. Note that you can identify these as expenses that can be reduced or limited, but they shouldn't be adjusted.

- **Advertising:** Owners often attempt to remove fees related to advertising because they feel the advertising campaign didn't bring in any business and was considered a wasted expense. But, developing successful advertising campaigns always involves risk. This is a business cost and can't be removed just because the campaign was unsuccessful. A new owner must continue to advertise and market the business, and many campaigns are unsuccessful. Instead, avoid running any risky advertising campaigns before you sell your business.

- **Cash Income:** Unreported cash income should be verified through other means. It's difficult to get paid for this in most cases.

Tips for Making Adjustments

It's important to remember that all adjustments should be concise and verifiable. The more thorough and accurate your documentation regarding your expenses, the better. If you're aggressive or inaccurate with one adjustment, most buyers will question the credibility of everything else you say from that point on. The more detail you provide and the more documentation there is to back up your adjustments, the more likely you'll sell your business quickly and for the best price possible.

If you're conservative, the buyer will assume you've been conservative regarding other issues as well, and the buyer may verify fewer of your representations during due diligence. On the other hand, if your adjustments are aggressive, the buyer may feel the need to perform more thorough and exacting due diligence.

Remember that value is a function of risk – the lower the risk, the higher the value. A buyer who's dealing with a conservative seller will view the transaction as less risky and may be willing to pay a higher multiple than if the buyer is dealing with an aggressive seller who potentially represents more risk.

The fewer the adjustments when selling your business, the cleaner your financials will look. Step back and look at your P&L. How many total adjustments do you have? Don't look at the total in dollars, for example, $436,950 in adjustments, but rather look at the total volume, as in, 14 adjustments in the most recent year. When a buyer first looks at your P&L, the total number of adjustments is one of many factors they will take into consideration when evaluating your business as a potential acquisition candidate. If your adjusted profit and loss statement is clean, with minimal adjustments, the buyer will assume that due diligence will be faster and less expensive, and they may be willing to pay more for your business as a result.

Your goal should be to reduce the total number of individual adjustments, not the total amount of adjustments. Adjustments less than $1,000 don't impact cash flow enough to have a substantial impact on the value of your company, so you should limit your adjustments to those that are greater than $1,000 for small businesses, or $5,000 for larger businesses.

A clean set of financial statements may justify a higher valuation because the buyer may perceive that fewer adjustments must be verified during the due diligence period. If you minimize the number of adjustments, the buyer will assume you'll be easier to deal with than other business owners and are running your business in an upright, above-board fashion. Collectively, these strategies build trust with the buyer, which reduces risk and maximizes value. It may also lessen the burden of due diligence for both you and the buyer.

While minimizing the number of adjustments is preferable, the ideal scenario is to eliminate adjustments altogether at least two to three years prior to a sale. This will increase the value of your business and improve the buyer's odds of obtaining financing for your business.

If you're not sure about an adjustment, keep it in your back pocket to use later in the negotiations. The strategies above don't prevent you from keeping "potential adjustments" in your back pocket to whip out as needed when selling your business. You can mention these adjustments later. Just don't put them in writing, and only mention them if necessary. Not putting them in writing prevents you from having to defend any adjustments that may be subjective.

If the buyer is performing due diligence and they uncover a few problem areas and attempt to renegotiate the purchase price, sit down and have a talk. Walk the buyer through the expenses you decided not to adjust. Tell the buyer you wanted to be as conservative as possible, and point out each expense you believe should be adjusted but which you chose not to.

If you want to maximize your purchase price, there's one trick you can employ – be conservative regarding your adjustments, but be aggressive regarding the multiple you choose when valuing your business. When doing so, you must develop a strong position to justify a higher multiple. You can often justify a higher multiple if you can demonstrate to the buyer that your business is lower risk.

> If you're aggressive or inaccurate with one adjustment, most buyers will question the credibility of everything else you say from that point on.

Here's an example to compare the effects of being conservative vs. aggressive when making adjustments to your financials:

A Comparison of a Conservative vs. an Aggressive Adjustment Approach		
	Business A	**Business B**
Net Income	$1,000,000	$1,000,000
Adjustments	$500,000	$300,000
EBITDA *(Net Income + Adjustments)*	$1,500,000	$1,300,000
Multiple	3.0	3.5
Asking Price *(EBITDA x Multiple)*	**$4,500,000**	**$4,550,000**

How to Produce a List of Adjustments

The best way to prepare a list of your adjustments is to export a "General Ledger" (i.e., a list of all transactions for the accounting year) from your accounting software to Microsoft Excel, a Google spreadsheet, or another similar program. This lists every transaction for each account on your P&L statement.

Once you've exported this to Excel, simply mark each adjustment with an "X" or highlight the entire row. The advantage of doing this is you'll have an organized, detailed report available for buyers when they perform due diligence.

Simply show buyers this report, and the buyer will be able to tie each adjustment to the specific entries in your accounting software. The buyer may also request the source documents, such as receipts for the transactions, so be prepared to produce detailed invoices or receipts if the buyer requests them.

Conclusion

The first step to valuing your business is to normalize or adjust your financial statements. Once you've done so it's a simple task to calculate SDE or EBITDA. And remember, SDE and EBITDA are the starting point for all valuations – every valuation starts with normalizing the financial statements. If you want to simplify the sales process and maximize your price, keep adjustments to a minimum several years before you begin the sales process. Otherwise, export a general ledger from your accounting system and highlight the adjustments to produce an organized, clean report that buyers can use to verify your adjustments.

CHAPTER 8

Measuring Cash Flow

"Business is all about solving people's problems – at a profit."

– Paul Marsden, British Politician

Introduction

Now that you've normalized your financial statements, let's take a deep dive into the two primary measures of cash flow that all valuations are based on for small to mid-sized businesses – seller's discretionary earnings (SDE), and earnings before interest, taxes, depreciation, and amortization (EBITDA). It's critical that you understand how SDE and EBITDA are calculated and which measure of cash flow is right for your business, before you attempt to value your business.

Seller's Discretionary Earnings

Seller's discretionary earnings, or SDE for short, is the most common measure of earnings used to value Main Street businesses. Once you know the SDE of a business, you apply a multiple to arrive at the value of the business.

SDE is defined as:

Pre-tax net income, which is the bottom-line profit that appears on P&L statements, plus:

- Owner's compensation paid to all owners, less the cost needed to replace a second or third owner

- Interest expense

- Depreciation and amortization

- Discretionary expenses such as auto, cell phone, meals, entertainment, and travel

- Adjustments for extraordinary, non-operating revenue or expenses, non-recurring expenses or revenue such as from a lawsuit, and flood damage

Sample SDE Calculation	
Adjustment	SDE
Pre-Tax Net Income	$300,000
Owner's Compensation	+$150,000
Interest	+$50,000
Depreciation	+$50,000
Amortization	+$50,000
Discretionary Expenses	+$100,000
Extraordinary, Non-Operating, Non-Recurring Expenses	+$50,000
Total SDE	$750,000

> SDE is the primary measure of cash flow used to value small businesses and includes the owner's salary.

Earnings Before Income, Taxes, Depreciation, and Amortization

Earnings before income, taxes, depreciation, and amortization, or EBITDA for short, is the most common measure of earnings for middle-market companies. EBITDA allows a buyer to quickly compare two companies for valuation purposes. Once you know the EBITDA of a business, you simply apply a multiple to arrive at the value of the business.

Here's the strict definition of EBITDA:

EBITDA = Earnings (or Net Income) Before Interest (I) + Taxes (T) + Depreciation (D) + Amortization (A)

EBITDA measures the profitability from the core operations of a business before the impact of debt (interest), taxes, and non-cash expenses (depreciation and amortization). It eliminates the impact of financing (interest) and accounting decisions (depreciation and amortization), which vary from company to company. This allows potential acquirers to compare two businesses on an apples-to-apples basis.

EBITDA is the primary measure of cash flow used to value mid to large-sized businesses and does not include the owner's salary.

Here's a description of each component of EBITDA:

- **Earnings (E):** This is the net income of the business after all operating expenses have been paid.

- **Before (B):** This refers to "earnings before ..."

- **Interest (I):** This includes interest from all debt financing, such as loans provided by banks. Different companies have different capital structures or varying levels of debt, which results in different interest payments and, therefore, net incomes. EBITDA allows you to easily compare two businesses while ignoring the capital structure of each business, which changes post-acquisition anyway.

- **Taxes (T):** This includes city, county, state, and federal income taxes. Income taxes vary based on a number of factors and are likely to change post-acquisition for the buyer. As a result, EBITDA includes taxes in its calculation. Note: Only income taxes are added back – don't add back sales or excise tax when calculating EBITDA.

- **Depreciation (D):** Depreciation is a non-cash expense. Methods of depreciation vary by company. Actual cash flow is based on real capital expenditures, not depreciation, therefore, depreciation is also added back.

- **Amortization (A):** Amortization is a non-cash expense and is the "depreciation" (technically "write-down") of intangible assets, such as patents or trademarks.

Sample EBITDA Calculation	
Net Income (Earnings, or "E")	$3,000,000
Interest (I)	+$500,000
Taxes (T)	+500,000
Depreciation (D)	+500,000
Amortization (A)	+$500,000
EBITDA	**$5,000,000**

SDE vs. EBITDA

SDE and EBITDA are two different ways of measuring the profit or cash flow of a business. The main difference is:

- **SDE:** The primary measure of cash flow used to value small businesses, and *does* include the owner's salary as an adjustment.

- **EBITDA:** The primary measure of cash flow used to value mid to large-sized businesses, and *doesn't* include the owner's salary as an adjustment.

SDE and EBITDA vs. Cash Flow

Are SDE and EBITDA the same as cash flow? No, they're entirely different concepts. Here's why – "cash flow" as a term is used loosely in the industry, and you should always ask for a definition whenever someone cites it. "Cash flow" can sometimes refer to SDE or EBITDA, as well as what appears on a business's "cash flow statement" or "statement of cash flows." Unfortunately, many small businesses don't prepare a cash flow statement, which is another reason to verify what someone means when they cite "cash flow."

How SDE and EBITDA Are Used

There are two primary reasons buyers use SDE and EBITDA:

1. **Easily Compare Businesses:** SDE and EBITDA are rules of thumb for comparing businesses. They are approximate measures of cash flow available to the buyer. The goal of calculating SDE and EBITDA is to make an apples-to-apples comparison between businesses. SDE and EBITDA facilitate comparisons across companies, regardless of industry.

2. **Estimate Earnings:** SDE and EBITDA are also used to estimate earnings when a buyer is initially evaluating your company as an acquisition target. SDE and EBITDA are rough estimates of free cash flow – an estimate of the amount of cash flow available to pay back interest or debt and fund the purchase of new equipment, also known as "capital expenditures." Once SDE and EBITDA are calculated, buyers will dig deeper into a multitude of other factors to calculate other measures of cash flow and the multiple, including the growth rate of your company, its gross margins, customer concentration, and hundreds of additional financial and non-financial factors. Once a buyer digs deeper, they will use other measures of earnings to assess your company and will make adjustments to account for interest payments and capital expenditures.

Benefits of SDE and EBITDA

There are many benefits of using SDE and EBITDA:

- **Commonly Used:** SDE and EBITDA are the most used measure of earnings to value small to mid-sized companies.

- **Straightforward Calculation:** SDE and EBITDA are simple to calculate.

- **Eliminates Non-Operating Variables:** SDE and EBITDA eliminate variables that may not impact the buyer post-acquisition, such as interest or taxes. The calculation also removes non-cash expenses, such as depreciation and amortization, so buyers can make their own estimates regarding the amount of these expenses based on when the money is actually expended, not when it's deducted for tax purposes.

- **Allows Comparison:** Because SDE and EBITDA are commonly used and straightforward to calculate, it allows one to easily compare a business's earnings with other businesses. This comparison also facilitates the use of comparable transactions to value a business.

The major difference between SDE and EBITDA is that EBITDA doesn't include the owner's salary.

Downsides of SDE and EBITDA

SDE and EBITDA aren't infallible, however. Here are their major downsides:

- **Rules of Thumb:** Expect buyers to dig deeper into your financials than just calculating SDE or EBITDA. It's important to note that these measurements aren't magic bullets. Just because your business has a high SDE or EBITDA doesn't necessarily mean it will be an attractive acquisition candidate to a buyer.

- **Inaccurate Measure of Cash Flow:** SDE and EBITDA aren't wholly accurate measures of cash flow for a buyer post-acquisition for the following reasons:

  - **Taxes:** SDE and EBITDA ignore the impact of income taxes. Theoretically, a company in a non-taxable state, such as South Dakota, may be worth more than a company operating in a state where they have to pay corporate income taxes.

  - **Depreciation:** Adding back depreciation for companies with significant depreciation and ongoing capital expenditures results in an inflated measure of earnings. SDE and EBITDA are misleading for companies with significant fixed or depreciable assets.

  - **Amortization:** The same can be said for amortization, as in the case of companies with significant amortizable intellectual property, such as pharmaceutical companies.

  - **Working Capital:** SDE and EBITDA ignore working capital needs by not accounting for working capital injections that might be required by the buyer, especially in the case of high-growth companies.

Using the Right Measure of Cash Flow

As noted above, the major difference between SDE and EBITDA is that EBITDA *doesn't* include the owner's salary. Let's explore this difference in more depth.

When To Use SDE

SDE is used to value small, owner-operated businesses. In most small businesses, the owner pockets all the profits of the business and may pay themselves a salary in addition to the profit. Most owners don't distinguish between the profits of the business and their compensation. Other business owners may choose not to pay themselves a salary and instead may take a "draw." In other businesses, an owner may be paying themselves less than what they would have to pay an outside manager.

> For example, a business owner may pay themselves a $40,000 annual salary when a more appropriate salary for their role, based on market demand, would be $150,000 per year.

Additionally, many business owners deduct numerous personal expenses, or perks, through the business that wouldn't be paid to an outside manager to run the business.

> For example, a business may be paying for an owner's personal vehicle, health club membership, vacation home, and personal travel expenses. It's unlikely a business would pay for these perks for an outside manager.

SDE addresses this problem by blending the profits of the business and the owner's compensation into one number. This is the total compensation that would be available to a new owner-operator of the business. In other words, this is what a new owner could potentially put in their pocket, regardless of how they decide to characterize the income – whether via profits from the business, perks, a salary, a draw, or dividends.

SDE makes sense to use when valuing a small owner-operated business. In most cases, distinguishing a business's profits and the owner's compensation isn't practical since most small business owners blur the line between "business" and "personal." Calculating an appropriate manager's salary for a small business is also more subjective than doing so for a mid-sized business.

SDE is normally used with businesses that have less than about $1 million in SDE. The SDE calculation is mainly used by business brokers since most business brokers sell businesses that are run by an owner-operator.

When To Use EBITDA

EBITDA is used to value mid-sized businesses that typically have an EBITDA of greater than $1 million per year, and that can be run by a manager. If the owner currently runs the business, the owner's compensation is normalized to market levels. For example, if the owner's current salary is $500,000 per year, but a more reasonable salary based on current market conditions is $200,000 per year, the owner's compensation is normalized to $200,000 per year.

If the current owner isn't paid a salary, an appropriate market rate salary is deducted when calculating EBITDA. The same is true if the current owner is underpaid. A market-rate salary for a manager or CEO is deducted when calculating EBITDA. Regardless of what the current owner pays themselves, the owner's compensation is normalized to current market levels, which range from $150,000 to $300,000 for most businesses in the lower middle market.

This normalization is necessary because if a private equity group or company bought your business, they would need to hire a manager, such as a CEO or President, to run the company, which is why a manager's salary must be deducted when calculating EBITDA. In a small business, an owner would keep the owner's compensation, but in a mid-sized business, the new owner would need to pay a salary to a manager to run the business.

> *For example, if the SDE is $1 million, and a competitor bought the business and paid a manager $200,000 per year to run the business, their EBITDA would be $800,000 per year ($1,000,000 - $200,000 = $800,000).*

It makes sense to use EBITDA when valuing mid-sized businesses because the majority of businesses in the middle market are purchased by other companies that must hire and pay a manager or CEO to run the business post-closing. EBITDA is mainly used by M&A advisors and investment bankers who specialize in selling businesses to private equity groups, competitors, and other companies.

SDE vs. EBITDA

This chart summarizes the differences between SDE, EBITDA, and Adjusted EBITDA:

SDE vs. EBITDA		
Adjustment	**SDE**	**EBITDA**
Interest (I)	Included	Included
Taxes (T)	Included	Included
Depreciation and Amortization (DA)	Included	Included
Owner's Compensation	Included	*Not Included*
Non-Recurring Income and Expenses	Included	*Not Included*
Non-Operating Income and Expenses	Included	*Not Included*

Here's an example that illustrates the differences:

SDE vs. EBITDA vs. Adjusted EBITDA			
Adjustment	**SDE**	**EBITDA**	**Adjusted EBITDA**
Net Income	$200,000		
Interest (I)	$100,000		
Taxes (T)	$100,000		
Depreciation and Amortization (DA)	$100,000		
Owner's Compensation	$300,000	N/A	N/A
Non-Recurring Income and Expenses	$100,000	N/A	$100,000
Non-Operating Income and Expenses	$100,000	N/A	$100,000
Total	**$1,000,000**	**$500,000**	**$700,000**

SDE and EBITDA Multiples

Are multiples the same for SDE and EBITDA? If the multiples for the business were the same, it would make sense to always value a business based on SDE because SDE includes the owner's salary and is, therefore, higher, which would result in the highest valuation.

Unfortunately, this isn't the case. Multiples of EBITDA are higher than multiples of SDE for the simple reason that a business that's run by a manager should sell for more than one in which the owner is working full-time. If the business is in a situation where either SDE or EBITDA could be used to value it, the choice doesn't usually impact value in the real world because the lower EBITDA figure will be offset by its higher multiple, or the higher SDE figure will be offset by its lower multiple. Here's an example to illustrate. Let's value the same business using both EBITDA and SDE:

> For this example, let's assume an owner's salary is $250,000 per year for this hypothetical business. This results in SDE of $1,000,000 and EBITDA of $750,000 ($1,000,000 - $250,000 = $750,000) if all other factors are the same. Let's then apply multiples based on SDE and EBITDA:
>
> $750,000 EBITDA x 4.0 multiple = $3 million asking price
>
> $1 million SDE x 3.0 multiple = $3 million asking price
>
> Because multiples are higher for EBITDA, the value of this hypothetical company is actually identical for both methods.

Of course, not all valuations across SDE and EBITDA will be this neat. What if, for example, the value based on SDE is higher than the value based on a multiple of EBITDA? Again, it might seem that it would make sense to value the business based on a multiple of SDE, but businesses sold based on a multiple of EBITDA usually include working capital, such as cash, inventory, accounts receivable, and accounts payable in the purchase price, whereas businesses sold based on a multiple of SDE do not.

Let's examine one final scenario that shows the difference of the multiple when it's applied to EBITDA versus SDE.

EBITDA vs. SDE: Multiples vs. Business Value		
	EBITDA	**SDE**
EBITDA	**$750,000**	**$750,000**
Owner's Compensation	*N/A*	*+ $500,000*
Total EBITDA/SDE	**$750,000**	**$1,250,000**
Multiple	*x4.0*	*x3.0*
Value	**$3,000,000**	**$3,750,000**
Working Capital	*+$750,000*	*$0*
Total Business Value	**$3,750,000**	**$3,750,000**

Again, obviously, the math doesn't always work out this perfectly. But, this example illustrates that the value is usually similar regardless of whether you use SDE or EBITDA.

Keep in mind that the owner's compensation represents the main difference between SDE and EBITDA. So generally, when valuing a business with less than $1 million in earnings, use SDE, where the owner's compensation is included. And when valuing a business with more than $1 million in earnings, use EBITDA, where the owner's compensation is excluded.

Deciding on the Year

Another key question when it comes to SDE and EBITDA is which year's SDE or EBITDA should my valuation be based on? Normally, a valuation is based on the last full year's SDE or EBITDA or the most recent twelve months – also called last twelve months (LTM) or sometimes referred to as trailing twelve months (TTM). In other cases, a weighted average may be used if the results are inconsistent from year to year or if business cycles are longer and predictable. Some value may also be placed on projected current year's SDE or EBITDA if the growth rate is consistent and predictable. Some buyers may attempt to use an average of the last three years' SDE or EBITDA, which can pull down the valuation if the business is growing.

Conclusion

Nearly all business valuations are based on some measure of cash flow. The two most common measures of cash flow are seller's discretionary earnings, and earnings before interest, taxes, depreciation, and amortization. The primary difference between the two is that SDE *includes* the owner's salary, while EBITDA does *not*. When valuing your business, it's important to determine which measure of cash flow is the right one to use. As a rule of thumb, for small businesses that are owner-operated and have less than $1 million in cash flow, SDE is the right metric to use. For mid-sized businesses that are likely to be acquired by a corporate buyer and generate more than $1 million per year in cash flow, EBITDA is the right metric to use.

CHAPTER 9

The 8 Essential Principles of Valuation

"Managers and investors alike must understand that accounting numbers are the beginning, not the end, of business valuation."

– Warren Buffett, American Investor and Philanthropist

Introduction

There are eight critical valuation rules you should understand before valuing your business.

Rule 1: Standard of Value Determines Methods Used

A standard of value is the definition of value that's being measured. This is a critical premise in any valuation and determines the specific methods used to appraise the business. Most business appraisals use fair market value (FMV) as the standard of value. Unfortunately, using the wrong standard of value may result in underestimating the value of your business.

Rule 2: Size Affects Multiples

The methods used to value businesses with less than $5 million in revenue are different from those used to value middle-market businesses with more than $5 million in revenue. You must use the right methods for the size of your business.

Rule 3: Valuations Aren't Exact

The range of possible values for a business is wider than for other investments, such as real estate. An experienced appraiser should explain to you how wide the potential range of values is for your company and what factors will have the greatest impact on its value.

Rule 4: Comparable Data is Limited

The ideal way to value your business is to determine what similar businesses have sold for. But, in the business world, there may have been few, if any, recent sales of businesses similar to yours. And even if there are, each business is unique and accurate information on comparable transactions is limited.

Rule 5: Valuations Are Based on a Hypothetical Buyer

An appraiser is making an educated guess as to what a hypothetical buyer might pay for your business. It's difficult to estimate the value of a business because you're guessing how a diverse group of buyers is likely to behave.

Rule 6: You Won't Know Until You Sell It

No pricing formula, expert estimate, or clairvoyant can accurately provide a sales figure that's exactly "right." You won't know how much your business is really worth until the day a buyer writes you a check.

Rule 7: Transaction Structure Impacts Price

In most transactions, some portion of the purchase price is contingent. The terms of your sale, such as the amount of the down payment, the repayment period, and the interest rate, can affect how much a buyer may be willing to pay for your business.

Rule 8: Your Situation Affects Value

Not only can the transaction structure affect the value of your business, but your personal needs also have the potential to affect your business's value. For example, if you aren't willing to stay for an extended transition period, this may close off several exit options and negatively impact the value of your company.

So with that overview, let's dive back into each rule in more depth.

Rule 1: Standard of Value Determines Methods Used

A standard of value is the definition of value that's being measured and determines the method used to appraise a business. A standard of value also reflects who the parties will be to the hypothetical transaction.

> *For example, synergistic value is the value if sold to strategic buyers. Investment value is the value to corporate purchasers. Intrinsic value is the value to financial buyers, such as private equity groups, and fair value is the value to minority partners.*

Why is the standard of value important? Because it determines the methods used to value a business. The same business can have two entirely different values if two different standards of value are used.

What's the right standard of value for your business? Next, I'll explain the two most common standards of value in the M&A world, and walk you through the process to help you determine which standard is most appropriate for your business.

Fair Market Value

Fair market value is the most common standard of value used when valuing or appraising a business. According to the American Society of Appraisers, FMV can be defined as:

> *"The amount at which a property would change hands between a willing buyer and a willing seller, neither being under any compulsion to buy or to sell, and both having reasonable knowledge of the relevant facts."*

Implicit in the definition of fair market value is the following:

- **Price:** The prevailing standard in business transactions is the *highest* price, whereas in real estate transactions, the standard is the "most *probable* price."

- **Willing:** The definition implies that both parties are willing and able to complete the transaction, have sufficient motivation, and are acting in their own best interests.

- **Compulsion:** FMV assumes the parties are dealing with one another at arms-length and aren't influenced by special motivations.

- **Knowledge:** FMV also assumes the parties are well-informed and possess knowledge of the industry, marketplace, and the opportunities and weaknesses of the business.

The real-world understanding of fair market value can be defined as:

> *The highest price a business might reasonably be expected to bring if sold using the normal methods and in the ordinary course of business in a market not exposed to any undue stresses. The market must be composed of willing buyers and sellers dealing at arm's length and under no compulsion to buy or sell, and both having reasonable knowledge of relevant facts.*

Implicit in the real-world understanding of fair market value is the following:

- **Current Market Conditions:** The valuation is based on the current state of the economy and industry.

- **Sufficient Time:** A reasonable period of time is given to properly and competitively market the business using channels customarily used to market similar businesses for sale.

- **Negotiated:** The buyer and seller will hammer out the price based on supply and demand and their unique negotiating positions.

- **All Cash or Equivalent:** Payment is made in cash or its nearest equivalent. For example, the buyer obtains bank financing and pays the seller in cash at closing. If creative financing is involved, an adjustment is made to the valuation.

From that definition of FMV, one might ask, "Why do values sometimes exceed or fall short of fair market value?" Here are a few examples why a business may sell for more or less than fair market value:

- **Unwilling Partner:** An unwilling minority partner refuses to sell and drives up the price of the business at the last minute, which the buyer pays to recover the time and energy they have invested in the transaction.

- **Compulsion:** The seller is forced to sell due to health reasons and doesn't have time to adequately prepare, market, and negotiate the sale, thereby leaving money on the table.

- **Insufficient Knowledge:** The seller failed to disclose that a venture-backed competitor just entered the industry, and the buyer failed to discover this fact during due diligence. The buyer paid a higher price than if they had reasonable knowledge of the relevant facts.

- **Insufficient Time:** A seller is forced to sell for personal reasons and puts the business on the market in haste, thereby receiving less than what they would have if the sale had been conducted in an orderly fashion.

- **Creative Financing:** The seller offered creative financing for the business, which represented an increased risk for the seller and resulted in a higher purchase price.

- **Synergies:** The buyer brought significant synergies to the table in the form of an expanded distribution network, which increased the purchase price by 20%.

Strategic Value

Strategic value, also called investment value, represents the value in excess of fair market value to a specific buyer of a business, usually a strategic buyer. The primary downside to strategic value is that you can't measure strategic value until you know who the buyer is because every buyer is able to extract a different amount of value from the transaction.

For middle-market companies, it's possible your business may sell for more than fair market value if it's purchased by a strategic buyer. But strategic value is impossible to predict. Why? Because you can't quantify the amount of the synergies until you identify the buyer. Many times, in fact, you can never quantify the synergies. That's because most buyers won't tell you the synergies they expect to gain from the acquisition so they can maintain their negotiating leverage. For middle-market businesses, the purpose of a valuation is only to establish a minimum floor price or fair market value. You can then only determine the true value, or strategic value, in the actual marketplace by establishing a competitive auction process.

The Importance of the Standard of Value

What standard of value is most applicable when valuing your business? The standard of value is a critical premise in any valuation because it determines the specific methods used to appraise a business. If you retained an appraiser to value your business and the appraiser used fair market value as the standard of value, you would know that the appraiser didn't take potential synergies into account. In other words, your business may be undervalued if you're using fair market value as the standard of value.

Alternatively, a direct competitor you're negotiating with might argue that you should only receive a 4.0 multiple because prevailing multiples in your industry are 3.5 to 4.5. In this case, you could point out that the majority of buyers in your industry are private individuals who bring no synergies to the table. The buyer you're negotiating with will be able to significantly decrease costs and increase EBITDA by 30% as a result of the acquisition. The buyer can afford a higher price due to the synergies.

Here's another example of the impact of synergies on EBITDA:

- **Without Synergies:** $2 million EBITDA x 4.0 multiple = $8 million value

- **With Synergies:** $2.6 million EBITDA (post-integrated) x 4.0 multiple = $10.6 million value

- **Result:** The value of the business increases by $2.4 million as a result of a 30% increase in EBITDA. But, the value of synergies that the seller receives is negotiated. The seller won't always receive 100% of the value of synergies.

In reality, the exact standard of value is a theoretical term exclusively used by appraisers. You'll rarely hear a buyer mention fair market value or strategic value, but an understanding of the premise upon which the standards of value are based is critical.

> The standard of value is a critical premise in any valuation and determines what methods are used to appraise a business.

Rule 2: Size Affects Multiples

The methods used to value a small business with less than $5 million in revenue are different from those used to value a middle-market business with more than $5 million in revenue.

Multiples

Middle-market companies with annual revenues between $5 million and $100 million commonly sell for four to eight times their EBITDA. But companies with less than $5 million in annual revenue typically sell for only a multiple of two to four. This is because a smaller business is inherently riskier. The business may not have a diversified customer base or produce enough cash flow to withstand a downturn in its market. Small businesses are more vulnerable to failure than middle-market businesses, so they sell at lower multiples.

ROI vs. Multiples

The riskier your business, the higher the rate of return your buyer will require to compensate for that risk, and the lower your multiple will be.

> *It's a simple formula – if your business is larger and less risky, an investor might decide they need only a 20% return, or a 5.0 multiple, to justify the risk. If your business is smaller, a 40% return, or a 2.5 multiple, may be required to justify the investment.*

Middle-Market Businesses Are Easier To Sell

You'll receive more for your business if you're seen as a middle-market company rather than a small business. There's another good reason to grow beyond that $5 million mark if you can – less competition for buyers.

> *For example, there are approximately 300,000 middle-market companies in the United States with annual revenues from $5 million to $1 billion. But there are more than 10 times as many small businesses with revenues of less than $5 million.*

> The riskier your business, the higher the rate of return your buyer will require to compensate for the risk, and the lower your multiple will be.

Rule 3: Valuations Aren't Exact

When obtaining a valuation, you're paying for someone's opinion. This opinion is subjective and subject to change if market conditions change or new information is discovered. A valuation simply represents what a hypothetical buyer is likely to pay for your business, according to one expert.

Valuation Is Mind Reading

In reality, during valuation, the appraiser is attempting to predict how a diverse audience with different preferences, views, and perspectives will behave. Doing this is inherently difficult because the range of possible values for a business is wider than for other investments, such as real estate.

Identifying Value Drivers

Nonetheless, an appraiser's opinion is helpful and can be a realistic starting point for planning your exit. One of the most important roles an appraiser will play is identifying the factors that will most heavily influence the value of your business. Knowing what these factors are will allow you to maximize the value of your business.

Rule 4: Comparable Data is Limited

The ideal way to value your business is to determine what similar businesses have sold for, but that's easier said than done. In residential real estate transactions, it's not difficult to find recent sales of homes similar to yours. In the business marketplace, however, there may have been few, if any, recent comparable sales.

Each Business is Unique

Additionally, each business is unique. Even if you're able to find a somewhat similar sale in your industry, the business won't be the same as yours in terms of location, sales volume, number of employees, or a host of other important factors. This means that even seemingly similar sales of businesses can dramatically vary in price.

Limited Availability of Accurate Information

Even in the unlikely event that you can find the recent sale of a company that closely resembles yours, you may not be able to access accurate information on the business and the transaction. Unlike sales of real estate, which leave a public paper trail, accurate information on sales of businesses can be hard to come by.

Incomplete Information

Watch out for incomplete sales information. Rumor and exaggeration often obscure the real facts behind a transaction. Attend any business event with others in your field, and you're sure to hear that so-and-so sold their business for such-and-such dollars.

> *For example, at a business lunch, you may learn that Emma received $10 million for her business. Even assuming this number has some truth to it – and it may not – you may not be told other important details. For instance, the reports of the sale price may not mention that Emma agreed to work for the buyer for three years, which was included in the purchase price, or that the price included the real estate. It could also be that Emma received only 15% of the purchase price upfront with the rest to be paid over five years, or that 80% of the price was based on an earnout.*

Rule 5: Valuations Are Based on a Hypothetical Buyer

Buyers don't always follow valuations. Rather, an appraiser is making an educated guess as to what a hypothetical buyer might pay for your business. That task is difficult since the potential universe of different buyers for your business is wide.

It's much easier to predict how sophisticated buyers will behave than unsophisticated buyers. Sophisticated investors hire professionals who share the same training and education, as well as uniform perspectives regarding what makes an intelligent investment. Their behavior and perspectives fall along a more narrow band than unsophisticated buyers.

That's why estimating the value of a small to mid-sized business is difficult – you're conjecturing how a diverse group of investors will think and behave. This is an inherently challenging task regardless of one's expertise and knowledge.

> An appraiser is making an educated guess as to what a hypothetical buyer might pay for your business. That task is difficult since the potential universe of different buyers for your business is wide.

Rule 6: You Won't Know Until You Sell It

A key task in selling any business is coming to terms with how much it's worth. Price your business too high, and you'll scare off potential buyers. Price it too low, and you'll leave money on the table.

No Valuation is Exact

If you expect precision in pricing your business, you'll be disappointed. There is no way to predict what the "right" sale price will be. So, while you need to price your business sensibly, you won't know how much it's really worth until the transaction is complete.

Start High and Negotiate

If you have a healthy small business, you'll probably pick an initial asking price toward the top of your range and then, if necessary, be prepared to back off a bit in negotiating the final price. If you own a middle-market business, you'll most likely go to market without an asking price. Regardless, you'll need to take into account the general economic climate, as well as trends in your industry, whether positive or negative. And, of course, if you have to sell quickly, you may be required to settle for less than you might otherwise receive.

Rule 7: Transaction Structure Impacts Price

In most transactions, some portion of the purchase price is contingent. It follows that the terms of the sale, such as the amount of the down payment, the repayment period, and the interest rate, can all affect how much a buyer may be willing to pay.

An installment sale can affect your sale price calculation in another important way – you may want to charge a higher interest rate if you'll be paid over a longer period of time rather than a shorter time since you'll be exposed to more risk during the repayment period.

Keep in mind that selling on an installment plan can benefit you because it often puts you into a lower income tax bracket than if you received the entire sale proceeds in one lump sum. So it's not just the value of your business that matters, but also what you put in your pocket. The overall transaction structure, such as whether your sale is positioned as an asset or stock sale, can significantly impact your after-tax proceeds.

Rule 8: Your Situation Affects Value

Not only can the transaction structure affect the value of your business, but your personal needs also have the potential to affect your business's value. How?

Poor health or financial pressures may force you to sell. If, for these or other reasons, you need to sell quickly, you'll probably have to accept less than the optimal sale price. Similarly, if you're unable or unwilling to work for the buyer, even for a short time after the closing, that fact may diminish the value of your business in the buyer's eyes. Many buyers prefer to have the seller stay on board during the transition period, and your business may be worth less if you aren't willing to stay after the closing.

Conclusion

Valuing a business isn't just about the numbers. Rather, there are several important concepts to understand before you attempt to value your business. The following is a summary of the most important rules regarding business valuations:

1. **Standard of Value Determines Methods Used:** The standard of value determines the methods used to value your business. The two most common standards of value are fair market value and strategic value.

2. **Size Affects Multiples:** You must use the right valuation method that's appropriate for the size of your business. Small businesses are valued using a multiple of SDE, and larger businesses are valued using a multiple of EBITDA.

3. **Valuations Aren't Exact:** Business valuations are a range concept based on what a *hypothetical* buyer might pay for your business.

4. **Comparable Data Is Limited:** Comparable transaction data is limited due to the unique nature of businesses and the private nature of the transactions.

5. **Valuations Are Based on a Hypothetical Buyer:** An appraiser is conjecturing what a hypothetical buyer may pay for your business. What a real buyer may pay can be significantly different.

6. **You Won't Know Until You Sell It:** You won't know how much your business is really worth until the day you close the sale.

7. **Transaction Structure Impacts Price:** How the transaction is structured can have a significant impact on the price you receive.

8. **Your Situation Affects Value:** Your personal needs can also impact the price you receive.

CHAPTER 10

Valuation Methods

"The value of a business is the cash it's going to produce in the future."

– Warren Buffett, American Investor and Philanthropist

Introduction

There's a feature on the online shopping and auction site eBay that allows registered sellers to research the prices of items. If you're trying to unload that glass vial of Mount Saint Helens eruption ash, for instance, eBay says you can expect to fetch about $10. A barely used Vlad the Impaler 7" action figure is $50, give or take. That Bruce Lee commemorative coin that's been hiding in the junk drawer for decades? Most are selling for $4 to $11.

One of the first steps in preparing your company for sale is to put a price tag on it. Unfortunately, when it comes to valuing a business, it's not quite as simple as entering a three-word description into a search engine and pressing "Enter."

So, if you're in the market for an objective opinion about the value of your business, you'll likely hire a professional. But what methods should they use in appraising your company? Do you need a formal, written appraisal, or is a verbal appraisal sufficient?

There are few objective standards for valuations when it comes time to plan the sale of your company. In this chapter, I offer several recommendations for hiring the right appraiser and making sure you receive an appraisal in a format that meets your needs.

Overview of Methods of Appraisal

Pricing a business is based primarily on its profitability. Profit is the number one criteria buyers look for when seeking a business and the number one factor buyers use to value one. There are other variables buyers may consider, but the majority exclusively look for one thing – profit.

That being said, there are two primary methods for valuing a business:

1. **Multiple of Seller's Discretionary Earnings (SDE) or Earnings Before Interest, Taxes, Depreciation, and Amortization (EBITDA):** Multiply the SDE or EBITDA of the business by a multiple. Common multiples for most small businesses are two to four. Common multiples for mid-sized businesses are three to seven times EBITDA.

2. **Comparable Sales Approach:** Research prices of similar businesses that have sold, and then adjust the value based on any differences between your company and the comparable company.

Before we dive more deeply into each of these methods, let's first explore how to select the right appraiser.

> Without hands-on experience buying and selling companies comparable to yours, an appraiser won't be in a position to advise you on what actual buyers in the marketplace are looking for and what you can do to improve the value of your business.

Selecting an Appraiser

When assessing the value of your business, you should consider the following questions:

1. Who will value my company?
2. What methods will that person use to value my company?
3. What form will the valuation take?

The envelope, please …

Choosing an Appraiser

Whoever values your business should have real-world experience buying and selling companies, whether they're a business broker, M&A advisor, or investment banker. They should also have had direct involvement in selling companies comparable to yours in size and complexity. Specific industry experience related to your business is helpful but not essential unless you own a business that operates in a highly specialized industry. The landscape is littered with professionals who possess the academic qualifications to appraise your business but who have never sold a company. These individuals can include accountants, CPAs, financial advisors, or business appraisers.

It's essential that your appraiser have real-world M&A experience. Without hands-on experience buying and selling companies comparable to yours, an appraiser won't be able to advise you on what actual buyers in the marketplace are looking for and what you can do to improve the value of your business. Before you choose an appraiser, ask them how many companies they've sold, and what percentage of their professional practice is devoted to buying and selling businesses versus other activities.

Choosing the Right Methods

Most business appraisers perform business valuations for legal purposes, such as divorce, bankruptcy, tax planning, and so forth. But these types of appraisals differ from an appraisal prepared for the purpose of selling your business. The methods used are different, and the values will be altogether different, as well. It's because of these differences in types of appraisals that finding an appraiser who has real-world experience is so important. Working with an appraiser who spends a significant amount of their time buying and selling businesses will help ensure you receive an appraisal that will stand the test of buyers in the real world.

Choosing the Right Form

Your M&A valuation can take one of two forms:

- **Verbal Opinion:** This typically involves the professional spending several hours reviewing your financial statements and business, then verbally communicating their opinion of value to you.

- **Written Report:** A written report can take the form of either a "calculation of value" or a "full report." While a calculation of value can't be used for legal purposes, such as divorce, tax planning, or bankruptcy, it can be used for selling a business.

Is a verbal or written report preferable? It depends. A verbal opinion of value can be useful if you're the sole owner and the report doesn't need to be reviewed by anyone else.

The limitations of a verbal opinion of value are:

- **Possible Confusion:** There's the potential for confusion or disagreement if there are multiple owners. If a disagreement does arise, supporting documentation for each side will be necessary to resolve the disagreement.

- **No Hard Copy:** You won't have a detailed written report to share with other professionals on your team, such as attorneys, your accountant, financial advisor, or insurance advisor.

- **Hard to Double Check:** It will be time-consuming to seek a second opinion since a new appraiser will have to start from scratch.

For these reasons, I recommend a written report, particularly if anyone else will be involved in the planning process.

I've been involved in situations in which CPA firms have valued a business, but had little documentation to substantiate the basis of the valuation.

> *In one case, the CPA firm's measure of cash flow wasn't defined – it was simply listed as "cash flow." This is a misnomer as there are few agreements regarding the technical definition of this term. As a result, any assumption we might have made would have led to a 20% to 25% error at minimum in the valuation of the company.*

By having a written report in which the appraiser's assumptions are documented, it's simple to have these assumptions reviewed or discussed.

Note: When hiring someone to value your company, you're paying for a professional's opinion, but keep in mind that this opinion may differ from a prospective buyer's opinion. Some companies have a narrow value range of perhaps 10% to 20%, while other companies' valuations can vary widely – sometimes by as much as 200% – based on who the buyer is.

By having your business valued, you'll be able to understand the potential range of values your company may attain and the factors that can impact the value. As an example, business appraisers' valuations often contain a final, exact figure, such as $2,635,568. Such precision is misleading in a valuation for the purpose of a sale. It's preferable to have a valuation that results in a more realistic price range, such as $2.2 million to $2.8 million. An experienced M&A professional can explain where you'll likely fall within that range and why.

Now, let's dive into the two main methods for valuing a business.

Method 1: Multiple of Earnings

Here's how you can value your business using the multiple of earnings method:

Step 1: Determine the SDE or EBITDA for the previous 12 months, or your latest fiscal year.

Step 2: Multiply your business's SDE or EBITDA by the multiple.

Example: $1 million EBITDA x 4.0 multiple = $4 million value of business

Common Multiples

Here are common multiples for Main Street businesses generating less than $5 million in annual revenue:

- **Retail businesses:** 1.5 to 3.0 times SDE
- **Service businesses:** 1.5 to 3.0 times SDE

- **Food businesses:** 1.5 to 3.0 times SDE

- **Manufacturing businesses:** 3.0 to 5.0 times SDE

- **Wholesale businesses:** 2.0 to 4.0 times SDE

Here are common multiples for middle-market businesses generating $5 million to $100 million in annual revenue:

- **Retail businesses:** 3.0 to 7.0 times EBITDA

- **Service businesses:** 3.0 to 8.0 times EBITDA

- **Food businesses:** 3.0 to 7.0 times EBITDA

- **Manufacturing businesses:** 3.0 to 9.0 times EBITDA

- **Wholesale businesses:** 2.5 to 7.0 times EBITDA

Note: Multiples vary with the current economic climate and market conditions. How do you determine the appropriate multiple? The easiest way is by researching comparable transactions. However, in many cases, comparable transactions may not be available. Without access to accurate information regarding comparable transactions, you must rely on a professional's experience, but the guidelines above can be a helpful starting point.

Which Year to Apply the Multiple To

Which year do you base the value of your business on? Generally, you should base the value on the most recent fiscal year or the most recent 12-month period. But if your business is experiencing an unusual uptick in revenue that's unlikely to recur, it may be more appropriate to base the price on an average of the financial results for the previous two to three years. Likewise, if your business is rapidly and consistently expanding, you may be able to justify basing the price on a blend of historical and current results. Either way, the decision regarding which year to base the valuation on should be representative of the results the buyer should expect moving forward. In most cases, this means basing the valuation on an average of the previous three years, the latest fiscal year, or the most recent 12-month period.

Multiples for Larger Businesses

Most mid-sized businesses are priced at four to eight times EBITDA. The multiple varies based on several factors, primarily the industry that a business operates in.

Larger businesses sell at higher multiples. To demonstrate:

- **Business A:** EBITDA of $1 million per year = 3.0 multiple, or an asking price of $3 million

- **Business B:** EBITDA of $5 million per year = 5.0 multiple, or an asking price of $25 million

- **Business C:** EBITDA of $10 million per year = 7.0 multiple, or an asking price of $70 million

The relationship between EBITDA and multiples is direct. As the SDE or EBITDA of a business increases, so does the multiple. Larger businesses are seen as more valuable by sophisticated investors because they're viewed as more stable, have more professional management in place, and are less dependent on the owner to operate. This simple, clear relationship between the size of a company and its multiple is widely accepted by both intermediaries and buyers.

> The relationship between EBITDA and multiples is direct. As the SDE or EBITDA of a business increases, so does the multiple.

Method 2: Comparable Sales Approach

The comparable sales approach is a method for pricing your business based on the prices of similar businesses that have changed hands, with adjustments made to account for any differences between your company and the subject or comparable company.

Buyers will dismiss you as unrealistic if you compare your business to Amazon, Facebook, Google, or other companies with market capitalizations in the hundreds of billions of dollars – that is, unless your company is also valued in the hundreds of billions of dollars. If you point out comparable transactions in your negotiations with a buyer, stick to comparisons with companies in your industry that are similar in size and market potential to your own.

Comparable Transactions Are Scarce

Unfortunately, finding truly comparable transactions is difficult. Typically, all parties involved in a sale wish to keep the price and terms secret, especially the buyer. Serial corporate acquirers do their best to keep the prices they pay confidential because knowledge of the valuation could drive up the price they will have to pay for future acquisitions. That's because future sellers could use this knowledge against them if details of their acquisition prices are known.

Reporting Data Isn't Mandatory

Public companies are required to disclose the price and terms of an acquisition via Form 8-K with the U.S. Securities and Exchange Commission (SEC) if the transaction is considered "material." No such requirement exists for privately held companies, which account for most deals in the lower and middle markets.

"Material" isn't defined, but is generally believed to include acquisitions in excess of $50 million. It can also be based on a percentage of the acquirer's revenue. For example, the transaction might be considered material if the target's revenue is greater than 5% to 10% of the revenue of the acquirer.

Transactions Must Be Relevant

If knowledge of larger transactions does exist, the data is often considered irrelevant unless the companies are similar in size to the target. Billion-dollar transactions have few similarities with companies in the lower middle market. Additionally, there are vast differences between valuing public and private businesses. As a result, it's important that comparable transactions be similar in size for the transactions to be considered relevant.

> Serial corporate acquirers do their best to keep the prices they pay confidential because knowledge of the valuation could drive up the price they have to pay for future acquisitions.

Information is Limited

Transaction databases do exist, but the information is limited and used primarily by appraisers who are valuing a business for legal purposes, such as divorce or estate planning. Also, few databases include the name or other identifying information of the subject company, so the information often can't be verified.

Using the Comparable Sales Approach

The comparable sales approach is often difficult to use because the prices of businesses that have been sold aren't readily available. The best source of comparable transactions is from a business broker, M&A intermediary, or business appraiser who has access to private transaction databases. There are several databases with comparable business sales, but the information tends to be sparse or incomplete, so you can't rely on this data entirely. Collectively, these databases contain about 100,000 transactions.

When researching deal activity in these databases, you can narrow down the transactions based on several criteria, such as industry, size, and geographic location, but you may be left with few to no comparable transactions.

For example, you may search a database using the following criteria:

- **Industry:** Food manufacturing

- **Size:** EBITDA of $1 million to $10 million

- **Location:** Southwest

If you search one of the databases with this information, you may be lucky to receive a handful of comparable transactions. But let's say you perform this search and uncover the following three transactions:

- **Transaction 1:** Granola manufacturer, $3.2 million EBITDA, Georgia, $12.8 million selling price

- **Transaction 2:** Chocolate manufacturer, $9.8 million EBITDA, Ohio, $42.4 million selling price

- **Transaction 3:** Breakfast cereals manufacturer, $1.2 million EBITDA, Wyoming, $4.9 million selling price

You may be left with the following questions:

- What were the terms of the transaction? Was the purchase price paid in cash? Was there a seller note? Was there an earnout?

- What was the growth trajectory of the business? Was it on an upward or downward path?

- Was the seller in distress?

- What did the price include? Did it include working capital?

- How was EBITDA calculated?

- Was the business sold to a related party?

- Was the business sold using a private auction, which would maximize the purchase price?

- Was the business sold to a financial or strategic buyer?

- Did the seller retain any equity?

- How much work in progress did the sale include?

- Did the seller stay on to manage the business?

- How strong was the business's competitive advantage?

- How competitive was the industry?

Unfortunately, you won't find answers to most of these questions in the databases. The best the databases can do is give you a taste of the range of potential multiples in an industry, and then you must make further adjustments based on dozens of other factors.

Alternatively, you can broaden your search terms by, for example, removing the geographical location criteria. As a result, you'd be left with transactions filtered by industry and size, which are the two most useful criteria. Even then, the transactions can consist of businesses that can be significantly different from one another.

Finding Comparable Data

When it comes time to sell your company, information on comparable transactions can be useful in defending your price.

Here are some additional tips for documenting comparable transactions:

- **Obtain From the Source:** Your best bet for documenting comparable transactions is to obtain the information directly from sources within your industry. The more information on each transaction you have, the stronger your case will be. If the transaction information appears in a reputable publication, your argument can be more convincing, as well. Sellers and advisors are more likely to share transaction information than buyers since buyers normally seek to keep the key details private so as not to drive up future prices. In other words, they don't want the information to be used against them.

- **Set Up Google Alerts:** Set up a content-notification service, such as Google Alerts, to give you a heads up regarding recently announced acquisitions in your industry, using the following:

  · **Industry keywords:** Software, tech, online business, and so on

  · **Size keywords:** Small, middle market, and lower middle market

  · **Acquisition keywords:** M&A, acquisition, acquire, and so forth

- **Attend Industry Events:** Attend industry events and network with well-connected influencers in your industry. Ask them if they know of any recent acquisitions or anyone who may have been a party to a recent acquisition.

- **Join Meetup Groups:** Attend industry-related meetup groups and network with those in your industry to form new relationships that may lead to helpful information.

- **Network With Professional Advisors and Investors:** Network with angel investors, attorneys, accountants, investment bankers, M&A advisors, private equity investors, and other professionals to obtain transaction information. Set up Google Alerts to alert you to tombstone ads that investment bankers and M&A advisors place on their websites after a successful transaction. Offer to pay professionals for their time, keeping in mind that the more successful the professional, the less likely they'll be to give away their time for free.

- **Prepare a Buyer List:** Prepare a spreadsheet with two tabs – one for potential buyers and one for possible sources of buyers. The buyer list should contain the following columns: company name, contact name, website, contact information, number of employees, revenue, completed acquisitions, and potential synergies. The possible sources tab should contain a list of the sources and any relevant contact information. Here are more tips for your buyer list:

  · **List size:** Your list should contain a minimum of 50 buyers and, ideally, at least 200.

  · **Company size:** Most companies on the list should be at least 5 times the size of your company.

- **Products and services:** The companies on your list should offer products or services complementary to yours.

- **Acquisitions:** Note if the company has recently made any acquisitions. If so, jot down any details of the transaction that you're aware of, including the name of the company, size, and more.

While transaction databases can be helpful, they should be used with care. Also, understand that the data they contain is limited, and you'll never know to what degree two businesses are comparable since much of the information can't be independently verified or further researched.

What's Included in the Price

When valuing your business, it's important to consider what assets are included in the price. The price should include all tangible and intangible assets used in the business to generate the cash flow your business produces, including all the equipment and assets required to operate your business on a daily basis. Following is a list of considerations:

- **Included Assets:**
  - Furniture, fixtures, equipment, vehicles, and all other hard assets used in your business

  - Leasehold improvements

  - Business name, website, email addresses, phone number, software

  - Business records, financial records, client and customer lists, marketing materials, contract rights

  - Trade secrets, whether registered or not, and intellectual property such as patents and trademarks

  - Transfer of licenses and permits

  - Training, covenant not to compete

- **Excluded Assets:**
  - Real estate and land – these should be priced separately

- **Working Capital:** Working capital is *not* included in the asking price for small businesses but *is* included in the purchase price for mid-sized businesses. Working capital consists of the following assets:

  - Accounts receivable (AR), which consists of any money owed to you by your customers for past work.

  - Inventory, but bear in mind the difference between equipment and inventory.

Equipment is fixed assets and consists of machinery, tables, chairs, vehicles, and other assets used in the operations of your business. Inventory is salable. For example, inventory consists of fuel for a gas station, food for a restaurant, clothing for a retail store, and so on. Inventory is consumable and must be constantly replenished.

- Accounts payable (AP), which is an assumption of accounts payable, short-term debt, and accrued expenses.

The formula for calculating working capital is as follows:

Accounts Receivable + Inventory - Accounts Payable = Net Working Capital (NWC)

> The price should include all tangible and intangible assets used in the business to generate the cash flow stream that's being sold.

Special Situations

Valuing a business isn't always a straightforward exercise. Here are several unique situations you may encounter.

Accounting for Synergies

There are five types of synergy calculations – cost savings, revenue enhancement, process improvements, financial engineering, and tax benefits. But the valuation methods mentioned above don't consider possible synergies that might be achieved. The value of synergies is impossible to calculate without knowing who the buyer is and having access to their financial statements. The value of synergies is also different for every buyer, meaning that the value of your business can differ substantially depending on who the buyer is.

Pricing a Business That's Losing Money

Let's say you have a manufacturing business that's breaking even, but you invested $1 million in it. Surely, it must be worth what you put into it, right?

Most buyers consider buying a wide variety of businesses. For this reason, the price of your business must be competitive with other investment alternatives available to buyers. Imagine you're a buyer – which of these businesses would you buy?

- **Business A:** Asking $5 million – the business is breakeven

- **Business B:** Asking $5 million – EBITDA is $1.5 million

The answer is obvious – 99% of buyers will purchase Business B. Always keep in mind that the number one thing buyers look for in a business is profit – specifically the ratio between the asking price and EBITDA – or the multiple.

Why are there businesses for sale that aren't profitable? Because they *aren't* profitable.

Yes, they're for sale, but they haven't sold. Why do you think you don't see many businesses priced right that are still on the market? It's because they've already sold – because they were priced correctly. The fact is that 80% to 90% of businesses are overpriced, so don't let the fact that there are overpriced businesses on the market deceive you.

Getting Paid for Potential

Do buyers of businesses pay for potential, or do they base their valuation strictly on SDE or EBITDA?

Let me explain what buyers want and why. To do that, let's start by establishing some truths:

1. The closer the potential is to being realized, validated, and revenue-generating, the more the buyer will pay for the potential in a business.

2. Buyers prefer a proven business with revenue and cash flow in which "unrealized potential" has already been realized.

3. Ideas in rough form are worth little to buyers.

Here are a few examples of potential:

- **Selling to a New Customer Group:** Acme Corporation believes they could dramatically grow their business by selling their existing products to a new customer group. The idea is just an idea at this point, and they have never sold one of their products to this customer group.

- **Creating a New Product or Service:** Acme Corporation believes it could dramatically increase revenues by introducing a new product to the marketplace. The product is just an idea and hasn't been developed yet, hasn't been user tested and validated, and hasn't generated any revenue.

- **Creating a New Product Idea:** Ralph has an amazing business idea for a new product. He has a business plan, but no progress has been made beyond creating the idea. The idea hasn't been validated, and no sales have been made.

- **Creating a New Business Idea:** Roger started a business that looks great on the surface. He spent over a million dollars building the business, but it generates no revenue and is currently breaking even. Roger believes his business has significant potential, but the business hasn't generated any profits yet.

These are examples you may see as potential opportunities, but when selling a business, you'll soon discover that most buyers will be willing to pay little for these types of potential.

Under what circumstances are buyers willing to pay for potential? If potential exists in your business, what can you do to get paid for it? Here are some general characteristics of potential:

- The idea is only a rough idea. There are no plans or data to back it up, and little has been executed. Implementation hasn't begun, and the idea hasn't been validated.

- The business, division, product, service, or idea hasn't generated any revenue.

If there's no proof the idea will generate revenue, it may be a good idea, but it's still just an idea. Buyers will be hesitant to pay for ideas unless they have generated revenue. As former Apple CEO Steve Jobs once said, "To me, ideas are worth nothing unless executed."

So, what are they willing to pay for? Buyers want:

- **Revenue:** Future revenue that's secured by a contract. But you'll achieve a higher valuation if you wait until the revenue from the contract is recognized on your financials before you attempt to sell your company.

- **Products in Development:** A product in development that has generated revenue. The stronger the validation, the more the buyer will pay. It's even better if you have a track record of developing successful products.

- **Synergies:** Buyers won't pay for synergies unless they have to. Generally, only larger companies pay for synergies and only in an auction in which they are competing with other companies to acquire your business.

But what about venture capitalists? Don't they buy ideas? Yes, but with a catch.

Venture capitalists buy more than an idea. They're also investing in a team that will execute the idea and turn it into reality. Venture capitalists don't buy a business outright. They normally make a minority investment in the business in which the ownership team will remain.

So venture capitalists aren't buying an idea. Rather, they're investing long-term in a business and a team that will stay in place to execute the idea. In earlier rounds, investors focus more on the strength of the team than the actual idea. If you expect to create a visionary idea and then sell that idea to a third party to execute, think again, because you'll get paid little for selling an idea that someone else will execute.

With that being said, here's my advice:

- If you have unrealized potential, point it out to a buyer. But the less polished and unvalidated the opportunity, the less you can expect to get paid for it.

- Treat ideas as icing on the cake. Use potential to motivate the buyer to purchase your business but don't expect to get paid for ideas if no revenue has been generated.

- To demonstrate the potential, crystallize it into a one-to-two-page business plan. Outline your assumptions and back them up with data. Better yet, run a series of experiments to validate your assumptions in the real world.

- If you believe a buyer may pay for synergies, consult with an M&A advisor. An M&A advisor may be able to determine if synergies exist and will be able to conduct a private auction in which multiple buyers are competing to acquire your company.

Keep in mind that while you may see potential in your business, potential alone isn't a solid basis for selling your company. What buyers want is actual revenue and profitability, so the more you can demonstrate the revenue-generating possibilities of your business's opportunities for growth, the more interested they will be in buying your company.

> If no revenue has been generated, most buyers will be willing to pay little for an idea.

Preserving and Increasing Value

Once you've calculated the value of your business, you should then plan how to both preserve and increase that value.

Preserve the Value

After you've established the range of values for your company, you should develop a plan to "preserve" this value. Note that preserving value is different from increasing value. Preserving value primarily involves preventing a loss in value.

Your plan should contain clear strategies to prevent or mitigate catastrophic losses in the following categories:

- **Litigation:** Litigation can destroy the value of your company. You and your team should prepare a plan to mitigate the damaging effects of litigation. Have your attorney perform a legal audit of your company to identify any concerns or discrepancies that need to be addressed.

- **Disasters:** Meet with your CPA, attorney, financial advisor, and insurance advisor to discuss potential losses from natural or man-made disasters that can be minimized through intelligent insurance planning. Examples include your permanent disability, a fire at your business, a flood, or other natural disasters.

- **Taxes:** You should meet with your CPA, attorney, financial advisor, and tax planner to minimize potential tax liabilities.

Important: The particulars of your plan to preserve the value of your company also depend on your exit options, which we discuss elsewhere in this book. Many elements of your exit plan are interdependent. This interdependency increases the complexity of the planning process and underscores the importance of a team when planning your exit.

Only after you've taken steps to preserve the value of your company should you begin to actively take steps to increase the value of your company.

Increase the Value

This plan begins with an in-depth analysis of your company, its risk factors, and growth opportunities. At this stage, knowing which type of buyer is likely to acquire your business is crucial.

Here are some steps you can take to increase the value of your business:

- Avoid excessive customer concentration.

- Cut back on disproportionate supplier dependency.

- Increase recurring revenue.

- Increase the size of your repeat-customer base.

- Document and streamline your operations.

- Build and incentivize your management team.

- Physically tidy up your business.

- Replace worn or old equipment.

- Pay off equipment leases.

- Reduce employee turnover.

- Avoid excessive employee dependency.

- Differentiate your products or services.

- Document your intellectual property.

- Create additional product or service lines.

- Develop repeatable processes that allow your business to scale more quickly.

- Increase EBITDA or SDE.

- Build barriers to entry.

A professional advisor can help you ascertain and prioritize the best actions for your unique situation to increase the value of your business. The advice in this book can be a useful starting point. Unfortunately, I've seen business owners spend three months to a year on initiatives to increase the value of their business, only to discover that the initiatives they worked on were unlikely to bring any value to a buyer.

Taking the strategic steps addressed in this book will get you well on your way to successfully selling your business and turning confidently toward your next adventure. The remainder of this book is focused on specific strategies you can implement to prepare your business for sale and increase its value.

Conclusion

When deciding to have your business valued, choose an appraiser with real-world experience buying and selling companies. You should also consider the form of appraisal that's most suitable for you – whether it be a written or verbal report. Finally, make sure the appraiser you hire uses methods buyers use in the real world.

There are two primary methods to value a business, and both are based on a business's profitability. There are other variables that buyers may consider when purchasing a business, but the majority exclusively look for one thing – profit. When valuing your business, focus on the two methods most buyers use to value a business:

- Multiple of SDE or EBITDA

- Comparable sales

Remember, when preparing your business for sale, there are two primary ways you can increase the price you receive – by increasing your SDE or EBITDA or by increasing your multiple. The rest of this book shows you how to do just that.

PART FOUR

Strategies & Tactics

CHAPTER 11

What Buyers Look For

"Money flows in the direction of value."

– Uche Ugo, International Brand Consultant

Introduction

Your business is one of your most valuable assets. If you want to maximize the value of that asset, it's critical to know what buyers of businesses want – and then build it – when you're preparing your business for sale.

The most important factor 99% of buyers look for is profitability. Few buyers will be interested in your company if it isn't taking in more money than it's shelling out. If your business isn't producing a profit, don't waste your money building systems that won't increase your profitability. Invest your money in sales and marketing instead. Only when your business is profitable should you invest in other optimizations.

> If your business isn't producing a profit, don't waste your money building systems that won't increase your profitability.

In addition to profit, let's examine what the two primary buyer types – individuals and companies – look for when buying a business.

Buyer Type 1: Individual Buyers

If your company is valued at less than $5 million, chances are high that it will be sold to an individual buyer.

Many individual buyers evaluate a business based on the income it can generate for them. Buyers of small businesses will consider buying any business they have the skills to operate that will provide them with a level of income that meets their goals. This type of buyer is generally looking for an income stream and will consider any type of business they're comfortable operating and feel they can understand and learn.

Individuals are more likely than corporate buyers to consider businesses in a variety of industries. For example, they may be open to considering a service business, an online business, a retail business, or a wholesale business. They may have worked in the marketing department at a Fortune 500 company and have skills that are applicable to a wide range of industries. Or they may be a serial entrepreneur looking for their next business. Outside of a preference for certain industries, individual buyers often have general parameters regarding a business, such as proximity to their home, work hours required, or licensing requirements – but rarely do they have more specific criteria beyond that.

These buyers usually prefer non-specialized businesses. If your business is highly specialized, requiring a rare set of skills, knowledge, or experience, the universe of potential buyers will be smaller than normal. As a result, your business may be difficult to sell due to the limited pool of potential buyers. The price of your business will often be lower as well.

> *For example, imagine you're selling your business, and the buyer must have highly specialized or unique skills to operate it. Imagine also that only 1 in 1,000 buyers has this unique combination of skills, abilities, and talents. How hard do you think it would be to find a buyer with this rare blend of skills and experience to buy your business?*

If the skills needed to operate your business aren't easily found in groups of people who can be readily identified and targeted, selling your business will be much more challenging. If running your business requires a rare blend of soft skills or personal attributes, finding a buyer will be more difficult. Hard skills are simpler to target because most types of people who possess hard skills have already been classified in some form – for example, engineers would be easy to target through trade publications.

If you own a highly specialized business, find out if there's formal industry training available for your business. Buyers without experience can benefit from this training and may be able to attend the training before taking possession of your business. You can also consider including this training in your business's purchase price. Including training in the purchase price makes your business more attractive to buyers as well as easing the transition for them. Including training can even potentially increase the value of your business.

Infrastructure

Infrastructure isn't as important to individuals because most will be involved in the day-to-day operations once they purchase your business and won't be dependent on infrastructure or a management team to ensure the operations run smoothly. If your business is small enough to appeal to an individual, it may not be necessary to invest a significant amount of money in building infrastructure before selling. But don't think you're off the hook – your business must still have enough infrastructure to ensure a smooth transition. But these types of buyers may require less infrastructure than corporate or financial buyers.

Numbers

Individuals are highly numbers-driven. If your business is likely to be sold to an individual, prioritize profitability over infrastructure until your EBITDA exceeds $1 million per year. If your business is valued at less than $5 million, it's usually still more beneficial to invest in sales and marketing to increase the revenue or profitability of your business than to invest in building infrastructure. To be sure, adding infrastructure helps, but most individual buyers prefer more cash flow over more infrastructure.

If the buyer is simply comparing your business's numbers to other businesses on the market, your business is replaceable. These types of buyers focus heavily on the numbers in the business because they're often looking for the highest return on their investment. They scour business-for-sale portals looking for businesses selling at the lowest multiple, which is calculated by dividing the asking price by your SDE or EBITDA. They're likely considering dozens of other types of businesses at a time.

> For example, if you operate a business with $1 million in EBITDA and are asking for $4 million, or a 4.0 multiple, that buyer may be comparing your business to another business with $1 million in EBITDA that's asking for $3.5 million, or a 3.50 multiple.

In order to maximize your business's price when selling to an individual, spell out why your business is unique. Differentiating your business is key to getting the best price. If a buyer views your business as replaceable, they have no reason to buy your particular business, especially if there is a similar one with a lower multiple. Making your business stand out will keep it from being reduced to a set of numbers.

Individuals are looking for an income stream and will consider any type of business they're comfortable operating and feel they can understand and learn.

Buyer Type 2: Corporate Buyers

Corporate buyers primarily consist of direct and indirect competitors and financial buyers, or private equity firms.

Competitors

Competitors will examine the extent to which they can replicate your business or generate a similar level of organic growth. It may be possible to replicate your product or service by starting a similar business from scratch, acquiring another company, or launching a new product line akin to what your company offers.

The more difficult it is for a competitor to simulate your business, the higher the multiple you'll receive. The degree to which a buyer can reproduce your business depends in large part on the industry in which you operate. Certain industries have low barriers to entry – a vending machine franchise, for instance, or a t-shirt business. Others have much higher barriers, such as companies in the telecom or ride-sharing space.

While other factors may influence the price, the degree to which your business can be easily replicated is one of the most important factors competitors consider when evaluating your company for purchase.

Competitors also compare the cost of investing in your business with the cost of other corporate development options such as joint ventures, partnerships, or strategic alliances. Note that this doesn't apply to private equity firms unless they own a competitive business in their portfolio.

All Corporate Buyers

Corporate buyers look for a business that's scalable or that has the potential to grow quickly. Corporate buyers love a scalable business in which the owner hasn't tapped its full potential. This usually involves an owner who is burned out or one who hasn't built effective sales and marketing systems – but one that has operational systems in place that allow the business to quickly scale once sales and marketing are ramped up. If you want to sell your business for the maximum amount possible, focus on building a business that's scalable from day one.

Corporate buyers are usually in the market for a business with a competitive advantage that's sustainable and not easily replicated. Individual buyers, by contrast, regularly purchase lifestyle businesses with no competitive edge. An individual buyer may purchase your company if you don't have a competitive edge, but many corporate buyers will not. Your business must have a competitive differentiation that a buyer can't easily reproduce. Otherwise, it will be difficult to sell your business to anyone other than an individual buyer.

Infrastructure

Companies also prefer businesses with strong infrastructure in place. The degree to which corporate buyers require infrastructure in your business depends on if they will be integrating your business with theirs or if they will run your business as a stand-alone entity post-closing.

- **Integrated:** Corporate buyers who will be integrating your company with theirs *generally* require less infrastructure in your business than if it will be run as a stand-alone business after the closing. In these cases, the buyer already has existing infrastructure and doesn't require your business to have a significant amount of infrastructure.

- **Stand-Alone:** Corporate buyers who will keep your business as a stand-alone entity will require more infrastructure than if they were integrating your business with theirs. They may not be interested in acquiring your business unless your company has adequate infrastructure in place and can continue to operate on a stand-alone basis without you. In some cases, this type of buyer may promote a manager at their corporate office to run your company as president. Still, your business should have a management team and systems in place to ensure that operations continue to run smoothly during the transition process.

Private equity firms expect to double or triple their investment in three to five years before selling the business again to another buyer. This is often possible only with systems and infrastructure in place, and installing these systems and infrastructure costs money. If your business lacks these systems, the buyer must invest money to build them. This capital will be deducted from the purchase price of your company when calculating potential returns and the price they can afford to pay. Building infrastructure takes time and involves risk, so a multiple of this investment may be deducted from the purchase price when calculating the price financial buyers can afford to pay.

Most private equity firms require that management remain to run the business after the closing. Partners in private equity firms focus their time on purchasing companies and don't become actively involved in the operations of their investments. So, either existing management must remain to operate the business, or the private equity firm must hire a management team to run the business after the closing. The only exception to this rule is when the private equity firm owns a portfolio company that competes directly with yours, and they plan to integrate your business with that company.

I have interviewed many partners at private equity firms and strategic buyers for my podcast, *M&A Talk*. If you'd like to listen to these shows to get a better feel for how firms evaluate a company, visit the Morgan & Westfield website at morganandwestfield.com and select *M&A Talk* (Podcast) under the Resources drop-down menu.

Institutionalizing Your Business

If your business is likely to be sold to a corporate buyer, you should first focus on institutionalizing your business. This primarily involves installing systems and developing a management team, and accomplishes three objectives:

1. Prepares your company for the next stage of growth.
2. Increases the value of your company.
3. Enhances the salability of your company.

Institutionalizing your business is accomplished through building systems and developing a management team. Let's explore both of these strategies.

Building Systems

Developing systems involves streamlining, standardizing, automating, and documenting all processes, controls, and systems in your business. By streamlining and documenting your key processes, you increase the chances of selling your business. It's also easier to attract valuable employees to your company when you have well-documented processes and clear job descriptions. A wonderful byproduct is that having well-documented processes makes managing your business easier. Finally, it increases the value of your company and improves the chances of selling your business.

Building a Management Team

Most businesses under $10 million in revenue lack a formal management team. Without professional management, corporate buyers are unlikely to pay a premium for your business. Unfortunately, building a professional management team requires a new set of skills for most entrepreneurs. When you first started your business, you likely performed most of the key tasks yourself. Once you reach a certain point in your business, you must build a team.

Building a team requires recruiting and management skills. You have to learn how to find and hire good people and how to get results from those people. Determine what position or positions would add the most value to your company. What does your company need most? Do you need a CFO, COO, VP of Marketing, VP of Sales, VP of Human Resources, or should you bring in an external president? By developing a formal management team, not only will your business be easier to sell, your revenues and profits will likely increase as well.

> Without a professional management team, corporate buyers are unlikely to pay a premium for your business.

What All Buyers Look For

While all buyers will place a different value on certain aspects of your business, there are some consistent aspects of your business that will appeal to buyers, no matter their type. Let's discuss them here.

A Growth Plan

Regardless of who is most likely to buy your business, you should prepare a short plan that outlines potential growth opportunities a new owner can pursue. Most buyers will ask why you're selling when you're at a supposed inflection point in your business. Your answer will either maximize or destroy your positioning. Ideally, you should be in the process of executing your growth plan, and the assumptions in it should be based on current data.

Prepare a short business plan with simplified financial projections. Highlight the major ways you can grow your business and include a short bulleted list for each growth opportunity. Here are some tips for preparing your projections:

- **Separate Revenue:** Don't lump all revenue streams together. Segment revenue by type.

- **Prepare Projections:** Include three sets of assumptions – low, medium, and high. Avoid so-called hockey stick business plans (unless you manufacture hockey sticks, of course). These are scenarios that show steep increases following periods of flat performances – similar to the shape of a hockey stick – and they diminish your credibility. Prepare your projections in a spreadsheet so the buyer can play with the numbers to determine the impact of any potential changes in the variables.

- **Provide Documentation:** Document and provide backup documentation for each key assumption. What's the basis for forecasting each source of revenue? What's the foundation for forecasting costs? Are they determined on a percentage of revenue, fixed costs subject to inflation, or something else? What are the assumptions behind capital expenditures over the coming years?

A Business That's Difficult to Replicate

How important is a unique business to buyers? Fungibility is the ability of individual units of a good or a commodity to be substituted for one another. Essentially, it means the goods are interchangeable.

For example, one $10 bill is interchangeable with any other genuine $10 bill or any combination of bills and coins that add up to $10. Fungible commodities include water, food, precious metals, and, possibly, your business.

So, what does fungibility have to do with your company? In business, a fungible asset is one that can easily be substituted for another asset. In the world of buying and selling companies, a fungible business is one that can be easily substituted by the acquisition of another business. For example, if a buyer is purchasing a business solely for the cash flow it generates, that buyer can consider a variety of different types of businesses that generate a similar level of cash flow.

Always prioritize profitability over infrastructure until your EBITDA reaches $1 million per year.

The following is a list of factors that can set your business apart, increase its value, and make it appear less replaceable to a buyer:

- A business that can be easily relocated

- An absentee business

- Advantageous contracts with suppliers, vendors, or other third-parties

- Cost advantages that are difficult to replicate

- Custom software

- Customer loyalty

- Distributor or supplier agreements

- First mover advantages in industries with network effects

- Government regulations that restrict competition due to high barriers to entry

- High switching costs for customers

- Intellectual property, such as patents or trade secrets

- Licensing requirements that prevent competitors from entering the market

- Long-term contracts with customers

- Minimal customer concentration

- Minimal seasonality

- Prime location with a long-term lease

- Proprietary technology

- Recurring revenue

- Repeat customer base

- Short cash flow cycle

- Significant barriers to entry

- Stable customer base

- Steady, long-term revenue growth

- Trained management team

- Website with high search engine rankings

When planning to sell your company, consider the extent to which buyers may view your business as fungible or replaceable. You want your business to be perceived as attractive as possible to the buyer so you receive the highest price possible. To do so, build a business that's unique or difficult to replicate. In other words, make sure your business isn't fungible so a buyer will choose to purchase your business instead of another one they may be considering. The less fungible a buyer views your business, the more it will be worth, regardless of who the buyer is.

Conclusion

When preparing to sell your business, it's important to understand the different buyer types, their criteria, and how you can best position your business to be as attractive as possible to the different types of buyers. Understand the degree to which each type requires systems and a management team before you go about building them. Each has a different set of preferences regarding the type of infrastructure, systems, and other elements they desire in a business.

Many buyers will consider a profitable business that lacks infrastructure. But few buyers will consider an unprofitable business that has significant infrastructure in place. Always prioritize profitability over infrastructure until your EBITDA reaches $1 million per year.

For most small businesses, developing a management team is the most critical factor in building a salable business. For other businesses, creating systems or increasing cash flow may create more value. There's no cookie-cutter formula. Knowing the potential types of buyers for your business can help you maximize your sale price and properly market your business to the right audience when the time comes, setting it apart from others like it.

CHAPTER 12

Products and Services

"When your work speaks for itself, don't interrupt."

- Henry J. Kaiser, American Industrialist

Introduction

Concentrations of risk in your products and marketing channels can give buyers pause. The value of a business, or any financial asset, is a function of the relationship between potential return and risk. The higher the risk, the lower the value. The higher the return, the higher the value.

One foolproof method for increasing the value of your business is, therefore, decreasing concentrations of risk. And reducing risk is usually one of the first steps you should take when preparing your business for sale because it often requires a significant amount of time.

The impact of concentrations of risk varies based on a specific buyer's appetite for taking chances and their perception of the risks present in your business. Every buyer will respond differently when presented with varying levels of risk. Some will back out entirely and pursue a less risky venture, while others may agree to move forward, but only if protective measures can be instituted or if the purchase price can be reduced to offset the risk.

Concentrations of risk can:

- Deter buyers from making an offer on your business.

- Reduce the value of your business.

- Lessen the chances of selling your business.

- Increase the thoroughness of the buyer's due diligence.

- Lower the amount of cash you receive at closing.

- Increase the amount of escrows or holdbacks.

- Strengthen the representations and warranties (reps and warranties) in the purchase agreement.

In most cases, concentrations of risk can't be quickly remedied and should be your first area of focus when preparing your business for sale. Addressing these concerns often takes a considerable amount of time and energy, but reducing these concentrations of risk can dramatically increase the value of your business and should be one of your top priorities when planning your exit.

This chapter explores two major concentrations of risk related to your products and marketing channels, and offers specific advice for minimizing the impact of each. Following the suggestions outlined here will not only improve the chances of successfully selling your business but will also boost its value.

> The value of a business, or any financial asset, is a function of the relationship between potential return and risk. The higher the risk, the lower the value. The higher the return, the higher the value.

Product Concentration

Product concentration is the degree to which your business is dependent on a specific product or service. For example, if you own a manufacturing firm and 90% of your revenue is generated from manufacturing one product, your business is considered to have high product concentration.

Tolerance for Product Concentration

How much product concentration will buyers tolerate? Generally speaking, buyers are much less concerned with product concentration than with customer or staff concentration. In fact, at Morgan & Westfield, we sell many businesses with product concentration in excess of 80%, and it isn't an issue much of the time. But in some cases, product concentration can be a deal killer.

For example, if you have an online business and 50% of your revenue is generated from the sale of one product – that's considered a short life span, and a buyer may consider this a deal killer.

Whereas the tolerance for customer concentration can be boiled down to a certain number – such as customer concentration greater than 20% may be considered too risky – product concentration can't. Instead, the risk associated with product concentration is assessed based on the underlying risks of your product. What's the typical lifespan of a product in your category? How susceptible is your product or service to obsolescence or new, innovative solutions? The risk of product concentration is considered on a collective basis and can't be boiled down to a specific number.

> *We sell many businesses in which 100% of the revenue is generated from one product or one service. In most cases, this isn't considered an issue by the buyer. On the other hand, an online business with one product that generated over 50% of their revenue and marketed solely through one channel, such as Amazon, proved to be unsalable due to high product concentration. It's the big picture that buyers consider, not isolated risks.*

Product concentration is considered a risk in industries that have a high degree of innovation and new product development, or if your product is susceptible to technological obsolescence – in other words, if a new product is likely to outseat your existing product, this poses a risk.

Reducing Product Concentration Risk

Product concentration risk can be mitigated if the buyer of your business intends to integrate your product into a wider suite of their existing products. With software companies, for example, buyers often add your software to their existing product line and distribution network, which can result in dramatically increased revenues. This enhances their existing customer relationships since they can offer a wider suite of available services. It also simplifies operations for the end-user, as they have fewer relationships to maintain. This can serve as a vehicle to establish new relationships by opening doors to new customers who have a need for your product. Collectively, a situation like this changes the buyer's perspective from one of mitigating risk to one of capitalizing on opportunity. By focusing on opportunity, you take the buyer's focus off risk.

Regardless, every business is unique. If you're unsure, an experienced investment banker or M&A advisor can often determine if product concentration will likely be an issue in your business.

Distribution Channel Concentration

Distribution channel concentration is the degree to which your business is dependent on a specific distribution or marketing channel. For example, if you have a tech or online business, and 90% of your revenue is generated from Facebook ads, your business is considered to have a high distribution channel concentration.

Tolerance for Distribution Channel Concentration

How much distribution channel concentration will buyers tolerate? Buyers are concerned with distribution channel concentration to the degree to which that distribution channel is considered stable.

> *I recently advised one client who had an eight-figure business that was dependent on one distribution channel – Amazon. If Amazon made just one minor change to their business model, this client could be out of business overnight. Because Amazon is still growing and innovating, and its policies continue to evolve, this is considered a riskier distribution channel than other channels.*

Ideally, your sales and marketing methods should be diverse, and your business shouldn't be dependent on any single channel. If you own the channel, all the better.

Reducing Distribution Channel Risk

The best antidote to these risks is to eliminate any dependencies your business has on third parties. If you're dependent on Amazon, Facebook ads, Google Maps, Yelp, or other marketing channels, strategize to see what you can do to eliminate these dependencies. A change in the ranking algorithm of these channels can have a disastrous effect on your business overnight. As an alternative, in some cases, it may be possible to sell your company to a buyer who already has a diversified array of distribution channels. If they purchase your company, your business would then have access to these distribution channels after the closing, and the risk would be mitigated as a result.

Founders are often the technical experts or inventors and lack sales, marketing, or business development experience. If that rings a bell, work to develop exposure and credibility in your industry – become a cited and published expert so a favorable light is cast on your company. Build social media traction and industry institutional thought leadership. Develop a wide variety of proven advertising tactics and materials to eliminate dependencies on marketing channels.

Sales Team Concentration

In addition to marketing-channel diversity, focus on building diversity across your sales team. Do you have one salesperson on your team who generates a significant percentage of your revenue? If so, it's possible this individual may intentionally jeopardize the sale and blackmail you for a large payday in exchange for them assisting with the transition. Lest you think this is unrealistic, I can tell you I've personally witnessed this more times than I can count on both hands. Work to build a diverse sales team and implement retention bonuses with your key salespeople to ensure they remain with the business after the closing.

Conclusion

Concentrations of risk can have a significant effect on the value of your business. Taking the time to address these risks can dramatically increase your business's value and improve the chances of a successful closing.

Addressing Concentrations of Risk is More Art Than Science

Assessing the potential impact of customer concentration risk is straightforward, but gauging the risk of staff, product, and distribution channel risks is more nuanced. If you want to maximize the value of your business and have a concentration of risk in products or distribution channels, I recommend obtaining the advice of an experienced M&A professional to assess your situation and help you strategize options for mitigating these risks.

Develop a Strategy for Reducing Risks

In some cases, these risks can be addressed by targeting specific types of buyers, such as individual, financial, or strategic buyers, or by implementing deal-protection mechanisms in the purchase agreement. Sometimes these risks must be addressed upfront before you put your company on the market. Regardless, it pays to understand the potential impact these risks can have on your business and to what degree it's necessary to address them before you begin the sale process.

CHAPTER 13

Financial

"Accounting is the language of business."

- Warren Buffett, American Investor and Philanthropist

Introduction

Note: *In this chapter, I use "EBITDA," "earnings," and "cash flow" to refer collectively to SDE and EBITDA.*

How does your company's financial performance compare with its peers? The stronger your financial metrics are compared with others in your industry, the more your business is likely worth, provided your metrics can be sustained in the long term. Let's explore the major financial metrics buyers will consider when evaluating your company.

Profitability

The number one thing you can do to improve your company's value is to increase your earnings. If earnings from your business are inconsistent or if there is a limited amount of cash flow, most buyers will consider this risky. This can result in potential buyers placing a lower value on your business, making it more difficult to sell. On the other hand, if earnings are consistent for your business, it reduces risk and improves value in the eyes of buyers.

Seller's discretionary earnings (SDE) and earnings before interest, taxes, depreciation, and amortization (EBITDA) are the starting point for nearly all negotiations in M&A. For most industries, SDE and EBITDA multiples are fairly predictable, and acquirers rarely stray from prevailing industry multiples.

For example, if your company generates $3 million in EBITDA, then most buyers will value your business at 4.0 to 6.0 times your EBITDA, or $12 million to $18 million.

How does a buyer determine where in the range you fall?

It's simple – they consider all of the factors other than SDE and EBITDA. In other words, nearly every buyer initially establishes a baseline value based on a multiple of your earnings, and then increases or decreases the price they're willing to offer within that range (e.g., 4.0 to 6.0 multiple) based on all the other factors. This means, the higher your earnings, the higher the baseline value of your company will be.

If you increase your EBITDA by 50% to $3 million from $2 million, the value of your company will increase by 50% as well. This means a range of $12 million to $18 million from $8 million to $12 million based on a 4.0 to 6.0 multiple. Not only will you put an additional $1 million in your pocket per year, but you'll also put an additional $4 million to $6 million in your pocket at the closing table.

One of your most important objectives, therefore, should be to increase your business's SDE or EBITDA. Every dollar increase in SDE or EBITDA increases the value of your business by its multiple.

For example, let's say your business is likely to sell at a 5.0 multiple. If you increase your EBITDA by $500,000 per year, you'll also increase the value of your business by $2,500,000 ($500,000 x 5.0 multiple = $2,500,000).

Here are several ways to boost your SDE or EBITDA:

Increase Revenue

The easiest way to boost your SDE or EBITDA is to bump up your prices because 100% of your price increase falls to the bottom line (i.e., SDE or EBITDA). If your company generates $10 million per year in revenue, and you increase prices by 5%, your EBITDA will increase by $500,000 per year ($10 million x 5% = $500,000), less any direct sales costs, such as commissions. If your EBITDA is $2 million, your EBITDA will increase by 25%, taking it to $2.5 million from $2 million. In essence, a 5% rise in prices can increase your EBITDA by 25%. All of your price increase, less any sales commissions, will increase EBITDA.

Another example, if your business generates $10 million in revenue and $2 million in EBITDA and is valued at a 5.0 multiple, or $10 million, and you increase prices by 10%, your new EBITDA will be $3 million, and the value of your business will be $15 million ($3 million EBITDA x 5.0 = $15 million). In this case, a 10% price increase resulted in a 50%, or $5 million, increase in the value of the company.

Other methods for increasing revenue primarily include creating new products or services or selling more of your existing products and services. But be careful before engaging in risky product development or marketing campaigns if you plan on selling in the next few years. Most buyers will generally *not* allow you to make adjustments for any marketing campaigns or product launches that were unsuccessful when calculating earnings. I recommend sticking to low-risk methods of increasing your revenue if you plan on selling in the next few years, such as increasing your budget in marketing campaigns that produce predictable returns. Avoid high-risk sales or marketing strategies, such as hiring a new sales manager or launching a new marketing campaign in which you have limited experience. These sorts of strategies can drain cash flow, which decreases earnings and, therefore, decreases the value of your business.

Decrease Expenses

Sometimes the easiest way to increase EBITDA is to reduce expenses. Decreasing your expenses is often easier than increasing revenue. Doing so also has the advantage of having an immediate impact on EBITDA and may be less risky than attempting to increase revenue. The only caveat here is to not reduce expenses that the buyer would view as unfavorable – standard insurance premiums should be maintained, for example, as should normal inventory levels.

You should pinch every penny for two to three years prior to your planned exit. For every dollar in expenses you cut, not only will you save one dollar, but you'll also receive three to seven, or whatever your multiple is, additional dollars at the closing table.

> *If you cut expenses by $200,000 for two years before the sale and the sale process takes one year (a total of three years), you'll put an additional $1.4 million to $1.8 million in your pocket – $200,000 (year 1) + $200,000 (year 2) + $200,000 (year 3) + $800,000-$1,200,000 (increased purchase price).*

As noted above, avoid making any large investments before selling your business, such as creating new products or services, or rolling out new sales or marketing campaigns that are high risk or that require a large up-front investment. These investments decrease profitability in the short-term, which decreases the value of your business. If you do make a large investment, organize all expenses related to the investment under a separate chart or account, so you can easily track these expenses and point them out to a buyer. Or better yet, stick to low-risk strategies for increasing your profitability.

As a general rule, you shouldn't invest in new equipment or other hard assets when you're in the process of selling your business unless it immediately increases your earnings. Why? Because you're unlikely to recoup your investment.

Buyers value businesses based on the SDE or EBITDA they generate. If the new equipment doesn't increase your cash flow, it likely won't pay for itself, and you shouldn't make the investment.

While the buyer may appreciate the new equipment, they're unlikely to assign enough value to it for you to justify the investment. If the buyer is considering two similar businesses at the outset, the age and condition of the equipment are just part of dozens of factors they may take into consideration when they're evaluating a business. At the same time, the cash flow your business generates nearly always trumps everything else, and buyers are always attracted to businesses that generate more cash flow.

If the equipment or investment immediately increases your revenue without having to market or sell a new product or service, perform a calculation to see if the investment and the resulting increase in cash flow will have a positive ROI for you. If it will, then you should make the investment, but this won't be true in the majority of cases.

On the other hand, if the investment immediately reduces labor or other costs, it may be a wise investment. If the investment will increase the profitability of your business by more than the initial cost, it makes sense to make the investment. To calculate how much the investment will increase profitability, multiply how much the investment will reduce labor costs and therefore increase your EBITDA, then apply your multiple.

> *For example, if an investment will reduce labor costs by $100,000 per year and your multiple is 4.0, the equipment will increase the value of your business by $400,000.*

If a new piece of equipment would simply be nice to have, or if it represents a new product or service line you could pursue, I recommend holding off on this investment. Point out the opportunity to the buyer and let them decide if this is something they want to pursue, and let them make the investment.

The number one thing you can do to improve your company's value is to increase your earnings.

Why Profitability Is So Important

To illustrate why profitability is so important, let's break down the sale process into action steps. When selling your business, there are two main steps when dealing with buyers:

1. **Attracting Buyers:** This first step involves confidentially marketing your business for sale and responding to buyers who request additional information on your business, such as through your confidential information memorandum, or CIM for short. At the outset, buyers consider a limited set of criteria when initially evaluating your business. At this stage, their main criteria is the profitability of the business they are considering.

   Few buyers take into consideration the investments you have made in new equipment or other capital assets at this stage in the transaction. In other words, investing in new equipment is unlikely to produce a higher response to your marketing campaigns. At this stage, most buyers' decisions focus on just a few criteria – your multiple, your competitive advantage, your growth rate, and perhaps a few other industry-specific measures.

2. **Convincing Buyers:** After you have attracted the buyer and they have responded, you need to convince them to buy. The buyer will look at a broader range of criteria once they're closely inspecting your business. One of the elements they will now consider is the current condition of your equipment. If a buyer doesn't make it to this stage, then your investment in new equipment is moot.

The buyers' main criteria they use to evaluate a business is the cash flow or profitability the business generates. Anything you can do to increase the cash flow of your business will end up having the most significant impact on its salability and value.

Revenue

Businesses with strong revenue growth are always highly desired by buyers. Buyers generally assume that financial trends will continue in most businesses. As a result, the revenue trends in a business are of particular importance to buyers and can have a tremendous impact on the value of your business. If revenue growth is consistent, the business will be perceived as having greater potential and less risk. As American businessman Martin Zweig is famously quoted as saying, "The trend is your friend" – at least, in this instance, when the trend is upward.

What are the growth prospects for your company? The higher the growth potential and prospects, the more your business will be worth. Businesses with high growth rates sell at higher multiples than businesses with flat or declining sales. Another method for increasing the value of your business is to increase its growth rate so that "projected SDE or EBITDA" is used to value your business instead of "current year's SDE or EBITDA." The value of your business is normally based on its most recent 12-month SDE or EBITDA – this is also known as trailing twelve months, or TTM. But if you've demonstrated strong and consistent growth, you may be able to negotiate a price based on a blend of historical and projected SDE or EBITDA.

Inconsistent or declining revenue, on the other hand, is considered high risk by most buyers and will always result in a low valuation. If revenue in your business is declining or inconsistent, you'll receive a far lower multiple than if your revenue is increasing or stable. If your revenue is declining or inconsistent, one of your top priorities should be to increase revenue. Declining revenue is a major concern for nearly every buyer.

> Anything you can do to increase the cash flow of your business will have the most significant impact on its salability and value.

Margins

Are your gross profit margins holding steady, increasing, or decreasing? How do your gross margins compare to industry benchmarks? If gross margins are high for your business, this helps improve its value if your lower cost structure is sustainable and if your margins show little variation from year to year. If gross margins are low or inconsistent for your business, this hampers its marketability and negatively impacts its value.

If gross margins are decreasing for your business, buyers view this as risky and will probe deeply during due diligence to determine the reason for the decline. If margins are decreasing in your business, make it one of your top priorities to stabilize your margins before you begin the sales process.

Recurring Revenue

If your business generates recurring revenue, this improves the scalability of your business and reduces risk for a buyer. Contractually recurring revenue is the number one value driver many buyers look for in some industries, such as software and tech businesses. Recurring revenue is viewed as more valuable than revenue generated from new sales, and buyers are willing to pay significantly more for a business that generates recurring revenue as opposed to revenue generated from new sales.

Examples of companies **with** recurring revenue include:

- **Netflix:** Monthly subscription fee

- **Spotify:** Monthly subscription fee

- **Apple:** Recurring subscription fees for Apple Music, iCloud, and other subscriptions

- **Accounting Software:** Subscription fees for QuickBooks, Xero, and other sites

- **Web Hosting:** Subscription fees for sites such as GoDaddy and Bluehost

- **Microsoft:** Recurring subscription fees for Office 365 and other programs

Examples of companies **without** recurring revenue include:

- Uber

- Lyft

- Airbnb

Note that there's a difference between *recurring* and *repeat* revenue. While it's good to have repeat revenue, it's unpredictable as a form of income. Recurring revenue is auto-debited from a customer's credit or debit card, or billed on a regular schedule, such as with cell phone bills, gym memberships, or online services. And companies of all stripes are catching on – the so-called subscription economy is believed to have grown at a 435% clip in the past decade.

Why the growth? Recurring revenue is more predictable and results in a higher customer lifetime value than non-recurring revenue. The higher the lifetime value, the more a company can afford to invest in acquiring customers, which reduces customer acquisition cost, and increases a business's scalability.

Not only should you focus on increasing recurring revenue, but you should also concentrate on customer retention. If your business suffers from high attrition, such as through low retention or high customer churn, your business will have a difficult time scaling. Poor retention can be caused by a number of issues, from product features to the overall user experience.

Fix any leaks in your metrics before you scale your business. Improve retention before attempting to increase recurring revenue. Nail down your value proposition before you attempt to scale. Nail it before you scale it.

Recurring revenue is viewed as less risky by acquirers than forecasted revenue based on new product sales, which buyers heavily discount. If the revenue isn't contracted, the owners may leave and take their relationships with them, or customers may leave during the transition phase due to the uncertainty an acquisition creates in the mind of the marketplace. As a result, contractually recurring revenue is the gold standard when buying a business.

Uncertainty can also kill sales in the pipeline for B2B businesses. Contracts ensure retention and offer the acquirer enough time to build trust with the customer post-closing. This means that businesses with contractually recurring revenue will sell at higher multiples than those with non-contracted revenue.

Following are tips for increasing recurring revenue:

- **Increase Pricing:** Test the elasticity of your pricing. The entirety of a price increase falls to the bottom line, net of direct costs such as sales commissions, and an increase in profitability will dramatically improve the value of your business. Here's an example of the potential effects on the value of a business of a 10% price increase:

  - **Before Price Increase:**

    - $10 million in revenue

    - $2 million in EBITDA

    - 5.0 multiple

    - **Valuation: $2 million EBITDA x 5.0 = $10 million**

  - **After Price Increase:**

    - $10 million x 10% price increase = $1 million in additional revenue and EBITDA

    - $11 million in revenue

- $3 million in EBITDA

- 5.0 multiple

- **Valuation: $3 million EBITDA x 5.0 = $15 million**

  - In this case, a 10% price increase resulted in a 50%, or $5 million, increase in the value of the company.

- **Offer Maintenance Contracts:** Convert your customers to an annual maintenance, or other long-term contract. Increase pricing and offer to grandfather legacy customers into your old pricing structure if they agree to sign a long-term contract.

- **Create Add-On Modules:** Offer a discounted price if customers purchase add-one modules. Let customers know in advance that you'll soon be increasing prices and offer to grandfather them into your old pricing model if they're willing to sign a contract.

- **Create Sales Incentives:** Reward salespeople based on the type of revenue they generate – contractually recurring revenue should be rewarded more than one-time, transactional revenue for example.

- **Track Metrics That Affect Recurring Revenue:** Create a dashboard that tracks key metrics for your business such as customer retention, customer churn, lifetime value (LTV), customer acquisition cost (CAC), months to recover CAC, customer engagement, and leads by lifecycle. The majority of key metrics have an effect on the amount of recurring revenue, either directly or indirectly, and tracking these metrics allows you to spot leaks in your funnel and optimize them.

- **Improve Retention:** Improve customer retention through product improvements.

Contractually recurring revenue is the gold standard when buying a business.

Learn More

If you haven't read Eric Ries's *The Lean Startup* (published by Currency, 2011), I recommend doing so. To improve retention, shortcut the customer feedback loop. Create either incremental or dramatic changes to your product in the form of minimum viable products (MVPs) through weekly sprints with your team and obtain early feedback on your iterations from your customers. Incorporate customer feedback into every weekly iteration. Your objective should be to quickly iterate to a solid value proposition that resonates with your user base. Once you've done so, you can begin priming the pump and scaling up your business.

Cash Flow Cycle

The cash flow cycle is the amount of time it takes a company to convert a sale to cash. Highly scalable companies have a short cash flow cycle. The shorter your cash flow cycle is, the more scalable your business will be. For example, if your business offers no or minimal terms to customers, this shortens the cash flow cycle, thereby improving its scalability and reducing risk. If your cash flow cycle is long, a buyer must make a significant investment in working capital to scale your business. As a result, they often include a deduction for an increase in working capital, which decreases cash flow and, therefore, the value of your business.

If your business offers significant terms to customers, this increases the cash flow cycle, thereby reducing its scalability and increasing risk. Has your business loosened terms to boost revenue in the short term? If so, this revenue will be discounted by buyers.

If you carry significant inventory levels, offer customized products, or offer your customers significant terms, your sales cycle will be longer. A long cash flow cycle limits the scalability of your business and requires that the buyer make large working capital injections to fund future growth. Both factors drive down the value of your business. While the cash flow cycle of your business is important, it's not nearly as important as the revenue and cash flow trends in your business that were described earlier in this chapter.

Working Capital Requirements

Working capital is defined as accounts receivable, inventory, and prepaid expenses, minus accounts payable, short-term debt, and accrued expenses.

If your business requires a lower-than-average amount of working capital, this increases the overall return on investment for the buyer and, therefore, its value. Corporate buyers will often make an offer that includes a set amount of working capital in the purchase price. Businesses requiring lower amounts of working capital are worth more than businesses requiring higher amounts, all things being equal. If your business requires a high amount of working capital, this must be factored into the purchase price, which decreases your net proceeds.

Many buyers factor the working capital into the total investment when calculating the multiple.

> *For example, if cash flow is $1 million per year and the business is valued at a 4.0 multiple, the business will be priced at $4 million. But, if the business requires $1 million in working capital (total purchase price = $4 million + $1 million = $5 million), then the multiplier will be 5.0 ($5 million / $1 million = 5.0) if working capital is included in the calculation.*

Because you must include working capital in the purchase price of your business if the buyer is a corporate buyer, it makes sense to reduce working capital as much as possible before the sale. For every dollar you decrease your working capital prior to the sale, you'll put an extra dollar in your pocket at closing time. But the changes you implement to reduce working capital must be sustainable in the long term.

Capital Expenditures

Capital expenditures, or CapEx for short, are investments made in capital equipment and other fixed assets. Capital equipment is depreciated because it's expected to have a useful life longer than twelve months. While depreciation is added back when calculating SDE and EBITDA, some corporate buyers subtract a reserve for capital expenditures when valuing your business.

If your business requires lower-than-average annual capital expenditures, this is a positive attribute for sophisticated or corporate buyers. A low CapEx makes your business more attractive to sophisticated targets. A high CapEx makes your business less attractive to sophisticated targets.

Carefully track your capital expenditures for five years prior to a sale, and be as frugal as possible with any capital investments you make in your business.

Financial Records

What kind of financial information do buyers ask for? Buyers typically ask for the following:

- Three to five years of profit and loss (P&L) statements

- Balance sheets

- Bank statements

- Federal income tax returns

- Year-to-date (YTD) comparison P&L statement

Owners who are serious about selling should organize their business's financial records for the previous three years, broken down in an easy-to-navigate format that can display the data by month.

Financial Statement Adjustments

SDE and adjusted EBITDA include adjustments such as your salary, perks, professional fees, rent, and so forth. Be as conservative as possible, making adjustments. When assessing the veracity of your adjustments, buyers may not explicitly mention their concerns, but they will discount the purchase price to offset any increased risk in adjustments that can't be verified. They will also question your credibility, and your aggressive stance might be considered an increased element of risk for them. As a result, they may be disincentivized from retaining you post-closing and may take actions to mitigate their risk, such as lowering the price, conducting more thorough due diligence, expanding the scope of representations and warranties, increasing the amount of holdbacks, or increasing the amount of seller notes, which may be subject to the right of offset in the event of fraud.

You want to be viewed as having strong management ability, judgment, and ethics. Your goal, therefore, should be to improve your credibility. As a result, you may receive a higher salary post-closing if they retain you and fewer purchase-price mechanisms designed to reduce their risk in the purchase agreement.

Minimize the Total Number of Adjustments

How do you do this? It's simple – minimize the number of adjustments you make two to three years prior to the sale of your company. The fewer adjustments you make, the lower the perceived risk to the buyer, and the more likely you'll receive a higher multiple. While this will cost you tax dollars, you'll receive a multiple of the earnings back in the form of an increased purchase price.

> When making adjustments, be as conservative as possible.

Pre-Sale Financial Due Diligence

How accurate are your financial and accounting records? Do your tax returns match your financial statements? Do you have any unreported income, such as unreported cash sales? Are your financial statements clear and accurate? Do you have strong accounting controls in place?

Is your business using LIFO, FIFO, or some other form of inventory accounting method? If so, has this dramatically affected the earnings? Has the recording of inventory been properly documented, or was inventory under or overstated in an attempt to manipulate earnings?

Are the financials prepared on a cash or accrual basis? If accrual basis, are the accruals being correctly done?

Just asking.

One of the most common deal killers when selling a business is inaccurate or incomplete financial records. Most buyers hire a CPA or accountant to help them perform financial due diligence. The accountant will evaluate all financial documents, and then reconcile the numbers between your financial statements and your bank statements, invoices, receipts, and tax returns to ensure they match.

With inaccurate financial records, you run the risk of losing a buyer. Why? Once the buyer discovers the defects during due diligence, the sale must be delayed to address the problems.

Sometimes, these issues take months to resolve. At this point, the buyer may have decided to move on, or may have decided your business is no longer a sound investment.

After spending many months finding a buyer, losing them over something that could have been corrected from the outset is a huge disappointment and a waste of valuable time, money, and resources.

Third-Party Review

Having your financial statements reviewed by a third party is always a wise investment. More than half of the business owners who approach me have at least some errors in their accounting work that need to be cleaned up prior to a sale. About 10% to 20% require a major overhaul. This is a scenario I encounter far too often.

If you aren't sure of the quality of your financial records, I recommend retaining a third-party CPA to take a look. This review helps spot potential issues a buyer may find and allows you to address them before you receive an offer.

The stronger your financial statements, the less risk buyers will perceive, and the more they may be willing to pay for your business. That's why you should hire a third-party accountant to thoroughly review your financial statements as early as possible in the process. Simplify your accounting records and consolidate your chart of accounts to make sure it accurately reflects your business and gives you the information you need to properly manage your business.

Having your financial records in order before selling your business also potentially speeds up the due diligence process, resulting in a higher chance of closing a deal. This is because a buyer who discovers issues with your financial records will most certainly conduct thorough due diligence, looking for problems in other areas, as well. And some of the time, they will abandon the transaction altogether.

Learn More

If you'd like to learn more about the process of financial due diligence and the quality of earnings (Q of E) analysis, visit our website at morganandwestfield.com and listen to my *M&A Talk* podcast with Bill Wiersema, *Cooking the Books*. In this episode, we discuss the details of the Q of E analysis, what can potentially go wrong during financial due diligence, and what you can do to prevent these problems.

Switching Accounting Systems

In general, I don't recommend switching accounting systems if you're in the process of selling a business. Although there are some exceptions, the majority of the time, I recommend staying with your current accounting system if you're planning to sell in the near future.

QuickBooks is currently the most popular accounting system for small businesses, but that's slowly changing with the introduction of more modern, streamlined cloud-based programs.

Switching to a new accounting system is a major project and should only be undertaken with professional assistance. While software companies claim they can smoothly switch you over, the truth is that without an accountant familiar with the process, the conversion can be painful and take months to perform properly. Switching to a new system in preparation for a sale may also complicate the due diligence process because your data is now located in two systems.

Switch to a new accounting system only if you're using an outdated system. Buyers prefer businesses with up-to-date infrastructure and systems in place, and your accounting system is one of the most important functions in your business. If you decide to switch, it pays to update your system using newer software on the market.

I strongly prefer cloud-based accounting software as it can be easily accessed by multiple people simultaneously. This facilitates the due diligence process since you can provide the buyer with a unique username and password to access your data on a "read-only" basis. Switching to a cloud-based system may speed up the due diligence process and possibly even make your business easier to sell.

But, do think twice before you switch accounting systems. It pays to consult with an expert before making a change.

Treatment of Debt

It's essential to understand what happens to debt when a business is sold. In some instances, the debt is absorbed in the transaction as part of the sale. If it isn't, do you need to pay off debt before you sell your business, or can it be paid at closing out of the proceeds?

The fate of any debt in the sale of a business is largely determined by how the transaction is structured. There are two ways to structure a deal – either as a stock sale or an asset sale. Mergers are a third way, but these are rare in the lower middle market.

The overwhelming majority of businesses that sell for less than $10 million are structured as asset sales, in which specific assets and liabilities are individually transferred from the buyer to the seller at closing via a bill of sale. In contrast, in a stock sale, the buyer purchases shares or membership interests and assumes everything the business owns or owes.

In the following section, I explain the differences between a stock sale and an asset sale and discuss the various ways debt can be handled at closing.

Stock Sale

A stock sale occurs when the buyer purchases the stock (or membership interests for an LLC) of your entity (corporation, LLC, etc.) and assumes everything your entity owns or owes, including its assets and liabilities. Only a minority of businesses that sell for under $10 million are structured as stock sales.

A buyer may decide to purchase your entity if they want to inherit something your entity owns that can't be transferred if the sale is structured as an asset sale, such as a lease or contract.

> *For example, some contracts are specific to a corporation, LLC, or entity, and structuring the transaction as a stock sale would ensure these pass along to the new owner, assuming the contract doesn't state that a "change in control" requires the consent of assignment of the contract.*

When structuring a transaction as a stock sale, you and the buyer determine what assets are being purchased and what liabilities are being assumed. At closing, you sign over the stock certificates to the buyer, and the buyer becomes the owner of your entity, making them an indirect owner of your entity's assets and liabilities.

Three exceptions to when liabilities, such as debt, will continue to be your obligation after the closing in a stock sale include when:

- The liabilities are personally "owned" by you as an individual, unless those liabilities are separately transferred.

- The buyer requires you pay all debt at closing.

- You agree to be responsible for the debt post-closing, even though your entity may be legally responsible, such as in a lawsuit.

Asset Sale

- In an asset sale, specific assets and liabilities are individually transferred from you to the buyer at closing via a bill of sale. The parties pick and choose which assets and liabilities they would like to include in the sale. Most asset sales include all assets required to operate the business and exclude all liabilities associated with the business. To affect the sale, the buyer usually forms an entity, and that entity is the purchaser of the assets.

- Most small business transactions are structured as asset sales because of the possibility of contingent or unknown liabilities. The amount of a contingent liability is unknown – thus "contingent." Therefore, the buyer can't calculate the amount of the liability. Examples of contingent liabilities include litigation or product liabilities.

- Asset sales are theoretically more complicated than stock sales because the individual assets and liabilities must be purchased and sold, but this concept usually only applies to larger transactions. In reality, asset sales are simple because the experts involved are used to this type of transaction structure. In a stock sale, by contrast, all you have to do is sign over the stock certificates. All other assets are automatically transferred unless they're owned by you individually.

Exceptions to When Debt Is Paid at Closing

There are a couple of exceptions to when debt may be paid at closing:

1. **Leased Equipment:** If equipment is leased by you individually, that lease or asset would have to be transferred separately, regardless of whether the transaction is structured as an asset sale or a stock sale.

2. **Successor Liability:** There is potential for successor liability in the purchase of a business, which means the buyer could assume the risk for certain liabilities. Successor liability occurs as the result of state (statutory) law and may allow a creditor to seek recovery from the buyer for liabilities, even if the sale is structured as an asset sale and even if the buyer didn't specifically agree to assume those liabilities. Successor liability is most common in the areas of product liability, environmental law, employment law, and for payment of certain types of taxes, such as sales tax. Because successor liability is a function of state law, the laws may vary significantly from state to state. Additionally, you could be subject to claims of creditors in states in which the bulk sale law is still in effect, such as California. As a result, regardless of the transaction structure, the buyer should perform extensive due diligence to avoid the possibility of successor liability. Additionally, the buyer will likely consider using an escrow company in certain states and include representations and warranties in the purchase agreement that require you to indemnify the buyer in the event of successor liability. Many middle-market acquisitions hold back a portion of the purchase price for a period of time after the closing to protect the buyer against the possibility of losses due to successor liability.

Options for Handling Debt at the Closing

There are three options for how to handle debt at the closing:

1. You can pay off the debt with cash prior to the closing.

2. The buyer could assume the debt.

3. The debt could be paid at closing through escrow out of your proceeds before they are released to you. For example, if you're selling a company for $10 million and you have $2 million in debt, escrow will deduct $2 million from the proceeds at closing, and the remaining $8 million will be paid to you at that time.

Conclusion

As Warren Buffett once said, "Accounting is the language of business." This statement is even more true throughout the preparation and sales process. When prepping your company for sale, it's wise to start with a review of your finances. Here's a summary of action steps you can take related to the financial aspects of your business:

- **Increase:**

  - Revenue

  - Recurring revenue

  - EBITDA

  - Gross margins

  - Profitability

- **Reduce:**

  - Number of adjustments to your financials three years prior to a sale

  - Expenses

  - Working capital

  - Cash flow cycle

  - Capital expenditures

- Normalize your financial statements

- Organize your financial records

- Prepare backup documentation for adjustments to financial statements

- Hire a third party to conduct pre-sale financial due diligence

CHAPTER 14

Customers

"A satisfied customer is the best business strategy of all."

- Michael LeBoeuf, American Business Author

Introduction

Your customers are a key asset to your business. When selling your company, the extent to which your customers add value to your company is determined by several factors. These factors can either add a tremendous amount of value to your business or serve to destroy value. This chapter outlines several strategies you can use to maximize value when it comes to your customer base.

Customer Base

Does your business cater to a strong, stable customer base that exhibits the ability and willingness to pay, such as with a Fortune 500 firm? The stronger your customer base, the higher the purchase price you'll receive.

Acquirers of B2B companies place a high value on relationships with large, established customers, such as Fortune 500 and blue-chip companies. They reason that if your product is good enough to satisfy the needs of these clients, the next challenge will be to scale your business by building a strong sales team and infrastructure.

Most acquirers view building an engaging product as riskier than scaling a company through sales and marketing efforts. National or Fortune 500 customers also hold a strategic value for certain buyers, as these relationships can serve as opportunities to cross-sell their entire product line to the company. Blue-chip customers are also valuable because it's easier to upsell to an existing account than it is to establish a new account.

> For example, Intuit, the parent company of QuickBooks, acquired Credit Karma for $7 billion. By acquiring Credit Karma, Intuit could market its other products to Credit Karma's 100 million registered users. It's much easier for Intuit to attempt to upsell 100 million existing customers that already have a relationship with Credit Karma than it would be for Intuit to acquire 100 million new customers.

Potential acquirers may purchase your company solely for the existence of relationships your company has with well-established customers. This allows the buyer to upsell your customers the additional products they offer, which provides a tremendous amount of value for the acquirer.

If you have a B2B business, seek to establish customer relationships with large, established companies. The more established your customers, the better.

If there's a strong product fit between your customer base and the acquirer's product line, it may be a prudent investment for the buyer to purchase your company solely for the value of your customer base, especially if time and lost opportunity costs are critical factors in your industry.

How diversified is your customer base? Your customer base should consist of not just early adopters, but also late adopters. For example, many software companies make fast progress initially as they sell to early adopters who are willing to take a risk on unproven software, but they stall once they've exhausted the supply of early adopters. Ideally, your business should have a balance of early adopters, the early majority, the late majority, and a handful of laggards.

Of course, small innovative companies' customer bases will consist primarily of early adopters and the early majority. But the more diverse your customer base, the better. Diversity among your consumers signals to the buyer that you're obtaining strong traction with your customer base and that you have a sound product fit.

Customer Contracts

Document your customer relationships by having your attorney prepare an agreement for your customers. You should do this even if there isn't a term to the agreement. Customers are a key asset to your business, and it's wise to document these relationships. This facilitates a smooth transition and reduces the possibility of any uncertainties by reducing the likelihood of the buyer losing those customers during the transition process.

If you already have customer agreements in place, have your attorney review them to ensure they're transferable upon a sale or to determine potential issues that a sale of the business may cause these contracts. In many cases, customer agreements aren't transferable. One common solution is to structure the transaction as a stock sale, but many buyers are unwilling to do this due to the possibility of contingent or unknown liabilities. Many third-party contracts also include a "change of control provision," but a stock sale would often be characterized as a "change of control" as defined under such a provision and would, therefore, require approval by the third party. One method for skirting change of control provisions is a "reverse-triangular merger," but this topic is beyond the scope of this section. If you decide to switch your customers to contracts, be sure to include a clause addressing assignability.

Customer Acquisition

How healthy are your customer acquisition metrics? Can your marketing methods be automated and scaled, or has your business depended too much on your personal selling, networking, or marketing efforts?

Customer acquisition cost is a double-edged sword. A high customer acquisition cost is good because it means your customer relationships are more valuable.

> *For example, if the average customer acquisition cost in your industry is $5,000 and you have 1,000 customers, it would cost a company $5 million ($5,000 x 1,000 = $5 million) to replicate the value of your customer base, assuming there's no overlap between your customer base and theirs.*

On the flip side, a high customer acquisition cost can be a negative factor because it limits the scalability of your business. The potential scalability of a business is limited by its customer acquisition cost. The higher the customer acquisition cost relative to the lifetime value of each customer, the more costly it is to scale the business.

> *For example, a business with a customer acquisition cost of $50 and a lifetime value (LTV) of $10,000 would be considered highly scalable, whereas a business with a customer acquisition cost of $1,000 and an LTV of $2,000 wouldn't be considered highly scalable.*

It's the ratio that matters – not the absolute numbers. Start tracking your customer metrics in a dashboard, and strive to create marketing methods that can be automated and scaled. Limit the amount of personal selling you do unless you'll stay with your business after the closing. Then track the metrics for each marketing strategy in your dashboard so you can establish projections based on assumptions that are backed up by your metrics.

Customer Sales Pipeline

Document your sales pipeline in your customer relationship management (CRM) system so the buyer can easily project your revenue. Keep track of your pipeline, along with the relevant metrics that will enable the buyer to project future sales. If your pipeline is strong before the closing, you're in a much better position to negotiate a high purchase price than if your customer sales pipeline is weak or undocumented.

Customer Database

A customer database, such as a CRM system, is valuable to buyers for several reasons. One reason is so the acquirer can market their products to your existing customer database. As previously mentioned, selling a product to an existing customer, or upselling, is easier than establishing a relationship with a new customer. Your CRM can also assist the buyer in projecting revenue after the closing, which can help justify a higher purchase price if your pipeline is strong.

A robust CRM offers buyers the ability to implement scalable methods for rolling out their product suite to your customer base. The more information your database contains, the better. Demographics or other targeted information also allow the acquirer to develop targeted marketing campaigns.

> *In the example of Credit Karma, it would be valuable for Intuit to know which Credit Karma customers own a business – Intuit could then develop targeted email campaigns offering those customers a free trial of QuickBooks or other solutions for small businesses. Intuit could also develop targeted campaigns based on the user's credit score – for instance, lines of credit could be offered for those with high credit scores, or credit-builder programs could be offered for those with low credit scores.*

Regardless, the more information your customer base contains that allows the acquirer to develop targeted campaigns, the more value the buyer will see in the database. Without this information, it's likely Intuit would alienate Credit Karma's customer base if they blasted out non-targeted campaigns on a frequent basis (e.g., nuns don't want emails about Viagra).

Customer Metrics

Maintain a centralized dashboard with your key metrics and monitor your metrics on a regular basis. Watch your customer acquisition cost, customer retention, lifetime value, and other key metrics. Then develop weekly sprints with your team to slowly improve those metrics over time. Track your metrics on a weekly or monthly basis in a spreadsheet to make sure they're improving.

> *For example, if your customer acquisition cost lowers to $900 from $1,000 and your customer lifetime value increases to $5,500 from $4,000, you can use these improved metrics as the basis for the assumptions in your projections to potentially justify a higher price.*

Documenting the assumptions in your projections allows you to more easily defend your asking price, which is based on your pro forma. Your projections are built on your assumptions – so documenting and tracking your key metrics lays a solid foundation for your projections.

Close Relationships

Reduce any personal relationships you have with any customers. Some customers may believe the only way they can do business with your company is by doing business with you. In their minds, their relationship is with you, not your company. When you leave, their business may leave. Buyers become nervous if you have close or personal relationships with customers. Minimize any personal relationships you have with customers by transferring these relationships to your staff to reduce this impact during the transition.

Customer Concentration

Customer concentration occurs when a small number of customers generates a significant percentage of your business's revenues. Here are some examples of how the amount of customer concentration is often expressed:

- The top customer generates 57% of the business's total revenue.

- The top 3 customers generate 27% of the business's total revenue.

- The top 5 customers generate 42% of the business's total revenue.

- The top 10 customers generate 3% of the business's total revenue.

The higher the customer concentration in your business, the more risk this presents to the buyer. On the other hand, the greater your customer diversity, the less risk a buyer will view in your business. In extreme circumstances, I've encountered businesses that couldn't be sold due to high levels of customer concentration.

Mitigate customer concentration risk before you sell your business, if you can. A high percentage of your revenue generated from a few customers presents a high risk to a buyer. If you lost one large customer, your business would experience a significant decrease in revenue. Buyers view a concentration of customers in your business as risky. I recommend developing strategies for mitigating this risk, such as asking your largest customers to sign long-term contracts in exchange for discounts.

There are other methods for mitigating this risk to the buyer, and they generally fall into the following two categories:

1. **Actions Prior to the Sale:** These include asking the customer to sign a long-term agreement and "institutionalizing" the client – that is, reducing the personal relationships you have with any customers.

2. **Deal Structure Mechanisms:** These include methods to assess the risk, such as customer surveys and interviews during due diligence, and mechanisms designed to reduce risk if a customer is lost, such as earnouts, holdbacks, or other contingent payments.

How much customer concentration will buyers tolerate?

Some buyers will tolerate customer concentration as high as 20% to 30%, but they will expect numerous deal-protective measures such as escrows, earnouts, or a reduction in the purchase price to offset the increased risk. If you have customer concentration above 30% to 50%, your business may be unsalable, unless you're willing to agree to a transaction structure that offers the buyer numerous protections if one of your customers leaves shortly after the closing.

While the exact figure depends on the industry, customer concentration generally becomes a problem once a customer generates more than 5% to 10% of your revenue. If the concentration level is below 5%, many buyers won't question the relationships. If it's between 5% to 10%, many buyers will begin to probe deeper and may start to consider measures designed to reduce the risk from customer concentration. If one customer generates more than 10% of your revenue, expect to include protective measures in the purchase agreement or be prepared to reduce the purchase price to offset this increased risk.

There are two methods for minimizing customer concentration risk:

1. **Reduce Customer Concentration:** This method only works in the long term and involves diversifying your customer base so that no single customer generates more than 5% to 10% of your revenue. If you're selling your business in the next year or two, this likely won't be practical. For example, if one customer generates 50% of your revenue, focus on obtaining new customers and reduce your dependency on that one customer. This obviously isn't possible in most cases in the short term, but many businesses can diversify their customer base over time.

2. **Mitigate the Risks of Customer Concentration:** This method involves instituting measures designed to reduce the risk of customer concentration to the buyer without actually reducing customer concentration and includes:

   a. **Long-Term Contracts:** Ask your key customers to sign long-term contracts. Offer incentives in exchange for signing a long-term contract, such as grandfathered pricing or other sweeteners, such as free support, discounts, or other add-ons.

   b. **Institutionalization:** Institutionalize your relationships with your customers. In other words, reduce the level of your personal involvement with the customers. If you have a strong personal relationship with a customer, slowly transition the relationship to some of your key employees who will remain with the business after the closing. But before doing so, make sure you've also implemented a retention plan with your key employees to ensure the customer relationship transitions smoothly to a buyer. If there's a risk that your key employees won't stay after the closing, such a strategy won't reduce the risk for the buyer.

c. **Deal Protective Measures:** Deal protective measures include escrows, earnouts, holdbacks, and other forms of contingent payments. You can't take action on these items prior to a sale, but you can be mentally prepared to accept such protective measures, or you can include specific proposals in your information memorandum designed to reduce the risk. By proposing specific mechanisms for reducing risk, the buyer will feel that you understand the risk inherent in customer concentration, and they will feel comfortable that you're prepared to address this risk. In most cases, an escrow, or holdback, is more appropriate for addressing customer concentration risks than an earnout and involves a portion of the purchase price being held in escrow by a third party. The amount held in escrow would then be released over time according to a schedule, assuming the customer is retained.

The higher the customer concentration in your business, the more risk this presents to the buyer.

Conclusion

Without customers, your business wouldn't generate any revenue. Your customers are, therefore, a critical component of your business. Here's a summary of tips for ensuring that your customer base adds value to your business:

- **Customer Base:** Build relationships with large, established customers. Gain a mix of different types of customers. Build a diverse customer base consisting of a critical mass of customers at various adoption stages of your business. Build sales infrastructure and a team that gives you the capability to acquire larger customers.

- **Customer Contracts:** Ensure customer contracts are assignable in the event of a sale. Develop incentives to convert customers to long-term contracts, such as grandfathered pricing or free add-on modules.

- **Customer Acquisition:** Track your customer metrics in a dashboard and work to improve them over time by building marketing strategies that can be automated and scaled.

- **Customer Sales Pipeline:** Track your sales pipeline in your CRM so buyers can project your revenue.

- **Customer Database**: Build a robust customer database that contains detailed information on your customers that will allow a buyer to develop scalable, targeted campaigns.

- **Customer Metrics:** Build a centralized dashboard to track your key metrics. Prepare a backlog of projects designed to improve and track the improvement of your metrics over time to serve as the foundation for your financial projections.

- **Close Relationships:** Reduce any personal relationships you have with customers before the sale.

- **Customer Concentration:** Minimize customer concentration. Institutionalize customers that generate a significant percentage of your overall revenue and reduce your personal involvement in these relationships.

CHAPTER 15

Operations

"Business has only two functions – marketing and innovation."

– Peter Drucker, American Business Author

Introduction

Preparing your operations for sale is a relatively straightforward task. This chapter includes several quick actions you can take to ensure your operations are in tip-top shape before you begin the sales process.

Suppliers

Diversify your supplier base if you're dependent on any one supplier. Buyers don't want a key supplier to hold them hostage, so consider ways to reduce your supplier dependency. Ask yourself the following – how are my relationships with my suppliers? How long have I worked with them? How much power do my suppliers have over me? If you're at all dependent on your suppliers, create a strategy for reducing your dependency before you put your business on the market.

Premises

You know what they say – you never have a second chance to make a first impression. The same goes for your business. Implement cosmetic enhancements that help improve your business's value. Perform quick and easy improvements, such as cleaning up the physical space. A couple of coats of fresh paint can never hurt, but don't go overboard – if your business appears too fancy, it may turn off some buyers. Consider hiring an interior designer to project the right image if you're in doubt.

> You never have a second chance to make a first impression. The same goes for your business.

Online Presence

Check your online presence and reviews to make sure you don't have any poor reviews. If you do, work to clean them up or push them lower in the search results. Poor online reviews can be a deal killer for many businesses, especially B2C businesses or those that rely on a strong online presence. If an online presence is important to your business, make sure your online image is as pristine as possible before you go to market.

Branding

You know how good your company is, but will your potential buyer? Gather any customer testimonials, credible customer lists, case studies, awards or recognition your company has received, and any involvement your company has had in community programs. Having this information organized and on hand will offer demonstrable proof from third parties that your business model generates value for your customers.

> If you own the real estate your business occupies, ensure your real estate is owned by a separate legal entity and your "Business Entity" should pay the going market rate to the "Real Estate Entity" to rent the premises.

Real Estate

If you own the real estate your business occupies, ensure your real estate is owned by a separate legal entity – the "Real Estate Entity," rather than your business – the "Business Entity." The "Business Entity" should pay the going market rate to the "Real Estate Entity" to rent the premises. This ensures your financials are more representative and allows you to value your business independently from the real estate.

Lease

Landlords are accustomed to businesses being bought and sold, so the news shouldn't shock them. Informing your landlord early on normally carries the benefit of being able to pre-negotiate the terms of the transfer. It's also possible your landlord might have a buyer in mind.

But landlords can be opportunistic and difficult to predict. Buyers like options, so don't sign or renew a long-term lease if you think a buyer may want to relocate your business. On the other hand, buyers also like stability, especially if your location is important. The best of both worlds is a lease that contains options to renew that are assignable. This gives you and the buyer both stability and flexibility. Still, there are downsides. Options to renew aren't always assignable and don't usually specify the amount of rent.

If you can, pre-negotiate an option to renew your existing lease. If location is important to your business, the buyer will feel more comfortable if a long lease term is guaranteed in the form of an option to renew. Buyers are uncomfortable with verbal assurances and prefer a written option to renew. You may consider talking to your landlord to obtain this option prior to selling your business, but make sure the option is transferable to the new buyer.

You should also contact the landlord early in the process to ask about their financial and experience requirements for approving a new tenant. Ensure the landlord is willing to renew your lease on favorable terms and that they won't opportunistically ask for a higher rate. Doing so will prevent this all too common problem from killing your deal.

Inventory

Compile a preliminary list of inventory that will be included in the sale. This helps eliminate last-minute surprises, such as underestimating the amount of inventory and, therefore, the amount of cash the buyer must bring to the closing table.

It's also important to liquidate any old, unusable or unsellable inventory. You'll likely end up giving it to the buyer for free, so liquidate it now and put the cash in your pocket. Doing this will simplify the counting of the inventory at the closing and help tidy up your facilities. Stale inventory that includes obsolete, out-of-favor, or overpriced items deters knowledgeable buyers, so get rid of it before you meet with buyers.

Equipment

Similar to inventory, before you put your business on the market, it's important to examine your business's equipment.

Prepare an Equipment List

Prepare a list of all hard assets that are part of the sale, including furniture, fixtures, equipment, leasehold improvements, vehicles, and any other physical assets. Keep the list in an easy-to-update format. There's no need to include values for each piece of equipment. In fact, this can work against you because the buyer can use your estimates to dispute the individual values or argue that the purchase price of the equipment should be allocated for tax purposes.

Perform an Equipment Inspection

Hire a third party to perform a preliminary equipment inspection to ensure all equipment is in proper working order. Repair equipment that isn't working properly or liquidate it if you no longer need it.

Purge Your Outdated Equipment

Liquidate or sell any equipment that's inoperable, outdated, or not used in your business. Repair or replace any broken equipment. Remove any assets from the premises that are not included in the sale. If the buyer sees them, they'll assume these assets are included.

Equipment Leases

Consider paying off any equipment leases. Deciding to pay off your equipment lease before selling your business is primarily a mathematical decision with one unknown variable – the multiple. Let's look at an example to illustrate the math behind the decision.

- **Example:**

  - Asking price = $3 million

  - EBITDA = $1 million

  - Business value = $3 million

  - Equipment lease payment = $20,000 per month

  - Paying off the lease will save the buyer $240,000 per year ($20,000 per month x 12 = $240,000 per year).

  - EBITDA will increase to $1.24 million from $1 million if the lease is paid off.

  - The value of the business will increase to $3.72 million ($1.24 million x 3.0) if the lease is paid off.

  - The difference between the two business values is $720,000.

- **Conclusion:**

  - If the payoff is less than $720,000, it will make economic sense to pay off the lease.

- The example above assumes the multiple will be 3.0. If the multiple is less or more, the formula will be different. Be conservative in choosing your multiple.

- Don't pay off your equipment lease until closing. You don't want to pay off the lease and then not sell your business.

- Consult your CPA to take the tax implications into consideration.

The bottom line is that it makes sense to pay off the equipment leases if the value of your business will increase more than the current payoff amount. The reverse is also true – it doesn't make sense to pay off the lease if paying off your equipment leases will increase the value of your business by less than the payoff.

Purchasing New Equipment

As a general rule, you shouldn't invest in new equipment or other hard assets when you're in the process of selling your business unless it immediately increases your SDE or EBITDA. Why? Because you're unlikely to recoup your investment. Buyers value businesses based on the earnings a business generates. If the new equipment doesn't increase your cash flow, it's unlikely to pay for itself.

> Don't invest in new equipment or other hard assets when you're in the process of selling your business unless it immediately increases your cash flow.

There are two ways to increase your business's cash flow:

1. **Increase Revenue:** If the equipment immediately increases your revenue without having to market or sell a new service, you should perform a calculation to see if the investment in the new equipment and the resulting increase in cash flow will have a positive return for you. This won't be true in the majority of cases.

2. **Decrease Expenses:** If the equipment immediately reduces labor or other costs, it may be a wise investment. If the new equipment will increase the value of your business by more than the cost of the equipment, it may make sense to purchase the equipment. The reverse is also true – if the new equipment won't increase the value of your business by more than the cost of the equipment, it doesn't make sense to make the investment. To calculate how much the new equipment will increase the value of your business, simply multiply how much the equipment will reduce labor costs and therefore increase your SDE or EBITDA, and then apply your multiple. For example, if the equipment will reduce labor costs by $100,000 per year and your multiple is 4.0, then the equipment will increase the value of your business by $400,000.

If the new piece of equipment would simply be nice to have, or if it represents a new product or service line you could pursue, I recommend holding off on this investment. Point out the opportunity to the buyer and let them decide if this is something they want to pursue, and let them make the investment.

Legal

Preparing your business for sale also means examining the legal footing of your business. Let's walk through what you should be looking for.

UCC Search

Perform a Uniform Commercial Code (UCC) search on your business to make sure there are no existing liens. Existing liens can lead to a delayed closing. If you have existing liens, see what you can do to clear them up prior to putting your business on the market.

Status of Entity

Ensure your entity (Corporation or LLC) is up to date. Not doing so can delay the closing.

Intellectual Property

Document any intellectual property included in the sale and gather the necessary paperwork to assist with the transfer. This can include trade secrets, recipes, proprietary products or services, trademarks, patents, and any other registered and unregistered intellectual property. If your employees or other contractors assisted in creating the intellectual property, make sure you have signed invention assignment creation agreements on hand. If your business has valuable intellectual property that hasn't been documented, consider consulting with an attorney who specializes in intellectual property.

Pending Litigation

Resolve any pending litigation or other legal matters – or even threats of litigation – as soon as possible before you put your business on the market. Even though you might offer to take full legal and financial responsibility for any negative consequences, many potential buyers will pull back, fearing the unknown – including how lawsuits and other disputes may affect the public image of your business. In short, if you can't reach settlements before you start to market your business, the salability of even a well-run, profitable business may be negatively impacted. Alternatively, if the litigation is frivolous or for a small amount, obtain a letter of opinion from your attorney to present to potential buyers and be prepared to hold back a portion of the purchase price in escrow.

Transition Period

The period when business ownership transfers to the buyer is an often overlooked yet important phase of the sales transaction. In worst-case scenarios, the buyer can fail due to inadequate training, and the business can close down, resulting in significant financial damages. In best-case scenarios, the transition will go smoothly and help ensure the new owner is successful. Here's how to set the stage for a successful transition.

The Importance of the Training Period

It can pay to help ensure your buyer is successful, and a training period can help you do just that. Most transactions involve seller financing, and when this is the case, the buyer needs to succeed to ensure you receive your payments down the road. The training period helps provide a smoother transition for the buyer's venture as a new business owner.

You likely have a good idea of how to run your business from an operational standpoint. A training period can be a fruitful time for the buyer to learn the "tricks of the trade," as well as some of the things that have made your business successful. Of course, every buyer or new owner wants to make the business their own, and in time, they should. But a short education of your business's basic elements can undoubtedly help make it a successful ongoing enterprise.

The Written Training Plan

You can dramatically increase the attractiveness of your business and reduce the buyer's perception of risk by preparing a written training plan for the buyer in advance. If the buyer lacks experience in your industry, the buyer won't know what the training should consist of, so work with the buyer to jointly create a plan. Unfortunately, most sellers take no preparatory steps to help ensure the transition goes smoothly for the buyer. Creating a plan will make the buyer feel much more confident that the transition will unfold as smoothly as possible.

You should begin creating a draft of the training plan before the sales process begins. The training plan should be designed to provide the buyer with the essential knowledge and skills to manage the business. While your employees can often train the buyer on the technical elements of the business, you must usually train the buyer in the managerial tasks. The training period is also a good time for the buyer to build relationships with key employees in the business.

Often, once this introductory period has passed, much of the training can be handled through email and phone conversations. The important thing is to establish the amount of time the buyer can expect to receive help, outlining limitations and expectations.

Each purchase agreement is as different as the next, and the training agreement is no exception. The specifications in each training agreement will be unique, as each business is unique. Every buyer comes into a business with a varied skill set and experience level, which will also factor into the particulars of the training agreement.

A well-thought-out list of any critical items or issues that should be covered during the training period will lead to a more effective transition and maximize the use of the time that was agreed to in the training agreement. It will also help to identify how long the training period needs to be.

I suggest putting the following into writing:

- A list of all topics to include in the training period: Customer service, office work, accounting and bookkeeping, legal, employees – including hiring, onboarding, and training.

- An agenda for procedures, tools, skills, and anything the buyer must be trained in.

- A timeline for the process as a whole, as well as timelines for each step in the process.

- Priorities for each item on the agenda.

- Details on how the training will be performed, such as in writing, in person, or virtually. Video recordings of highly technical or detailed processes the buyer can reference later may also be useful.

The training agenda should be as clear and defined as possible. A spreadsheet with each item marked as completed when it's finished should be kept on record in case there are problems down the road. The buyer should keep all training materials that the seller provides to assist during the transition period.

Here are some additional considerations when preparing the transition plan:

- **Operations and the Transition Period:** The day after the closing, the buyer may not have the knowledge, skills, and experience to begin operating the business immediately. You should also create a plan for who's responsible for running the business during the transition period to ensure a smooth hand-off.

- **People Involved:** Discuss who will execute the training. Employees can often assist with the process.

- **Additional Help:** Create options for your availability if any questions arise after the training period concludes. I recommend structuring this assistance on an hourly consulting basis at times that are most convenient for you. Much of this can be handled virtually – by phone, online meetings, and email.

- **Training Only:** These agreements are for training and consulting only, not for you to work in the business.

- **Specific Agreement:** The purchase agreement should contain a clause specifying a "training agreement" between you and the buyer. It should be specific regarding the length of the training, including how many hours and on what terms the training will be provided. Not doing so can lead to post-sale disagreements, and buyers sometimes sue sellers for failure to train them properly.

- **Document Completion of the Training:** Upon completion of the training period, it's important to have the buyer acknowledge in writing that the training period has been completed so there are no disputes. Failing to follow up on this crucial step opens the door for the buyer to default on payments by claiming that you failed to train them properly.

Length of the Training Period

The time dedicated to the training period depends on the type of business and the buyer's needs. If the business is a simple operation, several weeks of training time may suffice. However, a more sophisticated operation may require several months, or even years, of training. It's common to include a set training period in the purchase price and for the seller to offer an ongoing consulting agreement on an hourly basis if the buyer needs help beyond the formal training period. Much of the training can often be handled through online chats, emails, videos, and phone conversations once an introductory period has passed.

Conclusion

The training agreement is an important aspect of the business sale. The training period that you offer to the buyer can be an integral part of the new owner's success. Before stipulating the terms and conditions of the training agreement, give thought to what type of training is beneficial to the buyer, as well as the type of commitment you can reasonably offer. Clear and manageable terms are important so the needs and goals of the training period can be met.

Here's a summary of the actions you should take to prepare and improve your operations before you begin the sale process:

- Diversify your supplier base if you're dependent on any one supplier.

- Implement cosmetic improvements to your premises.

- Improve your online presence and online reviews. Push any bad reviews down in the search results.

- Gather customer testimonials and other awards or recognitions.

- If you own the real estate, move it to a separate entity and pay your business the going market rate.

- Negotiate options to renew your lease and make sure the lease can be transferred on the current terms.

- Prepare an inventory and equipment list.

- Purge your inventory and equipment, if necessary.

- Perform an equipment inspection and repair any broken equipment.

- Consider paying off your equipment leases. Perform a calculation to determine the ROI on doing so.

- Perform a UCC search and clear up any liens on your business.

- Check to make sure your entity is up to date.

- Document your intellectual property. Consider consulting with an attorney specializing in intellectual property if your business has valuable IP.

- Create a written training plan for the buyer.

- Resolve any pending litigation.

CHAPTER 16

Staff

"We don't hire smart people so we can tell them what to do.
We hire smart people so they can tell us what to do."

– Steve Jobs, American Entrepreneur

Introduction

Your employees are likely one of your business's most valuable assets. Problems with employees are a common deal killer when selling a business. It makes sense to carefully review any potential problem areas that may lurk with your staff and address them well before you put your company on the market. Many of these problems take a significant amount of time to resolve, so I recommend you work on this long before the sale.

> Problems with employees can be one of the most common deal killers when selling your business.

Ownership

If you own a business, don't make it difficult for a successor to replace you. The more valuable you are to your business, the less valuable your business will be to potential buyers. The ideal situation is one in which you're 100% replaceable. If you're irreplaceable, then most corporate buyers will expect you to remain with the business after you sell it.

Roles and Dependencies

Unfortunately, many business owners inadvertently make themselves irreplaceable in their business. Making yourself irreplaceable not only decreases the value of your business, but also makes it much more difficult to find a buyer that will be interested in assuming that risk. The easiest businesses to sell have a wide universe of potential buyers, can be relocated anywhere in the United States, and don't require their operators to have a highly specialized set of skills.

Absentee-owned businesses are worth much more than owner-operated businesses because the business isn't dependent on the owner, meaning the business can be easily transitioned to a new owner. Most absentee-owned businesses are successfully run by a small group of core employees or a management team. Assuming the employees in an absentee-owned business will stay after the sale, nearly anyone is qualified to purchase the business, at least from an operational standpoint. This greatly opens up the universe of potential buyers and increases the chances the business will be sold for top dollar.

As you streamline your business and make yourself replaceable, you'll build a business that's not only much easier to sell but also one that's simpler to operate. To streamline your business, you have to:

- Build a strong team of core employees or a management team.

- Build scalable systems into your business.

- Document your operations.

- Automate processes in your business using technology or other systems.

These methods of streamlining your business involve using either human talent or technology. But don't make the mistake of trying to rely solely on just people or technology. Most businesses must use both. In other words, not only must you have a strong and capable workforce and management team, you must also have systems and processes in place to support your team.

If your business isn't heavily dependent on you, this reduces risk for the buyer and greatly improves the marketability and attractiveness of your business for both sophisticated and unsophisticated buyers, and dramatically increases its value.

> The more valuable you are to your business, the less valuable your business will be to potential buyers.

If your business is heavily dependent on you, the buyer will consider this risky and will pay a lower multiple as a result. If this is the case, you should attempt to reduce any dependency the business has on any owners that won't remain with the business after the sale. You should do so by evenly re-distributing your responsibilities to your management team.

Multiple Owners

If more than one owner is actively working in your business, a buyer will need to replace all owners unless the owners are willing to stay with the business long-term. Replacing multiple owners will significantly increase risk for the buyer and will result in a lower purchase price, if they're willing to purchase the business at all. The advantage of only having one active owner in the business is that the buyer only needs to replace one person – the active owner. The fewer people the buyer must replace after the closing, the lower the risk, and a higher purchase price can be justified as a result.

If your business has multiple owners, you should seek to replace any owners who won't stay with the business after the closing. This dramatically reduces risk for the buyer. Alternatively, the owners can agree to stay with the business until the new owner can find and train replacements.

Owner Compensation

Are all owners of the business receiving a salary? If you're working 80 hours a week, it's unlikely that one salaried manager could replace you. As a result, a deduction must be made to the cash flow of the business to replace you with two employees, lowering its value. All owners should be paid a salary based on current market conditions, which should be based on what it would cost to hire a comparable employee in the current marketplace.

Other Partners

Seek the approval of all shareholders, partners, and decision-makers involved in your business. Consider whether everyone agrees to the time frame and the price, and if seller financing will be offered.

Don't underestimate the rights, power, and potential wrath of minority shareholders, whether they're voting or non-voting. Minority owners treated with disrespect can exercise their rights and powers and make things difficult for everyone involved. They can hire a lawyer and sue the company, causing considerable harm, even if they don't win in court. Majority shareholders are best advised to treat the minority shareholders as they would wish to be treated themselves. Ensure you have agreement from all minority shareholders before moving forward. Consult with an attorney if you don't. While they can be squeezed out in some cases, it's always best to mutually agree to a course of action.

All owners should be paid a salary based on current market conditions.

You should also seek the approval of your spouse. Under community property laws, a spouse may contest the sale even if they aren't an owner of the business because the ownership of the business may be considered community property.

Family

Selling a business in which your family members participate involves several unique considerations. Let's cover them here.

Working Family Members

If no family members are actively working in your business – advantage: buyer. That's because the buyer won't have to replace any family members who are working in the business after the sale.

If multiple family members are involved in your business, and some aren't willing to stay, the buyer may consider it excessively risky to attempt to replace these employees while also closing on the transaction. If so, replace any family members prior to the sale if they won't continue to work with the new owner. Alternatively, your family members can agree to remain working for the new owner until they find and train a replacement, but this represents more work and risk to the buyer, and you'll receive less for your business as a result. The fewer family members working in the business, the better. Buyers get nervous about buying a business in which a lot of family members are working because they must be replaced if they aren't willing to remain with the business after the closing.

Family Member Compensation

Are any family members working in the business without compensation? All family members actively working in the business should be paid market-rate salaries. If they're receiving payment below market rates, their compensation needs to be normalized to market levels when adjusting your financial statements, which decreases the value of your business. Having non-working family members on your payroll complicates due diligence and represents an additional risk to the buyer. If you have any family members who will be staying with the business after you sell it, formalize their roles and compensation and pay them a market-rate salary.

> Any family members actively working in the business should be paid market-rate salaries.

Do you have any family members on the payroll who aren't active in the business? If so, remove them from the payroll at least two to three years prior to the sale. While having them on the payroll won't be a deal killer, it will complicate due diligence because the buyer will need to confirm that the family member didn't spend any time working in the business. Keeping them on the payroll may raise additional suspicions and questions, so it's best to avoid this issue and remove any family members from the payroll if they aren't active in your business. The buyer may believe that if you had a non-working family member on the payroll, you may be taking other liberties in your business. They may worry that you're not running the business above board and may dig a little deeper in the due diligence process, so it's best to avoid this situation and keep these family members off the payroll.

Management Team

A capable management team dramatically improves the value of your company and makes it much easier to sell. Most small businesses lack a formal management team. Without professional management, your business will likely die without you. How long can your business survive without you? One year? One month? One week?

Unfortunately, building a professional management team requires a new set of skills for most entrepreneurs. When you first started your business, you likely performed most of the key tasks yourself. Once you reach a certain point in your business, you must build a team. Building a team requires recruiting and management skills. You have to learn how to find and hire good people and how to get results from those people.

Determine what position or positions would add the most value to your company. Who does your company need most? Invest in developing a formal management team. Not only will your business be easier to sell, but your revenues and profits will likely increase as well, and your business will be easier to manage.

If your business has a strong management team, this increases the universe of potential buyers you can market your business to, thereby improving the odds of a successful sale and the value of your business. How strong is your management team? Does your management team have a solid track record of achieving results? Do you have a trained and experienced management team in place? If so, your business will be worth more.

If your duties are heavily concentrated, some buyers may feel intimidated by the idea of having to fulfill your current roles and obligations, and your business will be worth less as a result. If you don't have a management team and aren't willing to stay to operate the business after the closing, your business will be difficult to sell to a financial buyer. On the other hand, your business will still be salable to the majority of individuals because most will plan on replacing you with themselves.

> A capable management team dramatically improves the value of your company and makes it much easier to sell.

Key Employees

Aside from customer concentration, the concentration in key employees is one of the most common areas of concern for buyers and is one of the most prevalent areas of risk in small to mid-sized businesses. The smaller the business, the more likely this will be a concern.

Toleration for Staff Concentration

Staff concentration in this context refers to the amount of dependency on any single employee. In a company that has one "general" and a hundred "foot soldiers," for example, there is high dependency. The degree to which this is a concern depends on the three types of buyers described next. They can be broken down as follows:

1. **Private, Wealthy Individuals:** These types of individuals are less likely to consider staff concentration an issue if they plan to be involved in the day-to-day management of the business and can step into your shoes and continue operating the business as you did. But this assumes that all of your employees will stay with the business after the closing – with the exception of you, the owner. If the buyer assumes your duties and your key staff are willing to stay post-closing, a concentration of employees is unlikely to be considered a deal killer by most individual buyers. If, on the other hand, you and your spouse work full-time in the business and you have a few family members involved who won't be staying with the business post-closing, this will be a concern for the majority of buyers. The primary exception to this will be direct competitors who have the capacity to replace you, or a husband and wife team with strong industry experience who will both be actively involved in the business.

> The degree to which key employee concentration is a concern depends on the buyer.

2. **Financial Buyers:** Most financial buyers only acquire businesses that have a team in place that can manage the business post-closing. If the business is heavily dependent on you and you aren't willing to remain with your business after the sale, it's unlikely you'll be able to sell your business to a financial buyer. The primary exception will be financial buyers who are planning to hire a CEO to replace you, or buyers who own a portfolio company in your industry and plan to integrate your company into their platform company. In these cases, they will be less dependent on your key employees.

3. **Strategic Buyers and Direct Competitors:** Selling to a strategic buyer or competitor is the simplest method for reducing the risk associated with staff concentration. But the degree to which this risk is mitigated depends on the extent to which the buyer will integrate your business and your products into their business. If the buyer plans to operate your business as a stand-alone business post-closing, a management team will need to be in place to run your business for the buyer after the closing, and the buyer may need to hire a manager or CEO to replace you. On the other hand, if the buyer plans to fold your products or services into their existing product suite, close your facility, or eliminate duplicate functions such as accounting, HR, and legal, a concentration in responsibilities is unlikely to be considered an issue.

Methods for Reducing Staff Concentration Risk

Reducing concentrations of risk in your staff requires developing strong management skills and building infrastructure, and can be broken down into the following strategies:

- **Distribute Responsibilities:** Evenly distribute responsibilities among your team, so your business isn't dependent on you or any individual – avoid high concentrations of responsibilities in any one individual.

- **Distribute Authority:** Evenly distribute decision-making authority within your firm. Make sure authority isn't highly concentrated in any one person.

- **Build a Strong Management Team:** Build a management team capable of developing and executing their own strategies and goals, and that has the authority to make their own decisions. Hire only experienced people with a demonstrated history of achieving results.

- **Hire Highly Capable People:** Only hire talented people capable of operating on an autonomous basis, and who don't depend on input from their senior managers to plan and execute objectives.

- **Implement a Retention Plan:** Develop and implement a retention plan to retain your key employees after the closing. The retention plan can consist of a cash bonus or equity incentives, such as phantom equity.

- **Sign Agreements with Key People:** Ensure you have signed employment contracts with your key people that address the issues of confidentiality, non-compete, and non-solicitation.

- **Eliminate Personal Relationships:** Reduce or eliminate any personal relationships you have with customers and delegate relationship-building evenly across your staff.

- **Build Trust Through Timely Disclosure:** Reassure your team that the transition provides an opportunity for continued career development and the potential for career advancement. Reinforce the role and value of the retention bonus.

I recognize the difficulty of implementing my advice here – every entrepreneur understands the value of building a management team. The issue isn't understanding its importance – the issue is actually building a strong team, and this is certainly easier said than done. I realize this is a Herculean task. But as an entrepreneur, you must understand that the more indispensable you are to your business, the more difficult your business will be to sell – and the less your business is worth.

If you just received a $20 million venture capital injection, chances are you can afford the best available talent and motivate your team with stock options and other incentives. Such scenarios tend to attract strong, autonomous, driven talent. But if you own a technology company in

Detroit, Michigan, that generates $4 million in revenue and you have no institutional investors backing you, you must learn to make do with less.

I understand the limitations inherent in a small business and empathize to a great degree with entrepreneurs struggling to make the leap to middle-market status. Many business owners are looking to sell because they can't make that transition from a small company that's highly dependent on themselves to a middle-market business run by an independent management team.

Other than retirement, this is perhaps the number one reason entrepreneurs sell their companies – because their business is dependent on them and they feel as if they "can't escape their own company." They have no time to relax, can't take vacations, and have a hard time letting go. It's a catch-22 – they want to sell because the business is so dependent on them, but they wouldn't sell if the business weren't dependent on them. What's the solution? Either way, the solution is to try to reduce your business's dependency on you.

Nonetheless, it's important to understand the circumstances in which a strong team is necessary and under what circumstances you can sell your business, despite high concentrations of risk in your team. It's also important to prioritize the actions you can take and the degree to which buyers see value in those actions. Understanding the high-level picture will help you prioritize your actions and determine to what degree you should attempt to reduce the risk and whether expanding this effort is worth the lost opportunity cost to you.

Assessing the potential impact of staff concentration is nuanced and depends on more variables than assessing the impact of customer concentration. Every situation is different, and it's best to obtain the advice of an experienced M&A professional to evaluate your specific circumstance. They can help determine the probability of selling your business without building a strong management team and help you prioritize actions you can take to reduce risks in employee concentration in the interim.

Learn More

Many excellent books have been written that can help you build a strong management team. I recommend the following:

- *Scaling Up* by Verne Harnish (Gazelles, Inc., 2014)

- *The New One Minute Manager* by Ken Blanchard and Spencer Johnson (Harper Collins India, 2016)

- *Ready, Fire, Aim* by Michael Masterson (Gildan Media LLC, 2008)

- *The Breakthrough Company* by Keith R. McFarland (Random House Audio, 2008)

- *Business Model Generation* by Alexander Osterwalder and Yves Pigneur (John Wiley and Sons, 2010)

- *The Founder's Dilemmas* by Noam Wasserman (Princeton University Press, 2012)

- *Who: The A-Method for Hiring* by Geoff Smart and Randy Street (Ballantine Books, 2008)

- *Ownership Thinking* by Brad Hams (McGraw Hill, 2011)

- *Scrum: The Art of Doing Twice the Work in Half the Time* by Jeffrey Victor Sutherland (Currency, 2014)

- *Work Rules!* by Laszlo Bock (Twelve, 2015)

- *Organizational Physics* by Lex Sisney (Lulu.com, 2012)

- *High Output Management* by Andrew S. Grove (Vintage, 2015)

- *Measure What Matters* by John Doerr (Portfolio, 2018)

New Employees

If you're planning to sell your business within the next two years, avoid hiring new employees for roles with a steep learning curve or roles that don't offer an immediate return, such as sales positions. Doing so can reduce your SDE or EBITDA, which will decrease the value of your business in the short term. Instead, stick to hiring for less risky positions in which the results are predictable, and where there is a low probability that the employee will be a poor investment.

Compensation

Are wages above or below the industry averages? If below, a buyer will need to increase compensation, which will decrease the cash flow of your business and, therefore, its value. Ensure all employee compensation is at current market levels. Deviations from the going rates can turn off potential buyers and will need to be normalized to market levels, which will reduce the value of your business.

Tenure

What is your annual employee turnover rate? Longer-than-average tenures reduce risk for the buyer and improve the attractiveness of your business. Shorter-than-average tenures increase risk for the buyer and reduce the attractiveness of your business. Shorter tenures or high turnover rates could signal problems with your corporate culture and are a warning flag to sophisticated buyers. If the buyer is concerned about the culture of your business, this can dramatically reduce its value in that buyer's eyes. If you're having problems with tenure, figure out the root cause and address it long before you begin the sale process.

Employee Manual

Prepare an employee manual or handbook. Employees are a critical resource of any business. An employee manual or handbook projects a positive image to buyers that your business is well-run. Employee manuals set clear expectations and boundaries with employees, make maintaining operations simpler, and facilitate a smooth transition. Having a manual also reduces perceived risk for the buyer and improves the attractiveness of your business in a buyer's eyes.

Informing Employees

Carefully consider when to tell your employees about the sale. Employees are just as worried about losing their jobs as the buyer is about keeping them. Employees often become nervous when they find out about a sale. Should you tell your employees about the sale? There are no hard-and-fast rules regarding when you should spill the beans.

If your company's culture is positive and you have trust with your employees, you may consider telling some of them about the sale.

If you have a larger-sized business and have an in-house controller or CFO, you will benefit from informing them because they will play a pivotal role in the sale process. It would be almost impossible to keep the sale a secret from your in-house controller or CFO during your preparations and due diligence. The process of selling your business will involve numerous financial requests, and your controller will quickly become suspicious if you request numerous financial documents in a row. You may want to talk to them directly and disclose the sale only to them. If you take this approach, I recommend asking them to sign a non-disclosure agreement to ensure they keep the planned sale confidential.

If your staff is large, I recommend keeping the sale a secret, with the exception of your key management team. It's nearly impossible for a large group of people to keep mum. While your staff may feel betrayed, you can simply explain to them that it would have been impossible for everyone to keep the sale a secret, and you were bound by a non-disclosure agreement, so you had no choice but to keep it under wraps until the sale became official. And while you're at it, this would be an excellent time to announce a bonus for all employees.

The Advantage of Telling Your Employees

If you decide to tell your employees, you can use this to your advantage during negotiations with buyers. You can mention to buyers that you have told your employees, and you can selectively let buyers meet with some of your top people. This helps the buyer feel more comfortable and lowers perceived risk. The lower the risk, the higher the purchase price that can be justified. This also helps your employees feel more comfortable since they have the opportunity to meet with prospective buyers before one is selected.

Deciding When to Tell Your Employees

Tell your employees as early as possible or as late as possible. Why?

- If you tell your employees early, you have plenty of opportunities to repair any damage that occurs as a result of your conversation with them. Some employees may jump ship. If this happens, you'll have plenty of time to replace them.

- By telling them as late as possible, the amount of damage that can occur between your conversation and the closing is minimal. In most cases, telling your employees as late as possible involves telling them the day of closing.

Deciding when to tell your employees also depends on the circumstances and culture of your company. If you have 10 to 50 employees and your culture is trusting, you may consider telling them in advance. The longer the employees know, the more opportunity you'll have to build trust and prepare them for the process. You should stress that you will only sell to a buyer who will retain them. Frankly, this shouldn't be a problem since nearly every buyer will want to retain your current staff in any event, with the exception of any duplicate staff if the buyer plans on integrating your company with theirs.

> Deciding when to tell your employees depends on the circumstances and culture of your company.

How To Tell Your Employees

The following are several suggestions for deciding how to tell your team:

- **Use a Tiered Approach:** If you decide to tell your employees, I recommend informing your top people initially, either individually or as a group. Once they're on board, you can meet as a team, and the other employees will look to see how the top people react. If your top people react favorably, the rest of the team will likely follow suit.

- **Ask Employees to Sign an NDA:** Consider asking your employees to sign a non-disclosure or confidentiality agreement. This agreement can be paired with a retention bonus and non-solicitation agreement. The non-solicitation agreement prevents your employees from actively recruiting your other employees or customers in the event they choose to start a competing company or work for a competitor. Ensure this agreement is assignable to the buyer.

- **Keep Things Positive:** Position your plans as a positive move for your employees. For example, a new buyer may invest heavily in your company, increase salaries, and make other improvements to your business. If you position the transition correctly, employees will view this as an opportunity rather than a threat. Your employees' primary fears are the loss of their jobs or major changes to their roles. If you can assure them that neither will happen and that they may benefit from the transition, your employees will feel more comfortable and will be more cooperative during the transition period. Informing your employees also makes buyers feel comfortable with your business, since telling them means that retaining your employees is no longer a point of risk for buyers.

Be Prepared for the Question

Regardless of how and when you decide to tell your team, you must be prepared in case one of your employees approaches you off-guard and asks, "I heard you're planning on selling your business. Is that true?" If this happens, you have two options:

1. **Play it Off:** "Yes, haha, of course. My kids are for sale, too. Buy one, get one free. Everything's for sale for the right price. Did you bring your checkbook?" In other words, you need a pre-planned story. If you choose this route, I recommend asking your spouse, a friend, or a family member to catch you off-guard and ask you several times randomly during the day as to whether your business is for sale. This way, you can practice and hone your response.

2. **Confess:** Your second option is to fess up. Again, there are no hard and fast rules. If you're unsure, use the first option and play it off. You can always come back and confess later on.

As you can see, one of the most difficult decisions to make during a business sale is the timing of when to tell your employees. You need to determine the best way to approach this for your situation and consider your relationship with your employees and personal advisors. Obviously, word will get out eventually, but if you maintain control of the timing and the process, you can use this critical stage to your advantage. Be prepared for the unexpected, consult with your advisors, and make plans to help the sale become a smooth and successful transition for everyone involved.

Retention Bonuses

If you do decide to tell your employees in advance, I suggest offering your key staffers a bonus for staying through the transition. The bonus should be substantial enough to motivate them to stay for a significant period of time following the transition, especially if you're financing a portion of the sale. Consider offering employees a retention bonus as compensation for signing a non-compete or non-solicitation agreement.

Amount and Timing

You can also consider releasing the bonus in stages for 6 to 12 months following the closing. A typical bonus is 5% to 20% of their annual salary and varies based on each employee's importance to the business. You shouldn't give the employees so much money that they can band together and start a competing business, but it should be enough to motivate them to stick around after the closing. Releasing this bonus in stages helps solve this problem.

Explaining the Purpose of the Bonus

Position the bonus as you are sharing your success with your people. If you position it as a "retention bonus," your employees may realize the leverage they have over you and may use that leverage to their advantage. Instead, you want to let your employees know that you'll share a piece of the pie with them because the company wouldn't be in a position to be sold without their loyalty and hard work.

Staff Related Agreements

Your employees are a key asset to your business. To maximize the value of your business, you must protect the nature of these relationships. You must also prevent your employees from potentially damaging the value of your business.

Employment Agreements

Make sure your employment agreements address ownership of intellectual property, and the notice period required when resigning.

Non-Competition Agreement

Consider asking employees to sign a non-compete agreement – if they're legal in your state. Sometimes employees threaten to leave when they hear that the company is being sold, and they threaten to open a competing business and steal your customers. A non-compete can prevent this. If you can't obtain a non-compete, ask for a non-disclosure and non-solicitation agreement at a minimum. But, check to make sure they're transferable in the event of a sale.

In certain states, non-competition agreements signed with your employees are illegal. If your business is located in a state in which employee non-competition agreements are illegal, with California being the most notable example, there are two primary alternatives for protecting your interests:

- **Non-Solicitation Agreement:** A non-solicitation agreement only prohibits an employee from soliciting your employees or customers.

- **Confidentiality Agreement:** At a minimum, all employees should sign a confidentiality agreement. An NDA or confidentiality agreement can prevent employees from disclosing trade or other secrets to new employers.

Collectively, a non-solicitation agreement and NDA serve as highly effective psychological deterrents. Often, deterrents are more effective than other means. Just ask any owner of a Doberman.

Here's what I mean – a fierce-looking dog may be all you need to protect your home. Similarly, in business, an NDA and non-solicitation agreement may be all you need to adequately protect your business, even if you never intend to sue an employee for breaching the terms of these agreements.

Non-Solicitation Agreement

A non-solicitation agreement only prohibits an employee from soliciting your employees or customers. It doesn't prevent them from competing with you, as long as they aren't soliciting your employees or customers. It can be a stand-alone agreement, or it can be included as a component of another agreement, such as an employment, non-compete, or non-disclosure agreement. Non-solicitation agreements are most common in service businesses that have strong customer relationships. These agreements may be legal in some states in which a non-compete is illegal.

This is often an effective enough means to prevent your employees from competing with you, as it may prevent a band of employees from grouping together and poaching your customers. Additional measures can be created to strengthen the non-solicitation agreement. Past or future bonuses can be retracted or withheld if they violate the terms of the agreement. For example, if five of your employees leave to start a competing business, you could withhold any bonuses or other payments if they violate the terms of your non-solicitation agreement.

Non-solicitation agreements can also serve as a form of protection if an employee decides to work for a competitor. But your agreements need to be properly drafted for these mechanisms to be enforceable.

Non-Disclosure Agreement

All employees should sign an NDA at a minimum. An NDA can prevent employees from disclosing trade or other secrets to new employers. It may also be so difficult for the employee to comply with an NDA that they may pass on certain job opportunities to avoid violating the terms of the agreement.

> *For example, if you employ someone who has access to trade secrets for creating your product and a competitor hires this individual, your employee will be prohibited from disclosing your trade secrets to their new employer. If their potential new employer learns of the NDA the employee has signed with you, they may pass on hiring this individual due to the risk associated with doing so.*

An NDA can protect other information as well, such as:

- Customer names

- Prospective client information

- Pricing information, if private

- Financial information

- Employee names, salaries, and benefits

- Intellectual property, such as software codes, designs, technical processes, and trade secrets

It's important to note that in order to protect the above information, your NDA should contain a clear definition of "Confidential Information." If you wish to protect specific elements of your business, clearly spell these out in the agreement. You should also check to make sure they're transferable or assignable in the event of a sale.

To maximize the value of your business, you must protect the relationships you have with employees. You must also prevent your employees from potentially damaging the value of your business. While most businesses use a non-competition agreement to prevent their employees from causing harm to their business, non-competes are illegal in certain states. If a non-compete is illegal in your state, or if asking your employees to sign a non-compete is impractical, then you have two sound alternatives – a non-solicitation agreement and a confidentiality agreement. Both tools can be successfully used to help ensure you protect the value of your business. I discuss this in more detail in the chapter on Confidentiality.

> Consider offering employees a retention bonus as compensation for signing a non-compete or non-solicitation agreement.

Conclusion

Here are the steps you should take with your staff before you put your business on the market:

- Reduce your business's dependency on you.

- Replace any co-owners or family members who won't stay after the sale.

- Pay all owners and family members a salary based on the current market rates.

- Seek the approval of all partners, as well as your spouse, to sell the business.

- Build a professional management team that can run your business without you.

- Ensure all employee compensation is at current market levels.

- Reduce key employee concentration or dependency of any key employees.

- Prepare an employee manual or handbook.

- Consider whether – and when – to inform your employees about the sale.

- Create a retention plan and bonus for key staff.

- Ask key employees to sign a confidentiality and non-solicitation or non-compete agreement.

CHAPTER 17

Team

"Knowledge speaks, but wisdom listens."

– Jimi Hendrix, American Musician

Introduction

Many middle-market acquirers are serial acquirers. Unless you're a serial seller (not killer), this fact of M&A life can put you at an immediate disadvantage. Serial acquirers have mastered the craft of acquiring companies and often leave no stone unturned. For middle-market transactions, the investor often brings a cadre of staff and advisors to the transaction.

That's where professional advisors – your deal team – come into play.

The purpose of qualified advisors is to make you and your management team appear as professional and trustworthy as possible by anticipating issues and preparing disclosures in a forthright manner. Your aim should be to achieve negotiating parity with the investors, to establish a level playing field. It's difficult, if not impossible, to do this alone, especially if you've never sold a company. Not only does your inexperience put you at a great negotiating disadvantage, but the fact that you have only one company to sell also puts you behind the emotional eight ball.

The antidote here is clear cut – an experienced team of professionals to help you lay out and execute your exit plan. A good deal team – or "dream team," as I like to call them – pays for itself. But how do you go about assembling your dream team? The best way to find experts you can work with is through referrals from trusted friends, colleagues, and associates who have personally worked with the advisor or advisors in question.

When putting together your team, you should take into account how much of the work you're willing and able to do yourself and how much you will delegate to others. If the sale is expected to be fairly straightforward and you want to limit your expenses, you may decide to take on many of the routine tasks yourself, using occasional expert help from a lawyer or accountant as needed. Otherwise, plan for your team to be intimately involved in the process. In this chapter, I'll show you how to turn a routine team into a dream team.

> A good deal team pays for itself.

M&A Advisor

You will spend 6 to 18 months or more with your M&A advisor, so it goes without saying that your M&A advisor's style should complement your own. For example, my style is straightforward and no-nonsense. I'm usually straight to the point, matter of fact, and waste little time in small talk. If you're looking for a talkative, salesy-type advisor, I'm not your man. If you're selling a business whose valuation is based on projections and hype, an M&A advisor who takes a more sales-based approach will be a better fit for you. Either way, look for an M&A advisor or investment banker whose style complements yours.

One of the primary advantages of hiring an M&A advisor lies in their role as an intermediary. Retaining an intermediary to negotiate on your behalf enables you to maintain goodwill and minimize conflicts with the opposing party. This is valuable when you will maintain an ongoing relationship with the buyer after the closing.

Negotiations regarding price can become contentious. An experienced M&A advisor keeps their cool during these discussions and insulates you from the stress of negotiating. This helps you maintain your focus on the business and minimizes interpersonal conflicts with the buyer. This is especially important if your transaction includes an earnout, which is a promise of additional compensation in the future if your business achieves specific financial goals.

Your M&A advisor will be instrumental in providing a preliminary range of value for your company and preliminary transaction structuring. They will also negotiate with the buyer regarding the high-level elements of the transaction and how the various components work together to form the overall transaction structure.

Experienced investment bankers treat negotiations as a win-win proposition as opposed to stating a position and firmly holding one's ground. An experienced intermediary can be invaluable in uncovering a buyer's true concerns and creatively structuring a transaction to meet both parties' needs.

They can also assess your business before you go to market and identify risk factors a buyer is likely to perceive, then outline a strategy for mitigating those factors. Ideally, you should build a relationship with your M&A advisor several years in advance, so they can strategically advise you on actions you can take to maximize the value of your business.

> You will spend 6 to 18 months with your M&A advisor, so it goes without saying that your M&A advisor's style should complement your own.

Types of M&A Advisors

Before we discuss the fees for M&A advisors, let's break apart that term into its three most common subtypes – business brokers, M&A advisors, and investment banks.

Business Brokers

Business brokers sell the majority of small businesses, or those priced under $5 million. There are anywhere from 5,000 to 10,000 full-time business brokers in the United States with a variety of backgrounds, from sales to marketing to finance. According to the International Business Brokers Association, many business brokers are former entrepreneurs with an average age in their mid-50s. The more experienced and knowledgeable a business broker is, the more likely they are to sell mid-market businesses, thereby effectively becoming an M&A advisor. Most business brokers are generalists and don't focus on one specific industry.

Most business brokers work on straight commission. However, the more experienced they are, the more likely they are to charge up-front fees. Many business brokers operate both in the Main Street market and in the middle markets.

Most solo brokers and office owners are full-time brokers, although there are a number of part-time agents who work in offices. It takes a significant amount of knowledge to sell a business, and there are few formal training programs available. Due to the low barriers to entry to become a business broker, many people enter the industry expecting to make a quick buck, but underestimate the amount of expertise that's required. As a result, many brokers quit within the first few years, so turnover in the industry is high.

M&A Advisors

M&A advisors specialize in selling mid-sized businesses, or those generally priced from $5 million to $100 million – there is no universally agreed-upon range – and they are simply known as M&A advisors. There are a few thousand M&A advisors in the United States, with the majority representing sellers, though there are some who work with buyers.

Most M&A advisors work solo or as part of a boutique firm. There are a few larger firms that specialize in the lower middle market, but they are in the minority. Some M&A firms focus on specific industries, although the majority are generalists. Many firms offer additional services, such as financing, recapitalizations, and management buyouts, but these constitute ancillary services for most firms.

Most M&A advisors charge an up-front fee, sometimes called a retainer, in addition to a success fee. Some may also charge a monthly retainer. Typical success fees range between 2% and 8%. Common fee arrangements include the Lehman and Double Lehman formulas, which command a higher percentage on the first million – let's say 8% – and a lower percentage on successive amounts, such as 6% on the second million, 4% on the third million, and so forth. I will go into more detail about this fee structure later in this chapter.

As a general rule, most M&A advisors are much more knowledgeable than business brokers because there is a higher level of knowledge required to sell a middle-market business than a small business.

Investment Bankers

Investment bankers specialize in selling larger businesses, typically those generating more than $100 million per year in revenue. You should be aware that the term "investment banker" is regularly and loosely used by M&A advisors to identify themselves due to the lack of a catchy moniker for those specializing in the middle market – "M&A advisor" sounds clunky.

Many of the bulge bracket firm's clients include publicly traded companies. Investment banking firms also offer many other services, such as asset management, trading, equity research, raising debt financing, IPOs, and banking.

There are fewer investment banking offices than M&A firms. Most investment banking firms are larger and have more support staff, though there are some boutique firms in the lower end of the market with between $100 million and $250 million in revenue.

Other Industry Professionals

There is a diverse array of other professionals involved in the sale process to some extent. They can be broken down into several categories.

Exit Planners

Interestingly enough, there is a large divide between those who sell businesses and those who prepare businesses for sale. The world of exit planners is a world of a fragmented collection of professionals. There is little crossover between those who prepare businesses for sale and those who sell businesses. In other words, those who help entrepreneurs prepare their businesses for sale don't normally help them sell the business, and vice versa. As a result, there is often a disconnect between exit planning and the actual exit for most entrepreneurs. Also, how can an exit planner advise the seller on preparing their business for sale if they aren't actively engaged in the marketplace and aren't familiar with the buyer's preferences?

Few business brokers and M&A advisors assist entrepreneurs in preparing their businesses for sale. Our hypothesis is that doing so requires a different mindset, a different set of skills, and different processes.

Commercial Real Estate Agents

Many commercial real estate agents sell businesses that include a real estate component, such as hotels, motels, or storage units. Some commercial real estate offices are active in the business marketplace, though the majority consider this a minor segment of their overall business. Most commercial real estate agents charge a 4% to 6% commission, with declining amounts as the purchase price increases. Most work on straight commission, though there are a few who charge up-front fees.

It's best to hire a commercial agent if you have a business with a substantial real estate component. For example, if you own a hotel, hire a hotel broker. There are many agents who specialize in hotels, motels, storage units, gas stations, and car washes. However, it may be difficult if you're located in a smaller state, as every state requires a real estate license to sell real estate. You may need to hire an out-of-state broker who can cooperate with a local broker. Most state real estate departments allow an out-of-state broker to cooperate with a local broker if they're not licensed in the state.

Business Appraisers

Most business appraisers only value businesses for tax or other legal reasons. They rarely sell businesses, but most will appraise a business for any owner, for any purpose, including for exit-planning purposes. In my opinion, it's best to hire someone active in the marketplace, or someone who sells businesses, as they will be able to best advise you on how to increase the value of your business, and their knowledge won't be purely theoretical. Appraisals can cost $1,000 at the lowest end for a verbal opinion of value, up to $5,000 to $10,000 for a company doing $5 million per year, and up to $20,000 or more for larger companies.

Fees

The fee structure is often different for Main Street and middle-market transactions. Here is an overview of typical fees charged for selling a business based on its size:

Small Businesses Priced Under $5 Million (Main Street)

- This market is primarily handled by business brokers.

- Most brokers charge a flat commission between 8% and 12% if the business is under $1 million and charge a lower fee for businesses priced from $1 million to $5 million. Most follow the Double Lehman or Modern Lehman formula, or some version thereof:

  - 10% to 12% on the first million, plus

  - 8% on the second million, plus

- 6% on the third million, plus

- 4% on the fourth million, plus

- 2% after that

- If a business sells at $5 million, then the fee would be: $100k + $80k + $60k + $40k + $20k = $300k.

- Most business brokers charge a minimum fee of $10,000 to $25,000, regardless of the sale price for the business. For example, if a business sells for $50,000, the broker's fee would be $25,000.

- Most business brokers work on straight commission. A minority of brokers charge an up-front fee, but the more experienced the broker is, the more likely they are to charge up-front fees, as a general rule.

- Most business brokers have no incentive to improve the value of your business due to the fee structure. A straight commission model incentivizes the broker to sell your business as fast as possible with minimal effort.

Mid-Sized Businesses Priced From $5 Million to $100 Million (M&A)

- Most M&A advisors charge up-front fees, in addition to a success fee. The up-front fee, usually called a retainer, varies from as little as a few thousand dollars to more than $50,000. Most advisors have a minimum fee in the range of $50,000 to $250,000.

- The most common fee structures are the Lehman and Double Lehman formulas.

  - Lehman Formula:

    - 5% on the first million, plus

    - 4% on the second million, plus

    - 3% on the third million, plus

    - 2% on the fourth million, plus

    - 1% after that

  - Double Lehman Formula:

    - 10% on the first million, plus

    - 8% on the second million, plus

    - 6% on the third million, plus

- 4% on the fourth million, plus

- 2% after that

- There are other variations on the Lehman and Double Lehman models. For example, some M&A advisors may begin at 8% on the first million and level out at 4%.

Business owners with businesses that sell from $100,000 to $1 million can expect to pay a higher percentage than businesses that sell for more than $1 million. Businesses that sell for more than $1 million often pay a commission that is less than 10% of the purchase price.

Questions To Consider When Hiring an M&A Advisor

Do they work solely on commission?

Intermediaries who work solely on commission are disincentivized from spending time. A flat commission model incentivizes them to sell a business as quickly as possible with the least amount of effort expended. If you don't want to be rushed, you may be more suited to work with a firm that charges up-front fees in addition to a success fee.

Firms who work on straight commission must pad their fees to account for the businesses they take on but don't sell. For example, if they have a 40% success rate, they must find a way to receive compensation on the 60% of the businesses they don't sell.

A straight commission structure can also cause bias and misalignment. The more time the broker invests in selling your business, the more they will feel the need to recoup their investment. A broker who charges an up-front fee for services will feel this pressure to a lesser extent, and your interests are more likely to be closely aligned with the broker's interests.

> Intermediaries who work solely on commission are disincentivized from spending time.

Does the advisor charge up-front fees?

Most professionals are fee-based, but due to the nature of an M&A transaction, few business owners would be willing to pay tens or hundreds of thousands of dollars in fees only to have a transaction fail at the last minute. As a result, most M&A advisors charge fees for services, along with a success fee on the back end. Up-front fees shouldn't be charged if no service is being provided. For example, if a broker requires a $5,000 retainer fee and doesn't provide any specific service for this fee, I recommend you keep looking.

The more experienced the broker, the higher the likelihood they will charge up-front fees, especially if they invest a significant amount of time in the process. Most M&A advisors devote considerable time in preparing and packaging a business for sale, and they're reluctant to do so without being paid up-front for their expertise.

Is there support staff, or do they do everything on their own?

The more professional offices have support staff and rely on a team of both internal and external experts. Selling a business is a difficult multi-disciplinary task that requires an enormous amount of skills in disparate areas. The most efficiently operated offices have developed scalable systems for the repeatable elements in the sale process, such as financial analysis, valuation, marketing, packaging, screening buyers, and closing, with each element handled by an expert in that process. The best operations I've seen perform like a surgeon's office, where the most experienced advisors handle the most complex tasks, while a variety of other staff members deftly execute well-documented and defined processes within a flexible framework.

The size of support staff can have an impact on the level of professionalism demonstrated by the firm and the quality and efficiency of your transaction. Generally speaking, the more support staff the office has, the higher the skill level of everyone involved. In this instance, it's better to specialize in specific areas than to be a "Jack or Jill of all trades."

Can they customize services, or is it an "all or nothing" model?

Every business is unique and should be handled as such. Ideally, your advisor should work within a customizable framework, but if all services are 100% customized, the process will become too inefficient. The ideal scenario is hiring a boutique office that exclusively focuses on selling businesses, has an experienced support staff, and also has a customizable framework.

Can they do exit planning, or do they only sell businesses?

Only a minority of business brokers and M&A advisors help business owners plan their exits. Exit planning primarily consists of helping the owner improve the value of their business over time. Some prepare a formal exit strategy and valuation, while others help on an ad hoc basis. It's a bonus if they can assist you in preparing your business for sale.

Is the firm local or national?

Most business brokers work on a local basis, while many M&A advisors work on a national basis. Ask yourself if their physical presence is necessary. In most cases, it isn't. Most business brokers only work locally because they feel it's necessary to physically meet with buyers. Many do this to protect their commission. If you don't need the broker to physically meet with buyers, you don't need to hire a local broker.

Does the advisor work full-time or part-time?

It goes without saying that you should only hire a broker or advisor who works full-time.

What are the terms of their agreement?

Here are some key additional terms and conditions you should consider:

- **Length:** Most brokers and M&A intermediaries require a one-year exclusive agreement, but you can sometimes negotiate a shorter term. On average, the process of selling a business takes 6 to 12 months. However, it can sometimes take much longer. The term of the agreement usually reflects how long it takes to sell a business.

- **The Tail:** Regardless of how long the exclusive agreement is, at the end of the contract, your broker or M&A advisor should provide you with a list of potential buyers acquired throughout the contract if your business didn't sell for some reason. You will then be obligated to pay a fee if you sell your business to one of those buyers following a specified amount of time after the expiration date of the agreement – called a "tail."

- **Cancellation:** Discuss contract cancellation rights with the firm you hire. Some agreements allow you to cancel at any time, while others don't.

What is an open agreement?

You may seek the services of more than one broker or M&A intermediary in an open agreement, or even sell the business yourself without paying a fee, but this process can create a lot of frustration for you. Businesses with open agreements can take longer to sell and may sell for lower prices since you don't have a dedicated professional working on selling your business. In addition, the more people you have marketing your business, the more likely a mistake can occur to threaten the confidentiality of your sale. Open agreements are still available in some industries and geographic markets, but they're rare and far less popular than exclusive agreements.

The Bottom Line When Hiring an M&A Advisor

You need someone you can trust. Whether you choose an exclusive or open agreement, your business sale depends on reaching the right buyer – that's really the bottom line. Interview as many brokers as you can and go with the broker you feel most comfortable with that also possesses the most experience.

M&A Lawyers

When selling your business, retaining an attorney to represent you is required unless your business is small – less than $1 million in purchase price. It's also important to bear in mind that no contract can provide complete protection for both parties. There are too many variables to anticipate and address. As a result, it's critical that your attorney remains flexible and is capable of balancing tradeoffs.

Do you need an M&A attorney to sell your business?

For middle-market transactions, the buyer often brings a team of dozens of staff and advisors to conduct due diligence. As a result of this imbalance, you should aim to at least achieve negotiating parity by hiring the best advisors you can afford. While an attorney isn't always a requirement in smaller transactions, they can be tremendously helpful. While many small transactions successfully conclude without an attorney, all sellers should hire an attorney and have them prepared to become involved in the transaction at a moment's notice. If the purchaser of your business is a corporate or financial buyer, your attorney will need to be intricately involved in the transaction.

> For middle-market transactions, the buyer often brings a team of dozens of staff and advisors to due diligence.

Roles and Documents

Here are the common roles most attorneys play, as well as the documents they need to draft in the sale of a business:

Non-Disclosure Agreement

While a standard non-disclosure agreement (NDA) works in most cases, I recommend your attorney draft a custom NDA if the sale is particularly sensitive, and you're approaching or negotiating with your competitors.

Letter of Intent

Your broker may often prepare the letter of intent if the buyer is an individual. The buyer's legal team usually prepares the LOI if the purchaser is a corporate buyer, private equity firm, or competitor. You will often need to involve your attorney if the buyer prepares the offer. In such cases, your attorney should be on standby and available to respond quickly when you receive an offer or letter of intent.

Due Diligence

The extent to which your attorney is involved in due diligence depends on how thoroughly the buyer conducts their due diligence. Your broker can often anticipate how thoroughly the buyer will perform due diligence based on their preliminary conversations with them. Often, they can let you know in advance if they feel your attorney will need to play a more involved role.

Purchase Agreement

- **Small Businesses:** As noted above, your broker may often prepare the purchase agreement and closing documents using their templates if the buyer is an individual or smaller competitor with less than $5 million to $10 million in revenue, which tends to be more common for smaller businesses. If so, you may optionally have your attorney review them.

- **Mid-Sized Businesses:** The buyer's legal team customarily prepares the purchase agreement if the buyer is a corporate buyer, private equity firm, or competitor – this tends to be more common for mid-sized companies. If that's the case, your attorney will need to be intimately involved in the negotiations of the key agreements. The purchase agreement is often prepared simultaneously while due diligence is being conducted, which gives the parties plenty of time to negotiate the agreement. On the other hand, the negotiations surrounding the letter of intent tend to be more time-sensitive.

Closing Process

Your attorney can also facilitate the closing process and wiring of funds if the buyer's attorney or escrow is unavailable to do so.

Other Roles

Your lawyer can also prepare or review the necessary transfer documents if you're selling a building or land.

Tips for Hiring an M&A Attorney

When hiring an attorney, you should look for the following:

- **Experience:** Your attorney should have acted in dozens of transactions and should dedicate a substantial portion of their time to M&A – the more, the better. Ideally, your attorney should spend more than half of their time specializing in M&A transactions.

- **Negotiating Skills:** Your legal advisor should also be an excellent negotiator. Often the negotiation on representations and warranties is tougher and more challenging than negotiating the price.

- **Soft Skills:** Find a lawyer who doesn't feel compelled to participate in or influence the commercial aspects of the deal, unless you specifically request otherwise. Your advisor should also be capable of offering solutions in risk management, such as creative deal structuring.

- **Fees:** Most professional advisors charge by the hour, while a minority charge a flat fee. Most of those that charge a flat fee understand the process enough to be comfortable quoting a set amount. Fees can range from $150 per hour to more than $1,000 per hour, and tend to be lower in smaller metropolitan areas and at smaller firms.

> Your attorney should have acted in dozens of transactions and should dedicate a substantial portion of their time to M&A – the more, the better.

Accountant or Tax Advisor

Your best source of accounting help is likely to be a Certified Public Accountant (CPA) because of the rigorous requirements for earning that designation. But a word of caution – not all CPAs are sufficiently qualified to provide all of the services you may need. Probe to see whether the CPA has experience in the purchase and sale of businesses. Ideally, your accountant should have experience both on the buy-side and the sell-side in a range of different-sized transactions.

One of the most common deal killers when selling a business is inaccurate or incomplete financial records. With inaccurate financial records, you run the risk of losing a buyer. Why? Once the buyer discovers the defects during due diligence, the sale must be delayed to address the problems. Sometimes, these problems take months to resolve. Other times, the buyer walks because they don't want to invest the time sorting out the problems. At this point, the buyer may have decided to move on or may have decided your business is no longer a sound investment.

Ask your accountant to perform a thorough review of your financial statements to ensure they're accurate and up to date. Talk to your accountant about your plans to sell your company so you can gain their cooperation. If your accountant is internal, inform them of your plans to sell in advance. You will be asking your accountant lots of financial questions, and they will quickly figure out your plans, even if you haven't told them.

Your financials should be clear and highly organized, with all backup documentation showing the breakdown of revenue by product, service, and customer type. You should be able to quickly answer questions about your financials, such as, "What's your average dollar transaction?"

Your accountant can also analyze your financials on both a cash and an accrual basis, and determine which method presents your business in its best light. Sophisticated buyers often request both cash and accrual-basis financials, so be prepared to answer questions regarding both formats.

This review helps spot potential issues that a buyer may find with your financial records and allows you to address them before you receive an offer. Having your financial records in order before selling your business also potentially speeds up the due diligence process, resulting in a higher chance of closing the sale. This is because a buyer who discovers issues with your financial records will most certainly conduct a more thorough due diligence, looking for problems in other areas, as well.

Finally, accurate financial records may maximize the sale price by attracting buyers who are more confident in your business. The more organized your business's financial records appear, the more likely you'll sell your business quickly and for top dollar. Clean financial records speed up due diligence and maximize the selling price of your business.

- **Your Accountant's Role:**
  - **Financial Statement Review:** I recommend you ask your accountant to review your financial statements, tax returns, and bank statements and correct any inaccuracies before you go to market.

  - **Working Capital Calculations:** For transactions larger than $3 million to $5 million, an accountant can also prepare working capital worksheets for your closing.

  - **Tax Advice:** An accountant can advise you on the tax implications of the sale. I recommend involving your accountant as soon as possible in the process, because you will have much more flexibility in tax planning and maximizing after-tax transaction revenues if you consult with your tax advisor during the exit planning process. Your accountant can estimate the federal and state tax consequences of selling your business under varying scenarios, such as whether you're selling your assets only or your entire entity, whether you'll be paid in one lump sum versus installments over time, and whether your estate plan should also be a consideration. They can also prepare tax returns associated with the sale, such as the income tax return of a corporation that sells its assets or the tax return of an individual who sells their shares or corporate stock.

- **Purchase Price Allocation:** Your accountant can assist in allocating the sale price among the various assets being sold by completing IRS Form 8594, the "Asset Acquisition Statement."

- **Transaction Structure:** Your accountant can help with reviewing the financial aspects of the deal, including structuring earnouts, seller financing, or other contingent payments.

Because your numbers are such a critical component of the process, it goes without saying that the role your accountant plays is critical. The purpose of external advisors is to make you – the owner – and your entire management team look as credible as possible by anticipating issues and preparing disclosure in a professional manner. Your accountant will go a long way toward helping you do just that.

> With inaccurate financial records, you run the risk of losing a buyer.

Franchisor

Franchisors are accustomed to the transfer of franchises within their systems. The sooner you tell them, the better, and there is little risk in doing so. In fact, franchisors may become distrustful if you don't inform them early in the process. Many franchisors also provide assistance during the sales process and may help in generating interest from buyers for your business.

Assistance

Contact your franchisor as early as possible in the process to determine what role they will play and what assistance they may provide in selling your business. Some franchisors offer extensive support, while others play a more limited role.

Ask your franchisor for a written description of the process of transferring your franchise. Some franchisors ask buyers to attend "discovery day," while others don't. Also, some franchisors require the buyer to complete the training before the closing, while others don't. Secure a list from the franchisor of specific financial and experience requirements that a new buyer will need to have.

Also ask for what training is offered to new franchisees, the amount of the training fee, and who pays the fee. Contact your franchisor to determine the amount of the transfer fee and who pays it.

Franchise Agreement

Contact your franchisor to verify that the terms of your franchise agreement and the size of your territory will remain the same after the sale. Take the assumptive route: "I want to verify that everything will remain the same when I transfer my franchise to a new buyer." If there is a change in terms – whether it be the size of your territory or the amount of your royalties – find out before you put your business on the market, so you can present these new terms to buyers. Ask if your franchisor will require a buyer to sign a new franchise agreement or if your existing agreement will be assigned. If it's assigned, ensure you're released as a guarantor on the agreement after the transfer.

SBA Franchise Directory

If your business is valued at less than $5 million, check to see if your franchise is listed on the SBA Franchise Register at sba.gov/sba-franchise-directory. If your franchise isn't listed on the SBA Franchise Register, a buyer won't be able to obtain an SBA loan to finance your business and will have to obtain a conventional loan. This will make the sale of your business significantly more difficult to finance. To solve this problem, ask your franchiser to go through the process of adding their franchise to the registry before you begin the sales process.

Franchise Disclosure Document

Obtain a copy of your Franchise Disclosure Document (FDD), and read the following two information sections from your FDD:

1. **Item 19:** Item 19 is a financial disclosure and, if promising, it can be used as a marketing piece when selling your business. Read Item 19 in-depth and learn more about the financial disclosures your franchisor makes. Item 19 sometimes also segments performers into quartiles. If so, attempt to learn who the top performers are in your system, so you can use this information with the buyer to demonstrate what's possible in your franchise system.

2. **Item 20:** Item 20 lists the number of transfers that have occurred in the franchise system over the previous years. A low churn rate is indicative of a healthy franchise concept. Item 20 can also be used as a marketing piece when selling your business. If the turnover rate in your system is higher, check with your franchisor to learn the reason behind the transfers, so you're prepared if a buyer brings this fact up during your discussions.

Other Specialists

Depending on the nature of your business and industry, other specialists may be employed during the process. Their level of involvement will impact the scope of negotiations. In some cases, retaining experts in advance can mitigate risk for the buyer. Here are some examples:

- **Environmental Factors:** You may want to consider hiring an environmental consultant if your business handles hazardous materials or is subject to environmental regulations. Buyers often hire environmental experts if they're purchasing land or buildings and suspect the property may be contaminated. Many jurisdictions impose strict liability for all past owners of real estate when environmental issues arise. Such issues represent a high level of exposure for the parties. Retaining a consultant in advance gives you time to discover and address problems before they arise with the buyer.

- **Employee Benefits:** Employee benefits are the next-largest area of risk exposure for buyers. If you have a pension plan, consult with experts in this area well in advance of the sale to ensure assets exceed liabilities, and that a smooth transition of benefits can occur in the case of other benefits, such as deferred compensation, profit-sharing, stock options, employee stock ownership, health insurance, and life insurance. In most cases, the plans will be terminated and you'll be obligated to fulfill the termination requirements.

- **Code Audit:** When purchasing a software company, most buyers retain a third party to perform a code audit to ensure the software code is clean and well documented. A wise seller will hire a third party to perform the audit and clean up the code before the company is put on the market. The results of the audit and resulting cleanup can then be used as negotiating leverage to provide the buyers with some level of comfort regarding the documentation, accuracy, and organization of the code.

- **Insurance Advisor:** Your insurance advisor will play a limited role in the transaction. Most insurance isn't transferable in an asset sale. But your insurance agent should be available to gather information regarding your existing policies and assist the buyer with obtaining new policies by communicating your coverage limits to the buyer. You should also make sure your current coverage is adequate. If it isn't, the buyer will deduct the cost to upgrade your insurance when calculating SDE or EBITDA.

- **Commercial Real Estate Agent or Attorney:** I recommend hiring a commercial real estate agent if you own the real estate and plan on selling it. The agent can assist with marketing the property for sale or determining an appropriate rental rate. Once you determine an appropriate rental rate based on current market conditions, be sure to pay your business this rate.

Tips for Hiring and Working With Your Advisors

Experience

When hiring a professional advisor, the number one thing you should look for is real-world experience in buying and selling companies. Ask how many M&A transactions they have worked on in the last five years and their role in each transaction. The more, the better. An "affordable" advisor lacking real-world experience will prove to be much more costly than the most "expensive" experienced advisors.

For example, it's common for CPAs to kill deals by offering their unsolicited opinion on a business's value. They may attempt to use logic that only applies to publicly traded companies, or they may use valuation methods, such as discounted cash flow (DCF), that don't apply to small to mid-sized companies. I have heard CPAs claim that an appropriate multiple for a business was seven to nine times EBITDA when, in reality, multiples were in the range of three to four times. Such opinions are common among CPAs. If a CPA or other advisor opines on your company's value, respond by asking how many transactions they have personally been involved in recently.

The best advisors have deep, relevant experience. They understand their client's business and industry, and are willing to be flexible to meet the needs of both parties. Negotiating the deal involves making numerous tradeoffs. Both you and your advisor must be prepared to be flexible and make concessions if you want to get a deal done. By the same token, your advisor should have the experience necessary to know when a buyer is unreasonable and when it's sensible to advise you to stand your ground.

This understanding is required if they're going to offer their opinion on the transaction structure, as opposed to simply accommodating your requests. The most valuable advisors play a technical role and have the requisite experience to add more value than just what they were retained for. This is particularly important when a transaction structure involves an earnout, one of the most complicated deal mechanisms to design. Don't pay your advisor to learn on the job – ensure you retain advisors who have significant experience drafting and negotiating earnouts. As a business owner, you likely have no practical experience negotiating an earnout. You must, therefore, solely rely on the advice of professionals. Close collaboration with your deal team is essential to creating a deal structure that minimizes your risks and maximizes your purchase price.

Negotiating the agreements for the sale of a middle-market business is a complex undertaking. Don't be shy when inquiring about qualifications. Ask what role your advisors envision themselves playing in your situation – some prefer to be in the background, while others prefer to be on the firing line.

Here's an example where the need for experience is clear. The reps and warranties in a purchase agreement can have significant implications for several years following the closing. In some instances, the liability you may incur in reps and warranties can be perpetual, such as in the case of environmental issues, the payment of taxes, or employment-related matters. One word in the agreement, such as a knowledge or materiality qualifier, can make the difference between a million-dollar recovery of damages and no recovery at all.

Experienced accountants and attorneys know what's customary and reasonable – and what isn't. The American Bar Association (ABA) compiles surveys of attorneys in the trenches based on what's considered reasonable in an industry. For example, the ABA study might indicate that 34% of M&A transactions under $10 million in purchase price include an earnout, or that the average escrow is for 18% of the purchase price. The ABA's studies are detailed and contain specifics on every critical element of a purchase agreement. An experienced advisor can spot when the opposing party is making an unreasonable request and will be able to couple your objectives with current standards of reasonableness. A good advisor will tell you when to fight and when to acquiesce.

The more experienced the professional, the more cost-effective they will be. For example, an attorney charging $600 per hour may be cheaper in the long run than your general business attorney with little M&A experience who only charges $250 per hour.

While your general business attorney may be sufficient for advising you regarding general business matters, M&A is not a general business matter. Your attorney should have significant experience negotiating M&A transactions. For another example, an inexperienced attorney may miss that your reps and warranties should include a basket (deductible) and a cap (maximum). On a $50 million transaction with prevailing norms regarding the reps and warranties (10% holdback and 1% basket), this could cost you $500,000 if problems arise after the closing. What if a problem arises after the closing with potential damages estimated at $600,000? With the inexperienced attorney and no cap, you would potentially be liable for up to $600,000. With an experienced M&A attorney and a $500,000 cap, you would potentially be liable for only $100,000. You may have saved $10,000 in attorney fees, but this could come at a cost of $500,000.

If your attorney forgot to include a cap, or the maximum amount of your indemnity, this one seemingly small oversight could cost you millions of dollars – $45 million or more in this case, if something terrible goes wrong.

If your business may be sold to a corporate buyer, such as a competitor or private equity firm, you can count on the fact that they will bring dozens of specialized experts to the negotiating table. Their team will run circles around you if your advisors are inexperienced. To be sure, this isn't the place to be cutting corners.

Of all the specialists you hire, your investment banker (or M&A advisor), and your M&A attorney are the most critical, and therefore should have significant M&A experience.

You should only hire an M&A advisor that specializes in M&A. If they're attempting to do multiple other things, there's probably a reason for that.

> When hiring a professional advisor, the number one thing you should look for is real-world experience buying and selling companies.

Knowledge of Your Business

Selling a business involves balancing numerous tradeoffs. Price is relative to the ratio of risk vs. reward. If the perceived risk is high, either a buyer will offer a lower purchase price, or seek to mitigate the risk through transaction structuring, such as earnouts or stronger reps and warranties. It's critical that your advisor understands your business from an operational standpoint, so they can see how the deal mechanisms a buyer proposes fit into the overall deal structure.

Your advisors should understand the risks inherent in your business, particularly the risks a buyer is likely to perceive. The perception of risks will vary from buyer to buyer. Understanding this enables your advisor to get a handle on how a buyer's proposals relate to the overall transaction structure and their perception of risk. Your advisor will then be able to propose alternative deal structures that meet both parties' needs.

Help your advisors understand your business from both an operational and a financial standpoint. Tell your accountant or attorney what your primary concerns are, and work with your advisor to meet your needs before becoming buried in legal or financial jargon. But don't lose sight of your objectives. Once your advisor understands your business and aspirations, you can work together to create package proposals that meet the buyer's needs, while also addressing the needs of your business.

Role

Allow your own experience to dictate the roles of your accountant and attorney. If you've never sold a business, be prepared for your advisors to play an instrumental role in the process. If you're a serial entrepreneur who has sold dozens of companies, your advisors may play a more limited role. Ask what role your advisors envision themselves playing in your situation based on your experience level. If you're hands-off, you'll want an advisor who can take charge and lead the transaction.

Appetite for Risk

Attorneys and accountants are conservative by nature. Find an advisor whose appetite for risk matches your own. Some advisors are excessively risk-averse. Likewise, some business owners are also risk-averse. You should employ an advisor whose risk profile matches your own.

Pre-Sale Due Diligence

Ask your attorney and especially your accountant to conduct pre-sale due diligence. This involves conducting due diligence before you put your business on the market, and will allow you to identify and resolve potential problems before you begin the sale process. If your accountant lacks M&A experience, it may be wise to hire an accountant who specializes in this. Conducting pre-sale due diligence may also lessen the scope of the reps and warranties in the purchase agreement and is, therefore, a wise investment.

Annual Audit

Finally, I recommend that you assemble your professional advisors for an annual meeting to perform an audit of your business. The goal of this audit is to prevent and discover problems early on and resolve them. As the saying goes, "An ounce of prevention is worth a pound of cure."

Your advisors are a valuable source of information. This annual meeting is an opportunity to ensure that they're all on the same page and that there are no conflicts among your legal, financial, operational, and other plans. An in-person or virtual group meeting enables you to accomplish this quickly and efficiently.

A sample agenda might include a review of the following:

- Your operating documents

- New forms of liability your business has assumed

- Any increase in value in your business and changes that need to be made, such as increases in insurance or tax planning

- Capital needs

- Insurance requirements and audit, and review of existing coverages to ensure these are adequate

- Tax planning – both personal and corporate

- Estate planning – includes an assessment of your net worth and business value, and any needed adjustments

- Personal financial planning

Conclusion

When you're in the market for a professional advisor to help sell your business, go with someone who's been there and done that. Preferably multiple times.

Here is a list of steps you can take to build a team to help you with the sales process:

- Hire an M&A advisor or investment banker well in advance to help prepare your company for sale.

- Retain an M&A attorney in advance to help you conduct pre-sale legal due diligence.

- Ask your accountant to conduct pre-sale financial due diligence on your business.

- If your business is a franchise, check with your franchisor in advance to ensure their cooperation, and make sure your franchise is listed on the SBA Franchise Directory, if applicable.

- Check with your insurance advisor to ensure you're carrying adequate coverage.

- Hire a commercial real estate agent to determine an appropriate market rent if you own the property.

- Assemble your professional advisors to perform an annual audit on your business.

CHAPTER 18

Buyers

"There is only one winning strategy. It is to carefully define the target market and direct a superior offering to that target market."

– Philip Kotler, American Marketing Author

Introduction

You can get a jump-start on marketing your business for sale well before you put your business on the market. How? First, you should strategically consider who is most likely to buy your business and then build a business most suitable for that type of buyer. Second, you should also begin to build a list of relationships and information on potential buyers for your company that will form the foundation for the marketing campaign to sell your company. In this chapter, I explain several important strategies you can immediately begin implementing that will dramatically improve the effectiveness of your marketing efforts once you decide to put your business on the market.

Targeted Campaigns

What's the most effective method for selling your business? Is a targeted campaign the right way to go? In this section, I'll explain the most common approaches for marketing companies for sale, and help you decide which method is best for you. This will help you understand the most effective strategy to sell your business and what, if any, prep work you should perform before you begin the process.

A key consideration for developing a marketing campaign to sell your business is the size of your company.

- **For Small Businesses:** Confidentially marketing your company on specialized portals is the most effective strategy. If your business will be sold using these portals, there is often no preparatory work you need to do.

- **For Mid-Sized Businesses:** I also recommend targeting additional potential buyers, such as competitors and other companies, through direct, targeted campaigns. If this is part of your plan, you can get ready for the sale by preparing a list of potential buyers who may be interested.

With a targeted campaign, your M&A advisor will reach out directly to potential corporate buyers – a "private auction" in the parlance of many M&A advisors. This involves compiling a list of possible corporate buyers and contacting them directly through emails, letters, and phone calls. Corporate buyers can also be targeted through select trade publications.

There are advantages and disadvantages to selling your company to a corporate buyer or competitor, so it's important to proceed carefully. Targeted campaigns aren't recommended for every company.

In this section, I explain how targeted marketing campaigns work and discuss their advantages and disadvantages. I also explain the different types of corporate buyers, discuss who is most likely to be interested in your business, and how you can build a list of these potential buyers in advance.

Advantages and Disadvantages of Targeted Campaigns

The following are several advantages of targeted campaigns:

- **Experience:** A buyer in your industry will already be familiar with your marketplace and will likely be motivated to purchase your business as a means of expanding their market share.

- **Knowledge:** They may be more knowledgeable about what it takes to purchase a business. This means the transaction may go more smoothly than would be the case with an individual buyer who has never owned a business.

- **Price:** In certain industries, a competitor or corporate buyer may pay significantly more for your business than an individual buyer.

There are a few disadvantages of targeted campaigns:

- **Confidentiality:** It can be risky letting your competition know that you want to sell your business.

- **Probability:** In some industries, the probability of selling to a competitor or corporate buyer may be low.

- **Price:** In certain industries, a competitor or corporate buyer may pay significantly less for your business than an individual buyer would. This situation is especially true if it's easy for the buyer to replicate your business at a lower cost than your asking price.

Determining if a Targeted Campaign Is Right for You

A key factor in determining if a targeted campaign is right for your company is the size of your business and the type of buyer who will buy it.

Size: Selling Small vs. Mid-Sized Businesses

- **Small Business:** Small businesses – generally those with less than $5 million in annual revenue or less than $1 million in EBITDA – are purchased by individuals 95% of the time. Companies account for the other 5% of such transactions. Targeted campaigns are suitable only for a select number of smaller businesses.

- **Mid-Sized Business:** Targeted campaigns are almost always suitable for middle-market businesses with EBITDA greater than $1 million per year.

Buyers: Individuals vs. Corporate Buyers

- **Individuals:** As I just mentioned, individuals are more likely to purchase small businesses. The most efficient and cost-effective method of contacting individual buyers is through targeted forms of media, such as web portals and trade journals, where individuals have identified themselves as potential buyers. In other words, this group of people has already been corralled for you, thus making the process more efficient and cost-effective.

- **Corporate Buyers:** Companies are more likely to purchase mid-sized businesses. Most corporate buyers are looking for businesses that generate at least $5 million in annual revenue. There are always exceptions, though. For example, in industries where growth is a zero-sum game, such as landscaping, competitors regularly acquire small businesses.

Types of Corporate Buyers

Here are the different types of corporate buyers you can approach when conducting a targeted campaign:

- **Direct Competitor, Different Geography:** The business is in the same industry and may be looking to expand into your area.

- **Direct Competitor, Same Geography:** The business is in the same industry and same geographical area as your business. This is common in "zero-sum" industries where the industry is no longer growing, and competitors are fiercely competing for market share, such as in commercial cleaning or lawn care. In these industries, it's often more cost effective to acquire a competitor than attempt to increase market share through advertising.

- **Indirect Competitor:** In this instance, the buyer may be interested in expanding into a new market or selling their products or services to your existing client base. For example, a food distributor may be interested in purchasing a food manufacturer. Rather than build a business from scratch, they may be interested in simply acquiring yours. If you choose to approach a company you think may have this synergistic potential, be prepared to clearly and concisely demonstrate the potential and competitive advantages of your business.

The Ideal Corporate Buyer

Here are the characteristics of the ideal corporate buyer you should pursue when conducting a targeted campaign:

- **Acquisitive:** The corporate buyer has made previous acquisitions. Approach only those targets that are ready, willing, and able to take action. You'll know this by researching the company and determining how many acquisitions it has made in the past five years. The more acquisitions or companies the corporate buyer has bought recently, the more likely it will buy another company.

- **Appropriate Size:** The corporate buyer should generate at least $10 million in annual revenue and be at least three times the size of your company. An overwhelming majority of smaller companies aren't ready, willing, or able to spend millions of dollars to purchase a competitor. There are exceptions, but in general only mid-sized and larger companies grow through acquisitions. Be particularly wary of smaller companies with revenue of less than $10 million per year that contact you. Why? Smaller companies tend to be busy putting out fires and chasing the next big customer rather than proactively creating a team focused on developing and executing an acquisition strategy. While these deals do sometimes happen, the ideal corporate buyer will generate at least $10 million per year in revenue and be at least three times your size. If your company generates $5 million per year in revenue, for example, the ideal buyer should generate at least $15 million annually in revenue.

Approaching the Right-Sized Companies

When conducting a targeted campaign, it's important that you approach the right-sized businesses.

Do small companies buy businesses?

Smaller companies typically grow organically by gradually increasing their marketing and advertising budgets. Most of them are chasing the next big deal or new big customer and don't have enough time or cash reserves to pursue acquisitions as a growth strategy.

Attempting to sell your business to a smaller company often proves to be an ineffective strategy that can waste an enormous amount of time.

EBITDA, EBITDA, EBITDA – again, the primary criteria larger companies use to determine if an acquisition makes sense is EBITDA, which is earnings before income, taxes, depreciation, and amortization. These companies look for a minimum annual EBITDA of $1 million to $10 million or more.

Why? The answer is simple – it takes just as much time to do a $1 million deal as it does to do a $25 million deal. Also, the professional fees involved in these acquisitions are similar regardless of the transaction's size, though the fees may be slightly higher for larger deals.

> *For example, a $1 million deal may command fees and expenses of $50,000 or more, which represents 5% of the deal size, while a $25 million transaction may command fees of $150,000 to $300,000, which represents 0.6% to 1.2% of the deal size. This means that the percentage of fees and expenses decreases as the size of the deal increases. Doing larger deals is, therefore, more cost-effective for the buyer.*

A company must invest in 25 businesses – each with a cash flow of at least $1 million per year – to have the same impact as buying a single company with an annual cash flow of $25 million. So, buying larger companies is more efficient, both from a cost and time perspective.

Attempting to sell your business to a smaller company often proves to be an ineffective strategy that can waste an enormous amount of time.

Process for Targeted Campaigns

When we conduct a targeted campaign through my company, we work with the seller to prepare a list of potential buyers, including corporations and competitors. We then send the buyers a copy of the seller's teaser profile to pique their interest and follow up with them to determine if they're viable potential buyers. The confidentiality of the business is maintained throughout this process, since the teaser profile doesn't disclose the identity of the company.

At Morgan & Westfield, the process is as follows:

1. Research and Compile the Buyer List

    a. The seller sends us a list of potential buyers.

    b. We research additional potential buyers and send the list to the seller for approval.

    c. We research and compile a spreadsheet of potential buyers' contact information.

2. Initial Outreach and Follow-Up

    a. We send the teaser profile to the potential buyers through multiple channels and request that they sign a non-disclosure agreement if they would like additional information on the company.

    b. We follow up with buyers who don't respond to the initial outreach using multiple contact methods.

3. Buyers Sign the NDA and Receive the CIM: We email the confidential information memorandum (CIM) to the buyer and answer any questions they may have about the business, and begin negotiations.

4. Negotiate Letter of Intent: We negotiate with buyers interested in submitting a letter of intent (LOI).

When you engage an investment banker or M&A advisor to sell your business, one of their initial tasks is to prepare this list of potential acquirers – ideally, the line-up should contain between 50 and 200 companies. Having a head start on this process puts you at a great advantage.

Many clients come to us who wish to sell their company. During our preliminary conversations, or when we perform an assessment of the company, we ask them who is likely to buy their company. Many business owners name 5 to 10 potential buyers and then draw a blank when asked to expand the list. Often, most of these buyers are either too small or too large to be suitable acquirers.

As a result, we're often left with just two to three potential buyers to approach. This won't work in most cases and puts us at a great disadvantage when trying to sell the company.

If you'd like to get a head start on this process, I recommend you begin building your buyer list now.

Prepare a Buyer List

The action of preparing a buyer list is a high-value activity that takes little time, but offers significant long-term value. This simply involves setting up a spreadsheet with a list of potential buyers who may consider purchasing your company. This can also include sources of information that can be used to prepare a buyer list – such as industry directories, publications, events, and so forth.

It's helpful if you prepare this preliminary list of companies you believe may be suitable candidates well in advance of the sale. Your M&A advisor can then expand the list and research contact information for each buyer.

The Right Size and Fit

A list of between 100 and 200 buyers is necessary to conduct a private auction. The preferred size of the list depends on the type of business and industry, but the ideal roster should have a significant number of names. Smaller lists may sometimes be sufficient if the interest level of the names on the list is high or if the companies have aggressively pursued you in the past.

In order to get the best price, it's necessary to create a carefully orchestrated frenzy of activity through a private auction. It's only through this bidding process that you maximize the price. The more LOIs you receive, the higher you can drive up the price. If buyers know they're the only buyer negotiating with you, they know they have you pinned in a corner. Not only will you receive a lower price, but you're also in a weak position and susceptible to renegotiations during due diligence.

In certain instances, it's possible to sell your company with a small list of buyers. But it's important to maximize your odds of success because so many things can go wrong. For most companies, a list of at least 50 targeted buyers is necessary, though typically a list of between 100 and 200 buyers is necessary to produce the 30 to 40 conversations required to receive 5 to 10 letters of intent.

Not only should the list be large, but the buyers on the list must be targeted – containing buyers who are a good fit in terms of both size and services and who are in a position to acquire you.

The buyer should be big enough, but not too big. If the buyer is too close in size to your company, they will be too risk averse – and such a transaction may represent too much of a gamble for the buyer. The larger the buyer, the less risk the transaction represents to them, and the easier it may be for them to pull the trigger.

The more concentrated the ownership of the buyer, the more true this is. Imagine if you were purchasing a company similar in size to your own. Get out your checkbook and write yourself a check for exactly what you wish to sell your company for. If you want $10 million for your company, write yourself a check for $10 million. Now, imagine writing a check of that size to acquire one of your competitors. Do you have the guts to make the leap? Now, try the same exercise but cross a few zeroes off the check. You'll still be circumspect, but your aversion to the risk has likely decreased.

The same holds true with buyers in the real world. I see too many entrepreneurs in sole negotiations with one buyer – and that buyer is the sole owner of a company similar in size to their own. In most cases, the owner can't stomach the risk and seeks to offset the risk by a large earnout or another form of contingent payment, or by driving the price down.

If you're desperate and not looking to maximize your price, such a strategy can work. But if you want to receive the highest price possible, it's important that the buyers on your list are the appropriate size.

While no magic number exists for determining the right size – the acquisition of your business should be able to move the needle for the buyer. Approaching companies generating $500 million in revenue likely won't work if you own a business generating $1 million in revenue, though there are always exceptions, such as Facebook's purchase of Instagram.

A $1 million acquisition takes just as much time, energy, and money as a $500 million acquisition. As a result, most buyers focus on acquisitions that can move the needle for them. If the acquisition is unlikely to make a dent in their business, they'll be unlikely to consider it. Yes, there are rare exceptions, but you shouldn't count on exceptions for one of the most important transactions of your life.

This truth applies to strategic buyers and financial buyers, such as private equity (PE) firms. Most PE firms have a series of funds operating simultaneously – and most funds have a lifespan of 10 years. While the timeline varies, they may launch a new fund every two to three years.

> In 2019, Blackstone, one of the largest private equity firms, raised the largest-ever private equity fund with $26 billion. To invest $26 billion, Blackstone would have to complete 2,600 acquisitions over a five-year period if the average transaction size were $10 million ($26 billion / $10 million = 2,600 acquisitions). To reach that target, they would have to complete two acquisitions per day, assuming 250 workdays per year or 1,250 days over a five-year period (1,250 days / 2,600 acquisitions = 2.08 acquisitions per day). Given that a typical private equity group considers 100 companies for each acquisition they make, they would have to consider 260,000 potential acquisitions to complete 2,600 successful acquisitions. In other words, they would have to consider 208 potential acquisitions per day. This obviously isn't feasible. It wouldn't be practical for a large private equity fund to consider acquisitions of this size because they would have to complete more acquisitions than would be possible.

This is a long-winded way of telling you not to approach Blackstone if you wish to sell your $10 million company.

But don't some companies acquire pre-revenue businesses? Yes, there are always exceptions, but again, you don't want to count on exceptions when selling your company.

Typically a list of between 100 and 200 buyers is necessary to produce the 30 to 40 conversations required to receive 5 to 10 letters of intent.

Other Factors to Ensure a Good Fit

In addition to size, the buyer of your company should offer similar products, sell to the same customers, or sell through the same distribution channels as your company. This accomplishes two important objectives:

1. It gives the acquirer sufficient motivation to complete the transaction.

2. It offers the possibility of synergies, which can drive the price up.

Sources of Buyers

I suggest first researching direct competitors, then any indirect competitors, and finally any companies in related industries. Industry catalogs are an excellent resource for generating ideas for potential acquirers.

Obtaining Contact Information

For larger companies, the best way to get the attention of a potential acquirer is by contacting the manager of a division whose area could benefit from a complementary product like yours. I call this individual an "internal champion."

Not only should the company be sufficiently motivated to complete the transaction, but the individuals involved in the transaction should be, as well. So, in addition to preparing a list of potential buyers, your list should also include the names and contact information of buyers in those companies who have decision-making power and could personally benefit from the transaction.

Impact on Valuation

How does the buyer list affect your valuation? The potential range of values for your company can vary widely depending on who the buyer is. When assessing the potential value of your company, it's important to consider who is most likely to acquire your company and their motivations for doing so. If the buyer is likely a financial buyer, the value of your business can be more accurately predicted. If, however, strategic value exists, the potential value range can be wide. Note that it's not necessary for your list to include financial buyers unless the financial buyer owns a portfolio company in your industry.

Acquisition Activity in Your Industry

It's also important to consider the acquisition appetite and actions of potential buyers on your list. How many acquisitions have they made? What prices have they paid, if this information is available? How common are acquisitions in your industry?

An ideal buyer has acquired multiple companies and has demonstrated the ability to actually complete transactions – not just talk about completing transactions. Selling your company to a buyer who has never purchased a company before is a risky proposition with low odds of success.

> If you want to receive the highest price possible, it's important that the buyers on your list are the appropriate size.

Differences in Process

The main difference in approaching potential acquirers is that negotiating with competitors tends to be more rigorous. You should have your attorney on standby to manage revisions to the non-disclosure agreement, letter of intent, and purchase agreement, if necessary.

To download a sample spreadsheet, or learn more about buying, selling, valuing a business, or dozens of other topics related to mergers and acquisitions, visit the Resources section of the Morgan & Westfield website at morganandwestfield.com/resources.

Targeted Marketing in Publications

An alternative to approaching buyers directly is marketing in publications, such as trade magazines. But this approach is most suitable for highly specialized businesses. If this sounds like you, I recommend preparing a list of potential publications you can use to market your business for sale when the time comes.

Here are some types of publications that might be suitable for marketing your business:

- Trade publications

- Other publications that target potential buyers for your business. For example, if you have a medical-related business, medical journals might be suitable.

- Online blogs or forums

- Any other publication whose readership consists of your target market

Finding Other Buyers

There are several additional categories of buyers you can target – individuals, financial buyers, strategic buyers, and people already involved in your business, such as managers, employees, or family members. By considering who may purchase your business in advance, you can begin to contemplate who some additional potential buyers may be and prepare a list of these people, so you have the names at the ready when the time comes to sell.

Consider People You Know

Sometimes, you don't have to go far to find the perfect buyer. Does anyone you know seem to be a possible candidate? Has anyone expressed interest in purchasing your company in the past? Here are some thoughts to consider:

- **Personal Connections:** There are people in your life who would like to own a business like yours. You'll never know who they are until you connect with them. Once you begin talking to the people you know for ideas, potential interests, and references, you may find that you have a world of opportunities at your fingertips.

- **Word-of-Mouth:** You can do a lot of marketing through your personal network. People love to share compelling stories. If your business is well known, word of mouth may be enough to spread the news when you begin marketing your business for sale, although you need to balance this with your desire for confidentiality.

- **Print, Direct Mail Marketing, and Advertising:** There are a number of areas where you can look to place a classified ad, such as trade publications or periodicals geared specifically to your industry. You may also want to consider a direct mail campaign targeted to a list of business owners or geared to a geographic area.

Selling to an Employee or Management Team

Often, employees or your management team may have aspirations to become business owners. Your own team may be a source of potential leads to buyers – or it may be the cause of conflicts and hold-ups if not handled properly.

Benefits of Selling to an Employee

Employees are familiar with your business operations, strengths, customers, competition, and unique advantages in the market. Your current managers, or people in their networks, may have distinct insider knowledge that allows them to quickly make a decision, which can be one of the most efficient sales experiences that any seller can hope for.

Drawbacks of Selling to an Employee

An employee may not have the financial resources necessary to buy your business and invest in its growth. It can be an adjustment to go from being an employee to being an owner, even for the most aspiring entrepreneur. To sell to an employee, you must often be prepared to finance all or part of the sale or arrange for a bank to finance the transaction.

Disclosing to your team members that your business is for sale may cause some disruptions. Employees may fear the upcoming change and leave their positions, or may even attempt to undermine the sale. If you begin serious discussions with the wrong person, the dynamic shifts from an employer-employee relationship to a business owner's relationship with a business owner. This can cause tension in the work environment throughout negotiations and ownership transfer, especially if discretion isn't maintained and confidentiality isn't respected.

Employee Stock Ownership Plans (ESOPs)

> An ESOP normally yields the lowest sales price and is often used only as a last resort.

Employee stock ownership plans are one way to integrate employee ownership in a company, often positively affecting the employees' commitment, dedication, and productivity. In some cases, selling to one or more employees may also have tax advantages.

Employee stock ownership plans are plans in which employees can buy shares of a company under specific terms. Not often seen in businesses with less than $5 million in annual revenue, ESOPs are complex and expensive to establish. They often require the specialized knowledge of accountants, tax advisers, and lawyers for ongoing re-examination and re-certification to keep the plan compliant with all regulations.

Although the process varies, typically, the ESOP plan purchases the stock of your company at its inception, using a bank loan. Employees can receive shares as compensation, like a 401(k), with the potential for the ESOP shares to vest immediately or over time, as with a pension plan. As employees reach retirement age, they will have options to diversify their ESOP holdings away from company stock or cash out.

An ESOP structure may make sense for your business, but these normally yield the lowest sales price and are often used only as a last resort.

Professional Contacts

There are many other contacts you can reach out to in order to broaden your marketing strategy. These professionals are in contact with potential buyers every day. Keep in mind that if you establish a relationship with any of these professionals and it results in a successful sale, it's best to compensate them for their help:

- **Accounting and Legal Professionals:** Close advisers, such as lawyers and accountants, get to know the business owners they work with and may be able to connect you with their clients or someone in their network. Most firms have specialized groups in focused industries – you want the information for the group that specializes in your industry.

- **Consulting Professionals:** These people are in close contact with senior executives and can be in a strategic position to connect you with buyers. When you're contacting a professional at a consulting firm, attempt to reach the most senior-level contact possible. Research their portfolio and industry specialties, and approach them with a professional introduction that clearly indicates why you're contacting them.

- **Industry Associations:** In your local community, in your state, and nationally, there are likely multiple associations for professionals in your industry. These organizations connect people in the same and overlapping businesses and bring them together through online forums, trade shows and events, and industry-specific publications. Learn the names of the major associations, and gain membership, if necessary. Reaching out to other members, advertising within the organization itself, or participating in an event could introduce you to a range of potential buyers.

- **Active and Retired Senior Executives:** Current or retired executives in your industry often have extensive networks and may be less conflicted about recommending potential buyers. Using your knowledge of your industry, both local and widespread, consider executives who may be able to refer you to others in their network or who may be potential buyers themselves.

Other Potential Buyers

Here are a few other areas to consider where you may find potential buyers:

- **Employees of Competitors:** A competitor's employees or management team may be interested in buying your company. Of course, it can be hard to find the right employees to approach. It's generally done by word of mouth, through local classified advertising, or trade press advertising. In some cases, more aggressive buyers will contact business owners either directly or through a broker.

- **Customers:** Often, your best customers are your biggest fans. They promote your business within their circle because they love what you offer. They may make large purchases on a regular basis – or may have approached you about business deals, offers, or opportunities in the past. Don't overlook this important group of potential buyers.

- **Suppliers:** It's common for businesses to acquire other businesses that they're already connected with. Rather than continuing to outsource the product or service to you, it can be more profitable and part of an acquisition strategy to bring your services under their corporate umbrella. Sometimes referred to as "vertical integration," this type of acquisition can complete the value chain for a company expanding into new industries or areas.

Conclusion

The key to maximizing the value of your business is to sell your company to the right buyer – that is, the buyer that's able to pay the highest price. What's the secret to doing this? You know what they say – you have to kiss a lot of frogs before you find a prince. The more potential acquirers you have lined up before you're ready to sell, the more likely you are to find your prince to buy your business. By compiling a buyer list in advance, you'll be in a much stronger position to ensure you sell to the buyer willing to pay the highest price.

Here are some tips for being prepared to market your business for sale when the time comes:

- Prepare a list of potential buyers with complete contact information.

- Prepare a list of sources of potential buyers, such as from trade shows and via industry catalogs or other publications.

- Compile a list of potential publications in which to market your business for sale.

CHAPTER 19

Financing

"The value of an asset in business is directly related to the ability to finance it."

– Unknown

Introduction

Note: This chapter primarily applies to "Main Street" businesses valued at less than $5 million. If you own a middle-market business valued at more than $5 million, the buyer will use other sources of financing to acquire your business. Most M&A transactions in the middle market include some component of seller financing, though the amounts are low, often 10% to 20% of the transaction size.

> If you own a middle-market business valued at more than $5 million, the buyer will use other sources of financing to acquire your business.

Buyers of small businesses have three major sources of funds to finance the purchase:

- Buyer's personal equity (i.e., cash)

- Seller financing

- Bank or Small Business Administration (SBA) financing

Let's examine how each of these sources of funds can affect your transaction.

Source 1: Buyer's Personal Equity

The buyer's personal equity is a key element in the acquisition of small businesses, usually to the tune of 10% to half, or even more, of the total purchase price. At the same time, most buyers of small businesses prefer to leverage their down payment. As a result, they tend not to pay all cash when acquiring a business. The buyer's cash injection is commonly about 20% if they obtain a bank loan – or anywhere from 40% to 90% if the seller agrees to finance a portion of the sale.

Source 2: Seller Financing

Nearly every small business is sold using either seller financing or some form of bank financing. If the buyer of your business can't obtain bank financing, it's highly likely you'll need to finance the sale, as few buyers are willing to pay all cash to acquire a business.

With seller financing, you receive a down payment and then periodic payments, usually monthly, until the buyer pays you in full. Seller financing is faster to arrange and requires less paperwork than traditional financing sources, such as bank or SBA financing. This means it's often the most suitable option if the buyer can't obtain SBA financing to purchase your business. When considering whether to finance the sale, evaluate the extent to which it will impact your purchase price and net proceeds. Financing the sale can affect the purchase price and your net proceeds as follows:

- **Interest:** Receiving interest payments increases your net proceeds.

- **Price:** Offering seller financing can maximize your purchase price. Buyers are willing to pay more for businesses that can be seller-financed. The more favorable your financing terms, the higher the purchase price you can justify.

- **Taxes:** The taxes due on a promissory note are normally due only after you receive the money, which can help lower your overall tax bill due to the progressive nature of the U.S. tax structure.

How does seller financing work? If your business is worth $5 million and you're willing to finance half of the purchase price, the buyer would put down $2.5 million in cash at closing and make payments on the remainder until the note is paid in full. Sellers typically offer terms of 3 to 7 years and interest rates of 5% to 8%.

Here are the advantages of financing the sale:

- **Lower Taxes:** You don't pay taxes until you receive the money, but be sure to structure the note, so it's "non-negotiable."

- **Higher Selling Price:** Businesses that include seller financing sell for 20% to 30% more than businesses that sell for all cash.

- **Higher Success Rate:** Businesses offered with seller financing are easier to sell than businesses offered for all cash.

- **Less Paperwork:** Less paperwork is required with seller financing than with bank-financed transactions.

- **Faster Process:** Arranging seller financing is quick and has a faster closing time than bank financing.

If you can't get your business pre-qualified for bank financing, you should decide early in the process of marketing your business whether you'll offer seller financing. This is because one of the most important components of the business sale is how the buyer plans to finance the transaction. An early question buyers have is whether or not you'll finance a portion of the sale.

Most sellers of small businesses want a minimum down payment of 50%, and most sellers offer terms ranging from 3 to 7 years. For middle-market businesses, these deal structures usually include a seller note amounting to 10% to 30% of the purchase price.

You must consider financing the sale of the business if you're serious about selling, especially if your business isn't pre-approved for bank financing.

Down Payment

Your decision regarding how much to finance must make sense from a cash flow standpoint. If your business makes a profit of $100,000 per month, then a note of $90,000 per month won't make sense because this will leave the buyer with only $10,000 per month in cash flow. The profit from your business must cover the amount of the note and also pay the buyer a living wage. If it can't, it won't work.

The following information is based on statistics from more than 25,000 business sales from BIZCOMPS, a database of M&A transactions.

- **Average Interest Rate:** Ranges from 5% to 8%. The interest rate is based on risk, not prevailing rates. Financing a business is risky; hence, the relatively high rates compared with interest rates on other assets in the market.

- **Average Length of Note:** Normally 5 years, but it varies from 3 to 7 years.

- **Average Down Payment:** Usually 50%, but it varies from 30% to 80%.

- **All-Cash Deals:** Less than 10% of businesses sell for all cash.

Amortization Period

Most notes range from 3 to 5 years. Common sense is the rule of thumb here. The cash flow from your business should cover the debt service. Let's examine a simple scenario:

The following scenario won't work because the debt service is too high:

Price of business:	$5,000,000
Down payment:	$1,500,000
Amount financed:	$3,500,000
Term:	2 years
Interest rate:	8%
Monthly payment:	$158,296/month
Annual payment:	$1,899,552
Annual cash flow from business:	$2,000,000
Minus annual debt service:	$1,899,552
Profit left over after debt service:	$100,448

In this example, the payment is 94% of the annual profit of the business. A more realistic scenario would be a 4- to 5-year term. Note that the term has a larger impact on the monthly payment than the interest rate. The payment should be less than a third of the annual cash flow of the business. It can be slightly higher if the cash flow of the business is stable from year to year. If the cash flow is inconsistent, build in some cushion and structure the note so the payment is lower to ensure the business can survive any downturns.

> The interest rate depends more on the amount of risk involved and less on the current cost of money.

The Interest Rate

Historically, interest rates charged on promissory notes have ranged from 5% to 8%. As noted above, the rate depends more on the amount of risk involved and less on the current cost of money. Some buyers point out that current interest rates on residential real estate mortgages are lower and argue that the rate should be competitive with these. I explain to buyers that such a loan is risky for the seller, and little collateral is available other than the undervalued assets of the business. If you default on your mortgage, the bank simply takes your home back. But if you default on a loan used to buy a small business, there often isn't anything to take back other than a struggling business.

Other factors that should be considered in determining the interest rate to charge include the total price of the business, the buyer's credit score, the buyer's experience, the buyer's financial position, and perhaps most important, the amount of the down payment.

Deciding To Finance the Sale

Should you offer seller financing for the sale of your business or wait to see if the buyer requests it? For small businesses, it's best to mention that you're willing to finance a portion of the price when marketing your business for sale. This sends the message to the buyer that you've given the matter careful consideration and are serious and realistic in terms of the sale. Buyers like to deal with prepared sellers. You'll also receive a greater response to your marketing campaign if you offer your business for sale with some form of financing vs. all cash. For mid-sized businesses, it's common to market a business without an asking price or terms.

Selling the Note

You can often sell the note after it has matured for 6 to 12 months. There are many investors who purchase these notes, which effectively cashes you out. Unfortunately, they often purchase the note at a steep discount, but there are few alternatives other than selling your note. If you would like to leave this option open, it's important to ensure that the note can be transferred or assigned to a third party.

Protecting Against a Default

Because you're financing a portion of the sale, you should think and act like a bank, and qualify the buyer before committing to them. I recommend obtaining a detailed financial statement, credit report, resume, and any other pertinent information you can obtain from the buyer as early as possible in the process. You should also select a buyer you think will succeed in your business from an operational standpoint.

If the buyer of your business is another company, ask the buyer about their previous acquisitions. Talking to the owners of companies they have acquired in the past may also be helpful. Depending on the size of the company, it may be prudent to perform due diligence on the principals of the company that are interested in acquiring your business.

Most of the problems I see related to seller financing originate from the seller accepting a low down payment. I consider a low down payment to be anything less than 30%. The solution is to ask for a down payment of at least 30% to 50% of the asking price. Why? Few buyers will walk away from such a large down payment.

A strong promissory note should also be drafted with clauses that directly address what happens in the event of a late or non-payment. A Uniform Commercial Code (UCC) lien should also be filed on the business to prevent the buyer from selling the business or the assets during the term of the note.

If the buyer is an individual, you may also be able to negotiate to collateralize the buyer's personal assets in addition to the assets of the company, but doing this can sometimes signal to the buyer that you don't have faith in your own business. Additionally, you can require the buyer to maintain specific financial benchmarks post-closing, such as maintaining a minimum inventory level and working capital, or specific debt-to-equity ratios. I also recommend you request access to monthly or quarterly financial statements, which enable you to spot and help correct problems early on. You should also remain on the lease during the duration of the note so you can take back the business if the buyer defaults.

> Because you're financing a portion of the sale, you should think and act like a bank and qualify the buyer before committing to them.

Key Points

If you aren't willing to finance the sale of your business, there's probably another seller with a reasonably priced business that's similar to yours who will. You must consider financing the sale of the business if you're serious about selling, especially if your business isn't pre-approved for bank financing.

Source 3: Bank or SBA Financing

Nearly 95% of bank loans for the acquisition of a small business are Small Business Administration loans. To be clear, the SBA doesn't actually loan money. Through its 7(a) Loan Program, the SBA helps small businesses access credit by guaranteeing loans made by banks in the event of a default. This limits risk for banks offering such loans, which encourages them to lend money to small businesses. By doing this, SBA financing can offer buyers attractive loan terms and interest rates while eliminating or reducing the need for you to carry a note.

For the buyer, this means a lower down payment, lower debt service, and higher net income. Because this is a government-sponsored program, there are formal guidelines that any bank must follow when offering an SBA loan.

The advantages of selling your business with an SBA loan include:

- You receive cash at closing

- Lower down payment required (typically 10% to 20% cash), which makes your business easier to sell

- Longer amortization period (typically 10 years) and lower monthly payment, due to the longer amortization period, which enables the buyer to purchase your business with a lower down payment

- Can be combined with other forms of financing, such as seller financing and 401(k) rollovers

- No fees to the seller

- The real estate associated with the business can be acquired and financed as part of the business acquisition and financing process

Disadvantages of selling your business with an SBA loan include:

- More paperwork

- Longer time frame

- More stringent requirements and guidelines

- Normally a variable interest rate, increasing the buyer's risk

- Higher closing costs for the buyer – 3.5% to 4%, which is regulated by the SBA

- SBA loans above a certain size require a business appraisal

- Buyers often have a high failure rate in obtaining SBA financing

Buyer's vs. Seller's Responsibility

Isn't it the buyer's responsibility to obtain a loan? Why should you get your business pre-qualified for an SBA loan? Isn't that part of what a buyer does?

Your business must produce enough cash flow to cover the monthly loan payments – and then some. SBA loans are pre-approved based on the cash flow available to support the debt service. The cash flow to repay the loan is generated from your business, so the pre-approval process depends on the cash flow your company produces. While the buyer bears some burden of responsibility, the principal responsibility lies with your business since your business is producing the cash flow to pay the loan. Most denials for SBA financing are related to issues regarding the business, not the buyer.

Here's an example:

Cash Flow

Annual cash flow =	$300,000
Less buyer's salary =	$200,000
Annual cash flow after buyer's salary =	$100,000

Price and Terms

Asking price =	$1,000,000
Down payment =	$200,000
Amount financed =	$800,000

Debt Service

Annual payment =	$109,008 (10-year term @ 6.5% interest)
Plus 25% debt coverage ratio (DCR) =	$27,252
Annual payment + DCR =	$132,260

Cash Flow After Debt Service

Annual cash flow after buyer's salary =	$100,000
Less annual payment + DCR =	$132,260

This business wouldn't qualify because the "annual cash flow after buyer's salary" of $100,000 isn't enough to support the "annual payment" + "cushion" (debt coverage ratio) of $132,260.

When pre-approving your company for an SBA loan, the lender may also review additional criteria. For example, if revenue has consistently declined in your business in recent years, your business may not be approved. Additionally, the lender may require an appraisal of your company. If the appraisal doesn't meet the lender's requirements, they may deny your loan. In summary, there are several reasons your business may not be pre-approved for an SBA loan.

If your business does receive a pre-approval, I recommend the buyer also get pre-approved as early in the process as possible. The lender will review the buyer's financial position, credit, management experience, and several other criteria. If both your company and the buyer have been pre-approved, you have a favorable chance of obtaining financing for the sale of your business.

Why Bank Financing Is So Hard to Get

There's one main reason why bank financing is hard to obtain to purchase a small business. In an effort to boost profits, business owners reduce income taxes by not reporting all their income or by deducting as many expenses as possible. This lowers the income that's reported on the business's tax returns, which in effect reduces the cash flow available to repay the debt service.

Banks, by nature, are conservative and must follow guidelines and procedures when granting a loan. Banks have a specific process when pre-qualifying a small business loan. They start by reviewing the federal income tax returns. Then they add back a minimum number of adjustments, which may include interest, depreciation, amortization, and the owner's salary. This resulting number is normally lower than the seller's discretionary earnings (SDE) or EBITDA of the business and is used to determine the maximum amount of debt service available to repay a loan.

Banks are also conservative in the adjustments they make to your financial statements. They don't add back all the perks you may be running through your business, such as personal travel expenses, meal and entertainment expenses, and other discretionary or personal expenses. The result is a lower level of cash flow available to cover the debt service.

Improving the Odds

The number one thing you can do to help ensure a buyer can purchase your business with the help of an SBA loan is to maximize your taxable income and minimize the number of perks you write off several years before you begin the sales process. Banks typically allow the following adjustments:

- Interest

- Taxes

- Depreciation

- Amortization

- Owner's salary

The higher your reportable income on your federal income tax returns, the higher the likelihood the bank will approve your loan. If you don't want to finance the sale, minimize the number of adjustments you make to your financial statements at least two years before you begin the sales process. If the income reported on your tax returns isn't high enough to cover the debt service, the buyer's salary, and a debt cushion, it's unlikely your business will qualify for a bank loan.

Handling a Denial

Do you need to reduce the asking price for the business if your business isn't approved?

A bank's or SBA denial of a loan often has little to do with the fairness of your asking price. Lenders are, by nature, conservative, especially when granting an SBA loan, so don't let a rejection dampen your enthusiasm. Loans are often denied based on subjective requirements that don't have a bearing on the actual value of a business.

> *I recently worked on a $2.7 million transaction, and the bank performed an appraisal that came in at about $400,000 less than what we accepted for the business. We had our appraiser critique the bank's appraisal, and we were able to get the loan restructured. Ironically, the bank's appraisal was performed by a "third party" – the same third party that several large broker networks recommend.*

Other Forms of Financing

The forms of financing mentioned above comprise about 95% of the financing options used for the acquisition of small businesses. Other forms of financing exist, but they haven't proved to be readily available and accessible.

If the buyer is a veteran, they may qualify for a VA loan. A buyer can also avoid taking out a small business loan altogether by utilizing existing retirement funds to finance a new business purchase. Because the buyer is buying stock as an investment in their own company, the buyer doesn't have to take a taxable distribution. The major advantage is that you receive cash at closing, and this process has a high success rate.

Common Transaction Structures

You can generally expect the sale of your business to take the form of one of the following transaction structures:

- **All Cash**

  - 100% cash

- **Seller Financing**

  - 50% cash down payment, 50% seller financing

- **Bank or SBA Financing**

  - 20% cash down payment, 80% SBA financing

All-Cash Deals

Is it possible to sell your business for all cash, or do you need to finance a portion of the purchase price? It's a common question. Many business owners want all cash when selling their businesses. No muss, no fuss. So, can you sell your business for all cash?

The short answer is "Yes." That's the long answer, too, but your chances of selling your business decrease, and the timeline for selling your business increases. That's because buyers always consider multiple options when buying a business.

> *It's unlikely the buyer is looking only at your business on the market. It's more likely the buyer is considering businesses for sale where the owner is willing to offer financing, or businesses that have been pre-approved for SBA financing. (SBA loans are generally limited to $5 million or less.) If the buyer is a company, they may be considering other corporate development options for growing their business.*

If your business has been pre-approved for SBA financing, you don't need to offer seller financing as a second alternative. You can limit your search to buyers who are interested in purchasing your business only with SBA financing. This means you will effectively "cash out" when you sell your business, with the exception of a small note you may be required to carry that is typically 10% or less of the purchase price.

Why Buyers of Small Businesses Don't Pay Cash

Buyers of small businesses are usually industry agnostic and may be pursuing businesses across multiple domains. About 95% of the time, buyers of small businesses priced at less than $5 million aren't looking to buy one specific type of business. Rather, they're usually considering companies in a variety of industries, such as service-based, retail, manufacturing, and so forth.

It's rare for small-business buyers to limit their searches to one particular type of industry. The primary exception is highly specialized businesses, such as professional service firms and other niche businesses that require a unique set of knowledge or skills.

> If your business has been pre-approved for SBA financing, you don't need to offer seller financing as a second alternative.

Buyers are often looking at hundreds of companies for sale. As a result, they have a wide variety to choose from and tend to migrate toward businesses that can be financed, either through the seller or the SBA. Buyers tend to dismiss business owners who are asking for all cash unless the business has been pre-approved for SBA financing.

Buyers consider sellers who are asking for all cash unrealistic, and are wary of sellers who want to take the money and run. They see this as a lack of faith in the business from the seller and as a warning sign that something may be wrong with the business.

Buyers prefer to leverage their money to maximize their returns. For example, a buyer who has $1.2 million cash to invest in a company is more likely to buy a business for $2.4 million as opposed to a business for only $1.2 million. Why? Let's examine the numbers behind the logic.

Consider the following example where I've assumed a 10-year ownership period for both Business A and Business B:

Maximizing ROI Based on Financing			
	Business A	**Business B**	**Notes**
Asking Price	$1,200,000	$2,400,000	
Down Payment	$1,200,000	$1,200,000	The down payment is the same for both businesses.
SDE	$400,000	$800,000	
Multiple (Asking Price/Cash Flow)	3.0	3.0	The multiple is the same for both businesses.
Annual Debt Service	$0	$200,000	Debt service is also tax-deductible, though I didn't account for this in the calculations.
SDE (After Debt Service)	$400,000	Years 1-7: $600,000 Years 8-10: $800,000	The debt used to acquire the business will be fully repaid in 7 years for Business B. After 7 years, SDE will increase to $800,000, which is double that of Business A.

Return on Investment	33.33%	33.33%	ROI is the reverse of the multiple (1.0/3.0 = 33.33%).
Cash-on-Cash Return	33.33%	Years 1-7: 50% Years 8-10: 66.66%	

Would you rather buy Business A or Business B? Both businesses require the same down payment of $1.2 million. But Business B is offering 50% financing. Business B also has a higher SDE, which means the buyer will put more money in their pocket, even after paying debt service.

Most buyers prefer Business B because it offers higher returns – both ROI and cash-on-cash. In other words, they're buying a business that will put more money in their pockets – $600,000 vs. $400,000 for the first 1 to 7 years – but for the same down payment of $1.2 million. Also, because Business B offers financing, this implies that the seller of Business B has more faith in their business, which is likely to make the buyer more comfortable.

One additional principle you should consider when calculating ROI is equity building. Business B builds significantly more equity in the long term. Let's assume that both owners sell their business after 10 years. The owner of Business A would receive $1.2 million for their business, and the owner of Business B would receive $2.4 million for their business, excluding any growth in value. Essentially, the owner of Business B used the cash flow of the business to pay for itself.

You've heard it before, but terms are often more important than price.

Exceptions to the Rule

As with everything in life, there are exceptions, and in business sales, there is one principal exception. Americans love financing just about anything they purchase. But in some cultures, buyers prefer to pay cash because they're philosophically, culturally, or religiously opposed to the idea of paying interest and being burdened by debt, even though the ROI may be higher. Additionally, some religions forbid charging or paying interest.

> *A few years ago, I was selling a gas station for a couple of million dollars. In a conversation I had with the seller, who happened to be from Lebanon, we discussed structuring the promissory note. I asked the seller his preferences regarding the interest rate. He told me 0%. I thought the seller misheard me, so I asked him again. He again told me 0% and that he was forbidden from charging or receiving interest payments. I later learned that some branches of Islam prohibit charging interest, even at low interest rates.*

This is most common in culturally diverse cities such as Los Angeles, Seattle, or Miami, in which a buyer may be open to paying all cash, though they often expect a discount. For these types of businesses, I recommend two prices – an all-cash price and a seller-financed price. The price difference usually needs to be about 20% to make sense. For example, you can ask $4.0 million all cash or $5.0 million with 50% down.

Isn't it the buyer's responsibility to obtain financing?

Yes, the buyer must also meet the requirements for approval, but your business must be able to generate sufficient cash flow to repay the debt service. A valuable criteria for any buyer is the availability of financing. Assets that can be financed are more easily bought and sold, and the markets tend to be more liquid for them than for assets where no financing is available. How many cars could Ford Motor Company sell if no banks would finance them? If you own a business and are willing to offer financing or if SBA financing is available, you can expect to sell more quickly and more easily than if you're asking for all cash.

What are the options if you still want all cash?

If you still want to ask for all cash, you have two options:

1. Have your business pre-approved for SBA financing, but remember, the maximum loan amount is $5 million. If your business is valued at more than $5 million, the buyer will have to obtain their own financing.

2. Ask for all cash, but discount the asking price by approximately 20%. My analysis of more than 25,000 transactions found that businesses that sell for all cash receive approximately 30% less than those that can be financed. You can start with a lower discount, perhaps 20%, and negotiate from there.

Conclusion

If you own a business valued at less than $5 million, I recommend considering your financing options in the following order:

1. **SBA Financing:** This offers the most lenient terms, including the lowest down payment and the longest amortization period. If you want to increase the chances a buyer will be able to obtain an SBA loan to purchase your business, maximize your taxable income at least two years prior to the sale. I estimate that over 95% of loans made to purchase a small business are 7(a) SBA loans. For this reason, I recommend first exploring if your business would qualify for an SBA loan.

2. **Other Options:** If your business can't get approved for SBA financing, you have two options:

   a. **Offer Seller Financing:** Consider seller financing if SBA financing isn't available, or if you prefer to offer seller financing due to other reasons, such as tax benefits.

   b. **Ask All Cash:** Finally, you can ask for all cash, but you should reduce the purchase price to account for the fact.

CHAPTER 20

Due Diligence

"By failing to prepare, you are preparing to fail."

– Benjamin Franklin, American Scientist and Statesman

Introduction

After you accept an offer or letter of intent for your business, the buyer will begin the sometimes arduous undertaking of due diligence. Due diligence is the process the buyer uses to gather and analyze information on your business to determine whether to proceed with the purchase. This period of time normally lasts 30 to 90 days. In most cases, the buyer can walk away from the transaction if they're unsatisfied for any reason during due diligence.

Nearly half of all transactions die during due diligence. Why? In many cases, buyers discover serious defects with a business when they dig deeper and decide not to proceed with the transaction as a result. In most situations, these problems could have been prevented by the seller in advance. By preparing for the due diligence procedure in advance, you dramatically improve the odds of making it all the way to the closing table. How can you do this? That's the purpose of this chapter. But before I explain how to improve your odds of success, let me give you some background information on the due diligence process.

The Purpose of Due Diligence

Businesses are complicated – there are hundreds of factors buyers must take into consideration when deciding if they'd like to move forward with the transaction. When evaluating a home for sale, buyers can quickly form an opinion on the value and suitability of a home and hire an inspector to conduct a home inspection. Homes and other tangible purchases often require little to no due diligence. But buying a business involves assessing many intangible factors that aren't readily apparent at first glance, and are more difficult to assess and evaluate. As a result of this increased complexity, purchasers of businesses go through a lengthy and thorough due diligence process before deciding to complete the sales transaction. This process begins when you accept an offer.

List of Documents and When They Are Shared

Here's what is commonly shared with a buyer ***before*** you accept an offer:

- Balance sheets

- Breakdown of sales by customer (with customer names redacted)

- Breakdown of sales by product type

- Confidential information memorandum (CIM)

- Equipment list

- List of key competitors

- List of monthly sales for the previous three to five years

- Profit and loss statements (P&Ls)

- Sales literature and brochures

- Summary or abstract of the lease (not the entire document)

Here's what is commonly shared with buyers ***after*** you accept an offer during the due diligence period:

- **Operations**
  - Advertising contracts
  - Inventory count
  - Marketing material
  - Operations manual
  - Premises lease
  - Supplier and vendor list
  - Supplier and vendor contracts

- **Insurance**
  - Health insurance policies
  - Liability insurance policies
  - Workers' compensation policies and history

- **Assets**
  - Description of any real estate owned
  - Equipment inspection report
  - Equipment leases
  - Inventory list

- **Financial and Tax**
  - Accounts payable schedule
  - Accounts receivable aging schedule
  - Annual personal property tax certificate
  - Backup data of adjustments to financial statements
  - Bank statements
  - Copies of existing loan or financing agreements
  - Customer or client agreements
  - Documentation for add-backs to financial statements
  - Federal income tax returns
  - Financial budgets and projections
  - Full accounting software file
  - General ledger or detailed list of all transactions and expenses
  - Merchant account statements
  - Payroll tax reports
  - Sales and use tax reports
  - Utility bills

- **Staff**

  - Benefit plans

  - Compensation arrangements

  - Detailed schedule of payroll expenses

  - Employment, agency, and independent contractor agreements

  - Job descriptions

  - List of outside contractors

  - Other employment-related agreements

  - Overview of personnel turnover

  - Schedule of owners, officers, employees, independent contractors, consultants, and their titles, length of service, and compensation benefits

  - Summary biographies of key management

- **Legal**

  - Articles of incorporation or organization

  - Business license

  - Certificate of status of good standing from the Secretary of State

  - Copies of licenses, permits, certificates, registrations, and other documents from all governmental authorities

  - Copies of all key contracts

  - Corporate or LLC by-laws or operating agreements

  - Corporate or LLC minutes

  - Description of environmental liabilities

  - Fictitious business name statement (FBNS or DBA)

  - Financing agreements

  - Information for copyrights

  - Information for patents

  - Information for trademarks and service marks

- List of liens against the business

- Other third-party agreements or contracts

- Pending lawsuits

- Phase 1 and 2 environmental studies

- Preliminary UCC search results

- Previous purchase agreement and related documents for business

- Resale permit

- Seller's disclosure statement

To download a complete due diligence list, or learn more about buying, selling, valuing a business, or dozens of other topics related to mergers and acquisitions, visit the Resources section of the Morgan & Westfield website at morganandwestfield.com/resources.

Why You Should Prepare for Due Diligence

Here are the major advantages of preparing for due diligence:

- **Prepares You Emotionally:** Due diligence can be a grueling time. You must be prepared to commit a substantial amount of time and energy to the process. Some buyers have the nefarious objective to wear you down, discover problems, and then renegotiate the terms of the transaction. By anticipating this possibility and preparing for due diligence so issues are uncovered and resolved before a buyer discovers them, you remain emotionally unattached to the process. That way, you can negotiate from a detached, objective perspective.

- **Increases Odds of Success:** Preparing your business for sale dramatically increases your chances of success. When you don't prepare for due diligence, it can turn into an expensive and time-consuming undertaking. Preparing for due diligence allows you and your team to correct problems in advance, and helps you avoid pitfalls to a sale before you expose your business to buyers, which improves your odds of success. With inaccurate information, you run the risk of losing a buyer. Once a buyer discovers defects during due diligence, the sale must be delayed to address the problems, which decreases the odds of closing the sale.

- **Speeds Up the Process:** Time is your greatest enemy. Time kills deals. Having your records in order before selling your business can speed up due diligence once you have a buyer, resulting in a higher chance of reaching the finishing line. By organizing the documents so they're ready for review, you'll help ensure the process is quick and straightforward.

- **Increases the Chances of Receiving an Offer:** Many times, buyers are reluctant to make an offer on a business because they don't want to risk the time and financial investment in performing due diligence, only for there to be an undisclosed problem. Preparing for due diligence mitigates these concerns for buyers. You also demonstrate to the buyer that you're serious when you take the time and effort to prepare your business for sale. Buyers prefer dealing with motivated, prepared sellers, and are more likely to spend time with a seller they know has adequately prepared for the sale.

- **Resolves Issues Before They Become Issues:** You can resolve many issues before a buyer ever learns of them with advanced warning of any unsettled problems. Preparing for due diligence enables you to work out problems before a buyer comes into the picture. A problem identified in advance that can be explained will keep your credibility intact. There's nothing worse than spending time and money preparing and marketing your business for sale and finding a qualified buyer, only to lose the buyer because of an unforeseen matter with your business that could have been resolved beforehand. This scenario happens more often than sellers realize because, despite working in their business full-time, owners are often unaware of seemingly simple issues. But those simple issues can have a material effect on a buyer's perception of the relative risk of your company if they aren't resolved in advance. For example, problems with financial records, if not addressed beforehand, usually trigger demands for a lower price, more restrictive terms, or may cause the buyer to walk away from the sale entirely.

- **Maximizes Your Sales Price:** Conducting pre-sale due diligence maximizes the value of your business by identifying issues early on to avoid complications that can affect your transaction. Accurate financial records also help to maximize the sale price of your business by attracting buyers who are more confident in your company. Simply put, the more organized your company's financial records appear, the quicker you're likely to sell your business and receive top dollar. A thoughtful evaluation of your business before the sale process begins will make the undertaking more manageable, efficient, and cost-effective for you.

- **Prepares Your Team:** Through the process of preparing for due diligence, members of your adviser team will come to know and understand your company as well as you do – and far better than a potential buyer. This understanding enables your transaction adviser to prepare a confidential information memorandum (CIM) and other marketing materials that fully describe and highlight the strengths of your business. You'll be in the strongest position to sell your business for the best price possible by being fully prepared to explain its intricacies and showcase its strengths.

- **Reduces Holdbacks:** In a holdback, the buyer seeks to protect themselves by "holding back" funds – that is, a portion of the purchase price – at closing. A buyer may be concerned about skeletons in the closet, or other unknown problems about your business. By preparing for due diligence, you reduce the buyer's perception of risk, which reduces the likelihood the buyer will request a large holdback.

- **Reduces Strength of Representations and Warranties:** In the purchase agreement, you will have to make factual statements regarding the condition of your business, covering nearly all aspects of your company. Reps and warranties in the purchase agreement assure the buyer that legal remedies will be available if you fail to disclose any material facts regarding your business that aren't discovered during due diligence. By preparing for due diligence, you reduce the buyer's perceived risk, and the buyer may propose less stringent reps and warranties as a result.

Length of Due Diligence

Due diligence can take any period of time, as long as both you and the buyer agree. The typical due diligence period for most small to mid-sized businesses is 30 to 60 days. The length of due diligence should be based on the following:

- **Availability of Information:** If you organize documents in advance and respond promptly to the buyer's document requests, the due diligence period can be shorter.

- **Turnaround Time:** If you provide concise, organized, and clear information in a timely fashion, you'll speed up the due diligence period.

- **Communication:** If you're more available to respond to the buyer's requests and clarify points of confusion, this may also shorten the due diligence period.

> The typical due diligence period for most small to mid-sized businesses is 30 to 60 days.

Preparing for Due Diligence

Ideally, you'll want to anticipate and resolve any issues before a buyer discovers them. Put yourself in the buyer's shoes and assess your business as early in the sale process as possible by performing your own due diligence.

While this is optimally done just before putting your business on the market, it's never too late to get started. You can even conduct pre-sale due diligence if your business is already on the market. If you haven't already done so, make this a priority. Have your financials reviewed and in order, and perform legal and operational due diligence on your business, as well.

Many business sales fall apart during due diligence when issues are discovered. If the buyer discovers problems that weren't disclosed, they can end up in an advantageous position, and you'll lose your negotiating posture.

As a result, this can entice the buyer to make demands and negotiate a lower purchase price. Make no mistake – each item the buyer finds fault with during due diligence enables them to claw back at the purchase price, if they don't abandon the transaction altogether.

Your goal is not only to sell your business and move on to the next phase of your life, but to receive top dollar. By conducting pre-sale due diligence, you help ensure you maintain your negotiating posture throughout the sales process.

Preparing for due diligence is straightforward. It involves assembling and organizing the documents that most buyers request and review. I recommend you prepare for due diligence as early as possible – ideally, at least six months before beginning the sale process. This will give you ample time to resolve any issues.

Know What to Expect

Here are some tips for preparing for due diligence so you're ready when the time comes:

- **Understand How Buyer Type Impacts Thoroughness:** Individuals are generally less thorough than companies in conducting due diligence. But some individuals can be especially thorough if they're detail-oriented, risk-averse, or have a CPA, attorney, or other professional advising them. Most companies are thorough, especially if they have completed multiple acquisitions in the past.

- **Pre-qualify the Buyer:** Be sure you pre-qualify the buyer before negotiating and accepting an offer. You want to be sure you're negotiating with a buyer who has the financial capacity to close the transaction.

- **Maintain Your Focus:** Be prepared to spend a significant amount of time and energy during due diligence. By the time you reach the due diligence stage, you may feel as if you're almost done, but this is a critical phase where the sale can be made or lost. You're only on the 50-yard line at this point – if you lose focus, the deal can die. There's still a lot of work to be done before the sale is completed. It's vital that you stay engaged and actively involved in due diligence in order to reach your ultimate goal of a smooth closing.

- **Avoid Exclusivity if Possible:** Keep your business on the market even after you receive an offer unless you've negotiated an exclusivity period with the buyer.

- **Tell the Buyer You're Prepared:** If you've prepared your business for sale and organized all the documents, be sure to mention this in early conversations with buyers. You could say something like this – "I'm a motivated, serious seller who has prepared my business for sale with the help of my CPA and attorney. I have all the necessary documents ready for due diligence, including tax returns, leases, equipment lists, financial statements, and more."

Since much of the documentation needed for due diligence is financial in nature, you should include your accountant or CFO in the process as early as possible. The more cooperation you have from your team, the smoother the process will go.

You should also retain a third party to examine your financials, such as profit and loss statements, balance sheets, and federal income tax returns. Have them scrutinize key ratios, trends, and other data, and provide you with a report of their findings. This helps spot potential issues a buyer may find with your financial records, and allows you to address these issues before you ever receive an offer.

> Each item the buyer finds fault with during due diligence enables them to claw back at the purchase price, if they don't abandon the transaction altogether.

Conclusion

I strongly recommend you invest time preparing your business for due diligence. Most business owners skip this step altogether. By preparing for this process, you'll significantly improve the chances of a successful sale and maximize the price you receive at the closing table. Additionally, demonstrating to the buyer that you've prepared for due diligence increases the buyer's confidence in your business and reduces their perception of fear.

Due diligence can be heaven or hell. If you have your financials in order and all is well from an operational and legal standpoint, chances are due diligence will be uneventful, and your business sale will take flight and bring you one step closer to the closing. If you're unprepared and the buyer finds things amiss during due diligence, you'll find yourself on the horns of a dilemma. Being prepared can go a long way in facilitating the outcome you want.

Here's an action checklist to make sure you're prepared:

- Compile all documents that buyers typically request during due diligence.

- Ask a third-party accountant to perform pre-sale due diligence on your company.

- Ask your attorney to make sure all your legal ducks are in a row before you begin the process.

To download an editable version of this due diligence checklist or learn more about buying, selling, valuing a business, or dozens of other topics related to mergers and acquisitions, visit the Resources section of the Morgan & Westfield website at morganandwestfield.com/resources.

CHAPTER 21

Taxes

"The older I get, the more interesting I find lawyers and accountants."

– Alex James, English Journalist

Introduction

One of the primary considerations when determining how to structure the sale of your business is taxes. If you don't handle this properly, Uncle Sam will come knocking on your door sometime after your deal closes. When selling your business, federal and state taxes can dramatically impact how much of the proceeds end up in your pocket.

The type and amount of taxes that must be paid are directly impacted by four major factors:

1. **Your Entity Type:** Whether your company is a sole proprietorship, partnership, LLC, corporation, or other type of entity.

2. **Transaction Structure:** Whether your sale is structured as an asset sale or stock sale (mergers are rare in the lower middle market).

3. **Allocation of Purchase Price:** How the purchase price is allocated among various classes of assets, such as inventory, accounts receivable, equipment, goodwill, land, or buildings.

4. **Your State of Residency:** You must often pay personal and corporate state income taxes in addition to federal income tax on the gains from the sale of your business.

The section that follows provides general information about the main differences among the various elements of the transaction as they pertain to business sales, so you're prepared when the time comes to sell your business. Always consult with a qualified attorney or tax professional when considering how to structure your transaction. A review of the concepts discussed here will give you a head start before you meet with your tax advisor.

Asset vs. Stock Sale

When buying or selling a business, an M&A transaction can generally take one of two forms – it can be structured as an asset sale or a stock sale. Technically, there's a third way – a merger – but mergers are rare for private companies. Fundamentally, there are few differences between the two transaction structures, but the tax implications can be significant, which, of course, impacts your after-tax proceeds.

- **Asset Sale:** In an asset sale, your entity (corporation, LLC, or other) sells the individual assets of the business it owns, such as furniture, fixtures, equipment, and customer list, to the buyer (usually the buyer's entity). In an asset sale, your tax rates depend on your type of entity and how the purchase price is allocated, with some of the price being taxed at ordinary income tax rates and some of it being taxed at long-term capital gains tax rates. The taxes due on the sale of a business are higher for you if the sale is structured as an asset sale than as a stock sale.

- **Stock Sale:** In a stock sale, you – say, John Smith, as an individual – sign over the actual ownership, or shares, of your entity (corporation, LLC, or other) to the buyer. This would be similar to owning a share of Ford Motor Company and selling this share of stock to another individual. In a stock sale, the majority of the gains are taxed at long-term capital gains tax rates.

> You can assume your transaction will most likely be structured as an asset sale if the value of your business is less than $100 million.

If the value of a business is less than $100 million, chances are your transaction will be structured as an asset sale. From the buyer's viewpoint, an asset sale is usually more desirable due to certain tax advantages and the avoidance of any unknown legal risks on the part of your entity. From your viewpoint, asset sales are usually less desirable because hard assets may be subject to ordinary income tax rates, which are higher than capital gains tax rates.

Why Most Transactions Are Asset Sales

The majority of small transactions are structured as asset sales for two primary reasons:

1. **Tax Purposes:** If buyers purchase your entity (corporation, LLC, or other), they inherit your tax basis. But, if they purchase your assets, they can often begin depreciating those assets again and experience more advantageous tax benefits. Asset sales dominate smaller business sales because the buyer can write up the value of the assets and depreciate the costs, which lowers the amount of taxes they must pay after the closing. On the other hand, in a stock sale, the buyer inherits your tax basis (there are minor exceptions) and receives fewer tax benefits.

2. **Risk Mitigation:** If the buyer purchases your entity, they're inheriting unknown legal risks associated with your entity. These are known as "contingent liabilities." For this reason, buyers prefer to form a new entity that doesn't have any unknown risks.

The bottom line is that you can assume your transaction will most likely be structured as an asset sale if the value of your business is less than $100 million.

Entity Types and Tax Implications

The type of entity you have can also impact the tax implications of your transaction. The following is a description of the major entity types and the impact on taxes.

Sole Proprietorships

If your business is structured as a sole proprietorship, the sale can only be structured as an asset sale. Selling a business that's structured as a sole proprietorship is treated as the sale of a collection of assets. The taxes you pay will be based on capital gains tax rates for some assets and ordinary income tax rates for other assets. The tax rate will be determined by how you allocate the sale price, which is covered below.

Single and Multi-Member LLCs

Single-member LLCs are pass-through entities – there is no tax on the LLC itself. Sales of these entities can be structured as a sale of assets or as a stock sale, although technically, it's a sale of the membership interests in the LLC.

Regardless, the sale is treated and taxed as an asset sale, though some rare exceptions exist, and the tax rates depend on how the purchase price is allocated. LLCs may also be subject to higher self-employment taxes than S Corporations, so consult with your CPA prior to the sale. If you have elected for your LLC to be taxed as a C Corporation, different rules apply.

Partnerships

If your business is structured as a partnership, the sale can only be structured as an asset sale. A partnership is a pass-through entity, which means that only the members pay taxes – the entity doesn't pay taxes. Taxes are paid at both capital gains rates and ordinary income tax rates, depending on how the purchase price is allocated.

S Corporation

If you own an S Corporation, the sale can be structured as an asset sale or a stock sale. If it's structured as an asset sale, your tax rates will primarily be determined by how you allocate the purchase price for tax purposes. If it's structured as a stock sale, the majority of the proceeds will be taxed at capital gains tax rates, with some minor exceptions – amounts paid directly to the owners, such as through non-competition agreements or consulting agreements, may be subject to income taxes.

If your business is structured as an S Corporation, there is no double taxation at the federal level, which is the primary advantage of an S Corporation over a C Corporation. State income taxes may also vary from state to state. For example, some states (hello, California) only have income tax rates and don't have capital gains tax rates.

If your S Corporation was recently converted from a C Corporation, the sale may be structured as if you were still operating as a C Corporation. The IRS has created a 10-year look-back period for this situation. If this might apply to you, consult a CPA.

C Corporation

Your business is a C Corporation unless you or your shareholders have filed Form 2553 with the IRS electing to be taxed as an S Corporation. If the sale is structured as an asset sale, the C Corporation will sell its assets and you'll face two levels of taxation. This is known as double taxation – once at the corporate level when the corporation sells its assets, and again at the individual level when the corporation distributes the proceeds to its shareholders in the form of a dividend.

There are two primary methods to avoid double taxation:

1. Structure a portion of the sale as the sale of the owner's personal goodwill, which isn't legally classified as a personal asset. Check out the legal case *Martin Ice Cream Co., 110 T.C. 189 (1998)*.

2. Structure the sale as a stock sale, which is primarily subject to capital gains tax rates, though non-competition, consulting, and earnout agreements may be subject to income tax rates if they're paid directly to the owner.

If your business is structured as a C Corporation, consult with a CPA experienced in structuring the sale of companies well in advance of the sale. You have many options available to you, such as structuring some of the sale as a bonus or salary, negotiating the sale as a stock sale, or forming a trust. But, some of these options must be implemented well in advance of selling your business.

Allocation and Taxes

Allocating the purchase price, or total sale price, of a business among the various assets of the business, or asset "classes," is necessary for tax purposes when you sell your business. This is the case regardless of whether the sale is structured as a stock sale or an asset sale – part of the purchase price can be allocated to non-compete or consulting agreements in a stock sale.

Frequently, the allocation of the purchase price can become another area of negotiation after the price, terms, and conditions of the sale have been agreed upon. In most cases, what's good for you is bad for the buyer, and vice versa, which can lead to contentious negotiations.

In the end, it's crucial that both you and the buyer compromise and meet somewhere in the middle to satisfy your respective goals. Once again, an agreement is required because both allocations must match and be entered on a specific IRS form – Form 8594.

Unfortunately, business transactions have been known to come to a halt because a buyer and seller can't agree on how to allocate the purchase price. This is more likely to happen when the negotiations have been contentious. The allocation of purchase price sometimes becomes the final straw, causing a buyer and seller to abandon the transaction.

Arming yourself with the information in this chapter will help ensure you don't get blindsided by an element that's often an after-thought until the very end in many negotiated transactions.

> Consult with your tax advisor well before the sale to mitigate potential tax implications.

Why Allocating the Purchase Price Is Necessary

Both the seller and the buyer are required by law to file Form 8594 with the IRS. This form requires that both parties allocate the purchase price among the various assets of the business being purchased so you can calculate Uncle Sam's cut, and the buyer can calculate their new basis in the assets.

This form must be filed with each of your tax returns at the end of the year. Most tax advisors agree that the allocations should match on both your and the buyer's forms. While there is no legal requirement that the allocations match, most tax advisors agree that a match decreases the chances of an audit.

The Purpose of IRS Form 8594

IRS Form 8594 breaks down the assets of the business being purchased or sold into seven classes, or categories. Each type of asset is treated differently for tax purposes. It's important that you carefully consider how you'll classify each individual asset, as it can have significant tax and financial implications for both you and the buyer.

Specific allocations are referenced on the IRS form and are broken down as follows:

- **Class I:** Cash and Bank Deposits

- **Class II:** Securities, including Actively Traded Personal Property and Certificates of Deposit

- **Class III:** Accounts Receivables

- **Class IV:** Stock in Trade (Inventory)

- **Class V:** Other Tangible Property, including Furniture, Fixtures, Vehicles, etc.

- **Class VI:** Intangibles, including Covenant Not to Compete

- **Class VII:** Goodwill of a Going Concern

The seller usually seeks to maximize amounts allocated to assets that will result in capital gains taxes while minimizing amounts allocated to assets that will result in ordinary income taxes. The buyer, unfortunately, usually seeks exactly the opposite, which is why negotiations over the allocation can often be so contentious.

Stock vs. Asset Sales

Where stock sales are concerned, the majority of the purchase price is normally allocated to the value of the stock. The remainder is allocated to the value of any non-competition agreements, consulting agreements, or any other assets personally owned by you, and not the entity.

In a stock sale, the buyer doesn't receive a step-up in basis and inherits your existing basis in the assets. This is one of the reasons that asset sales dominate smaller business sales – because the buyer can deduct, or depreciate, the cost of the assets they acquire in the near term, which reduces the buyer's income taxes. On the other hand, with stock sales, there are no immediate tax benefits to buyers concerning stock purchases. For you, a stock sale is advantageous because you only pay long-term capital gains tax rates on stocks held for more than one year.

Common Allocations

The following is an overview of the most common allocations I see:

Class I: Cash and Bank Deposits

- **Allocation:** None.

- **Reason:** These assets aren't normally included in the purchase. If they are included, they're listed at face value.

Class II: Securities, including Actively Traded Personal Property and Certificates of Deposit

- **Allocation:** None.

- **Reason:** These assets aren't normally included in the purchase. If they are included, they're listed at face value.

Class III: Accounts Receivables

- **Allocation:** Normally valued at face value, if included in the purchase price.

- **Reason:** As a result, there's no gain for you and, therefore, no tax due on the amount allocated to this asset.

Class IV: Stock in Trade (Inventory)

- **Allocation:** Normally valued at your original cost.

- **Reason:** As a result, there's no gain for you and, therefore, no tax due on the amount allocated to this asset.

Class V: Other Tangible Property, including Furniture, Fixtures, Vehicles, etc.

- **Allocation:** Normally valued at current market value or "replacement value." Note that the buyer may have to pay sales tax on the amount allocated to this class of assets, although this depends on your state.

- **Reason:** Any gain on the sale of tangible property is taxed based on ordinary income rates to you, and the buyer can begin to depreciate these assets based on their stepped-up value.

Class VI: Intangibles, including Covenant Not to Compete

- **Allocation:** Normally less than a few percentage points of the purchase price.

- **Reason:** You must pay ordinary income taxes or long-term capital gains taxes based on the amount allocated to intangible assets depending on whether the non-compete is considered compensatory or a capital gain.

Class VII: Goodwill of a Going Concern

- **Allocation:** The balance of the purchase price is normally allocated to goodwill.

- **Reason:** Goodwill is treated at long-term capital gains tax rates for you, and the buyer can amortize goodwill over a 15-year period.

Once the parties agree to the allocation, it's usually attached as a schedule to the purchase agreement and signed at closing. The parties then file IRS Form 8594 at year-end, ensuring that IRS Form 8594 matches the allocation provided in the purchase agreement.

You and the buyer will each have a unique perspective when it comes to allocating the purchase price. Each allocation category will have a different effect for you and the buyer. It's important to give the allocations careful consideration because these differences can amount to significant tax and financial repercussions for you. You should weigh the advantages and disadvantages of each allocation because this will significantly affect your bottom line.

Conclusion

Tax implications can have a significant impact on the realized value of a business to both the buyer and the seller. Consult with your tax advisor well in advance to mitigate the tax impact of the sale. Consider how a sale is going to be structured from the outset, and keep in mind that advanced planning is essential to maximize the selling price of your business.

CHAPTER 22

Confidentiality

"What is told in the ear of a man is often heard 100 miles away."

– Chinese Proverb

Introduction

When it comes to selling your business, time is your friend before your business is for sale and your enemy once your business is on the market.

The longer it takes to sell your business, the higher the probability of a leak. Why is that a bad thing?

Once the cat is out of the bag and word of the sale leaks, the narrative may become distorted and impossible to control. Employees who learn about the sale through indirect means become distrustful. Customers may jump ship, and competitors may attempt to poach your employees and customer base.

Doesn't a non-disclosure agreement (NDA) ensure confidentiality?

A signed NDA alone doesn't ensure confidentiality any more than an ADT sign prevents a burglar from breaking into your house, but it's a critical component. NDAs do prevent leaks in most cases. But the longer it takes to consummate a transaction, the higher the probability that word will get out prematurely. The real purpose of a confidentiality agreement is to prevent a leak, but it's not the only tool in your arsenal you should use. A well-drafted confidentiality agreement should be combined with additional actions for maintaining confidentiality.

In this chapter, I reveal several strategies you can implement to help keep the sale of your business a secret from your customers, employees, and competitors.

> When it comes to selling your business, time is your friend before your business is for sale and your enemy once your business is on the market.

Reasons for Maintaining Confidentiality

There are three primary reasons for maintaining confidentiality:

1. If employees learn about the sale, they may become nervous regarding their job security. As a result, they could begin to look for employment elsewhere. In other instances, employees can feel betrayed and could form a small coalition to compete directly with you.

2. Both existing and potential new customers may learn of the possible sale and become nervous that a new owner will substantially change the business model or increase pricing, so they may begin looking for alternative solutions through competitors.

3. Competitors may use knowledge of the sale to poach both employees and customers of your company.

Let's explore strategies you can use for maintaining confidentiality.

> The longer it takes to sell your business, the higher the probability of a leak.

Strategies To Implement Before the Sale

The following is a summary of the major strategies you can use to maintain confidentiality *before* you put your business on the market.

Prepare for the Sale

The longer it takes to sell your business, the higher the probability of a leak. The more time you spend preparing your business for sale in advance, the more quickly your business will sell, which minimizes the possibility of a leak. To preserve confidentiality, you should ideally prepare for the sale years in advance, which helps ensure a quick, problem-free transaction, thereby minimizing the possibility of a leak and its consequential damage.

Control the Narrative

As anyone who has played the "telephone game" as a child knows, rumors quickly mutate, and once they become viral, the narrative is impossible to control. Rumors are like a bell – you can't unring them.

Controlling and managing the disclosure process puts you in a position to frame the discussion in a positive light, which allows you to:

- Minimize the possibility of damage.

- Retain the trust of your key people by telling them of your plans before anyone else.

- Frame your story in a cohesive, compelling fashion that aligns your interests with those of your employees.

Once word of the sale leaks, the narrative may become distorted and impossible to reframe. Employees who learn about the sale through indirect means become distrustful. Rebuilding trust with your employees can take years. And unfortunately, if you're in the process of selling your business, you don't have the liberty of time to rebuild trust with your employees. Therefore, you're at a great disadvantage for the remainder of the sale process because you've lost trust with your team and lost the ability to use your team as an asset to build trust with the buyer. Buyers become nervous when there's a lack of trust between owners and employees, and this has caused many deals to derail or outright fail.

Inform Employees

Employees understand there's a point in the life of every entrepreneur when it's time to let go. New ownership makes sense at key stages in the life cycle of many businesses, which often spells opportunity for a driven employee. In most cases, the only way an employee's career can grow is if the business grows. Most entrepreneurs reach a stage where they're "milking the cow" and no longer have the desire to grow the business, which limits employees' growth. To ambitious employees, this can be demotivating. New ownership can provide these employees with new opportunities.

Employees resting on their laurels may be understandably nervous about the prospects of a new owner. In many cases, buyers have told me that they found some employees seemed to be barely working in the business yet were receiving full salary and benefits. A transition can be an excellent means of purging the business of "dead weight." To be sure, the majority of employees are honest and hard-working, but there are always exceptions.

If the buyer is a larger company, they may provide a pathway of growth for employees through opportunities outside the organization. Imagine if 3M bought a $20 million company. Which situation would offer an ambitious employee more opportunity? A career at the $20 million company or a position in any one of countless divisions at 3M? New ownership may also bring capital to the table to expand the business, which could represent another opportunity for superstar employees. In nearly all acquisitions, the buyer desires to significantly grow the business post-closing and is willing to take significant risks in doing so. This offers your best employees opportunities – so make sure they understand the potential.

Draft a Non-Disclosure Agreement

NDAs prevent leaks of confidentiality in most cases. But the longer it takes to consummate a transaction, the higher the probability of a leak. In most cases, a leak is careless, and the offending party isn't intentionally harming your business. Who among us has never accidentally let something "slip"?

The real purpose of a confidentiality agreement is prevention, but it's not the only tool you should use. A well-drafted confidentiality agreement should be combined with additional actions for maintaining confidentiality. As an example, for highly sensitive information released to competitors, it may be wise to enter into a separate agreement, or a multi-part NDA, that addresses the disclosure of that information.

Strategies To Implement During the Sale

The following is a summary of the major strategies you can use to maintain confidentiality *after* your business is on the market.

Control How Information Is Released

Controlling what and when information is released is foundational to maintaining confidentiality. Here are several strategies for controlling what and when information is furnished to potential buyers:

- **Redact or Aggregate Information:** Consider sharing highly sensitive information in summary form in which key information – such as customer or employee names – is redacted.

- **Release Information in Phases:** Release information to buyers in phases as the sale progresses and as transaction milestones are achieved, such as completion of financial due diligence. At each milestone, request that the buyer sign off on its completion. For example, names of key customers or employees should be released only at the tail end of due diligence, or after the purchase agreement is negotiated and executed.

- **Develop Category-Specific Strategies:** Highly sensitive information subject to misappropriation by the buyer could be summarized, shared with neutral third parties, or shared only in summary form with the buyer. You should exhibit extreme caution in areas of unprotected trade secrets and other non-registered IP.

- **Set Up an Electronic Data Room:** If you're negotiating and conducting due diligence with multiple parties simultaneously, it may be wise to release all information through an electronic data room, which tracks who accesses information and provides you with controls, such as limiting the ability of buyers to download or print information.

- **Create a Document Trail:** Email as much information as possible to create a document trail in the event litigation needs to be pursued. This documentation can provide you with leverage in the event of threatened litigation, such as when the opposing parties weigh the potential merits of a case before initiating a lawsuit. Since the evidentiary burden is on the disclosing party in most confidentiality agreements, the more documentation you have, the more leverage you'll have to reach a quick resolution in the event of a breach.

Control Who Information Is Released To

If you're releasing sensitive information, you can often limit who this information is released to. Let's examine strategies for doing just that:

- **Thoroughly Screen Buyers:** Thoroughly screen all buyers financially before releasing any information. Direct competitors should be screened with extra diligence. Due diligence is a two-way street – verify your buyer's financial position during due diligence before releasing sensitive information. Verify how many acquisitions they have previously made and request to talk to several CEOs of their past acquisitions. If you encounter warning signs, immediately slow down and dig deeper. In the case of private, supposedly "wealthy" individuals, request a credit report or hire a private investigator to perform a background check if suspicions are raised. In one case, we sold a staffing firm to a private, wealthy individual who stole the funds he used to purchase the business from a trust, of which he was the trustee. While such cases are rare, if doubts are raised, trust your gut and dig deeper.

- **Release Sensitive Information to Neutral Third Parties:** In the case of extremely sensitive information, it's possible to appoint third parties to review the data and prepare a summary report to present to the seller. In one large transaction we handled at Morgan & Westfield representing the seller, two customers accounted for 40% of the annual revenue. The buyer was concerned due to the risk associated with the high concentration of revenue, but the seller was unwilling to let the buyer talk directly with the customers. We hired a third-party firm to perform customer surveys and prepared a summary report to present to the buyer.

- **Limit Information to Select Parties:** Alternatively, you can limit information to specific people or departments within the buyer's organization, such as the buyer's CPA, attorney, or CFO. When doing so, I recommend that the third party also sign a non-disclosure agreement. However, the terms of the agreement may need to be modified as follows:

  > *"Buyer agrees that select evaluation material will be provided only to Buyer's outside advisors, and that Buyer shall not disclose such information to Buyer's employees in its marketing, research and development, technology or finance departments."*

- **Use the Attorney-Client Privilege:** Omit documents from the data room that are subject to attorney-client privilege, such as those that might be relevant to recent litigation. In other words, if you're in the process of litigation, disclose any documents pertinent to the litigation exclusively through your attorney. Note that in the event of a successful transaction, the buyer may share a common interest with the seller if the buyer becomes a "successor defendant." But this privilege isn't guaranteed, especially if the transaction is unsuccessful. It's therefore wise to limit disclosure of any litigation-sensitive information exclusively through your attorney to retain the attorney-client privilege.

Handle Breaches Immediately

In the event of a breach, immediately call the offending party. Assess their reaction to the news and their tone – listen to their story before taking any dramatic action. In most cases, the other side will apologize and immediately take steps to correct the action, such as firing the employee who initiated the breach or calling the customer to reconstruct the narrative of the story.

When a breach isn't clear, a phone call may serve to raise the other party's awareness of the issue, and in most cases, the story will quickly disappear. Send a short email to confirm your conversation and any actions they have agreed to take. This creates a paper trail in the event you need to pursue litigation in the future.

Who Else To Inform

Who should you tell about the sale? Let's cover some key stakeholders:

Professional Advisors

Telling your professional advisors is almost always a safe bet, assuming they're true professionals. They're used to their clients selling their businesses and are unlikely to be surprised. Additionally, professional advisors, such as accountants and attorneys, don't like surprises, and getting them involved early in the process may prove to be of great benefit.

Landlord

Landlords are also accustomed to businesses being bought and sold, and the news shouldn't shock them. Your landlord may potentially have a buyer in mind. Informing your landlord early on normally carries the benefit of being able to pre-negotiate the terms of the transfer.

Franchisor

Franchisors are also accustomed to the transfer of franchises within their systems. Again, the sooner you tell them, the better, and there is little risk here. In fact, franchisors may become distrustful if you don't inform them early on. Many franchisors also provide assistance during the sales process and may help in generating buyers.

Family

I recommend informing only those closest to you, especially if you live in the same house. Keeping the sale a secret from your nearest family members will be nearly impossible. If your family members work in the business, this should be handled with caution.

Friends

Tell only your closest friends about your plans, as most will have a difficult time keeping their lips sealed. If you trust and share a close bond with a friend or two, this friend may be a safe person to talk to during the process, providing emotional stability for you during the transition.

Employees

Knock over the easy dominoes first. In other words, pick out one or two key employees who you believe will be comfortable with your plans and can keep a secret. Then, tell the remainder of your employees if you have a small business, or only your management team if you own a larger business. In my experience, about 20% to 30% of business owners inform their key employees.

Suppliers

Don't inform your suppliers unless you believe they would be a valuable source of potential buyers. Telling your suppliers is risky because they are also likely to do business with your competition and are likely to spread the word.

Conclusion

Maintaining confidentiality is a critical component of selling your business. A confidentiality agreement is one of many strategies to preserve confidentiality. A well-drafted confidentiality agreement should be paired with the strategies recommended above to ensure confidentiality is maintained throughout the sales process.

- Prepare for the sale to ensure the sale unfolds as quickly as possible, which minimizes the possibility of a leak.

- Control the narrative by deciding in advance how to handle disclosing the sale to your key stakeholders.

- Consider informing your employees about the sale – couple this with an NDA and retention bonus plan.

- Control what and when information is released to potential buyers by redacting information, reducing information in stages, developing separate strategies for different categories of information, using a data room, and using email to create a paper trail.

- Control who information is released to by thoroughly screening buyers, releasing sensitive information to neutral third parties, and using the attorney-client privilege.

- Handle any breaches immediately.

- Consider informing others involved in your business about the sale, such as your landlord and franchisor.

"My favorite thing is to go where I've never been."

– Diane Arbus, American Photographer

One of the most worthwhile investments you can make in your business is in the form of time – putting in the time to properly prepare your company for sale. Laying the groundwork to showcase your business in the best possible light will pay dividends even if your planned sale is years down the road.

I don't have to remind you that your company is one of your most valuable assets. And by investing the time now to prepare your business for sale – whether next month or two or more years from now – you'll add to the value of that asset. Diligent preparation will result in several perks, including:

- The value of your business will increase.

- You will improve the chances of a successful sale.

- You will speed up the sales process.

- Your negotiating position will dramatically improve.

- Your business will operate more efficiently, which is a plus, even if you decide not to sell.

By preparing your business for sale, you'll be ready to sell at any time. In many cases, unsolicited offers are the most attractive offers you will receive. By following the guidelines put forth in this book, and summarized here, you'll ensure your business is in the best position possible to take advantage of an unexpected opportunity.

Deciding To Sell

Planning the sale starts with the decision to sell. The following are suggestions for making this immense decision a little less difficult.

Making the Decision

The process of preparing your business for sale and then selling it should be based on your specific circumstances and reason for selling.

For professionals who regularly buy and sell businesses, the decision is far less traumatic than for an independent owner. For independently owned businesses, the decision to sell is often emotional and gut-wrenching. Selling a company will bring about major life changes for most entrepreneurs. If you own a small family business, planning for the sale and thoroughly exploring your motivations are key to ensuring a smooth transition.

Committing to the process once you've decided to sell is critical. It's therefore wise to fully explore your reason for selling before you begin to prepare your business for sale. Your motives will figure into the specific improvements you should make to your business and will also determine the extent to which you want to be involved in your company after the closing.

If you're burned out, for example, you're unlikely to have the drive and patience to commit to longer-term goals, such as building a management team, so instead, you may choose to focus on short-term objectives that have a more immediate impact. Or, you may wish to retire, but retain an ongoing part-time role in your business after the closing. On the other hand, if you've simply "had enough," it's unlikely you'll want to play a continued role. Likewise, if you want to diversify your wealth, you have a different range of exit options available to you than if you're already diversified. If you want to sell because you have a more promising opportunity you want to pursue, the process of preparing your business for sale will differ than if, say, you're going through a divorce.

Regardless, it's important to fully explore your reason for selling because this will serve as the foundation on which you'll make other critical decisions moving forward. Your motivations will also open up potential exit opportunities, or may close them.

Proper preparation goes far beyond cleaning up your financial statements from the past three years. You'll need to be both intellectually and emotionally prepared to effectively manage the sale. Taking an active role in the process and maintaining a cool head will help ensure the transition goes as smoothly as possible.

Using a Decision-Making Framework

Deciding to sell your business will be one of the most important decisions of your life. Use the framework outlined here for making this determination:

- **Goals:** Start by first considering your objectives and lost opportunity costs. This is the foundation of your decision and allows you to place all other factors within the context of your long-term aspirations. A myriad of considerations come into play when deciding to sell your business, and taking into account all of the factors at once can be overwhelming. Be honest with yourself about your long-term goals. The risk of making a hasty decision is that your decision may not align with those aspirations. You may back out of the sale or regret it altogether if you moved forward prematurely and the sale doesn't help you accomplish your goals.

- **Internal Factors:** Address the emotional or internal factors of a sale – namely, those relating to happiness. This step takes substantial time, especially if you're a novice in-depth soul-searcher. Ask yourself if you're happy. Really happy. Is your business making you unhappy? Would selling your business make you happier? Entrepreneurship is a struggle. No entrepreneur is ecstatic all of the time. Look at yourself objectively and determine if a change might make you happier – but beware of trading one set of problems for another. Would you keep your business if it made you happier? Would you keep your business if you could restructure your schedule and spend 80% of your time on high-value activities you enjoy and less time on minor details? If so, restructure your business to focus on your strengths and on what you love to do. If you've lost passion and have a strong gut feeling you need to make a change, develop a definite plan to exit your business sooner rather than later.

- **External Factors:** Once you've thoroughly explored your emotional objectives, consider the external factors, such as the timing of selling your business and the state of competition in your industry. Be particularly aware of the timing. Avoid selling in a severe economic or industry recession if possible. Your revenue should be stable and preferably growing by the rate of inflation or more. Is competition becoming stronger in your industry? Are new venture-backed entrants threatening your market share? Do you have enough capital to fight a competitive industry war? Are indirect competitors threatening to permanently change the structure of your industry, such as what happened in the taxi business thanks to Uber, the hotel industry thanks to Airbnb, or the newspaper industry thanks to the prevalence of online news? All these factors can affect timing, which is a critical factor when planning your exit.

- **Value and Exit Options:** Only after considering your goals, and both the internal and external factors, can you commit to the process. It's smart to have an idea of how much your business is worth and the steps you can take to increase its value. It's best if you and your business are prepared at all times for the unexpected buyer, and that you regularly take steps to increase the value. The buyers most likely to pay the highest price are those who approach you directly out of the blue, so be ready for them. Most entrepreneurs lack the experience to determine the exit options most suitable for their business and industry, so consider having a third party perform an unbiased assessment of your business to help you determine the exit options that will unlock the most value. Only then should you explore the additional facts related to the decision, such as timing, value, exit options, and salability.

Deciding To Sell or Double Down

If you're in a highly competitive industry, you typically need to invest cash back into your business to stay in the game. Instead of taking money out of your business, you must put money back into your business – perhaps the exact opposite of what you want to do at this stage in your life. As a result, you face a critical decision. Do you sell now and get out while you can, or double down? The answer depends on you and the state of your industry. You must look both inward – to yourself – and outward – to your industry – for the answer.

Look Outward: Start by gathering information on your industry, and withhold your judgment while doing so. Stick solely to the task at hand – data collection. Think objectively without the need to weigh the facts or assess their impact. Once you've gathered the necessary information, your M&A adviser can help you analyze and synthesize it. Be honest with yourself in assessing the state of your industry – don't let your heart fool your intellect.

Look Inward: Once you've examined your business and industry, it's time to look inward – to yourself. While analyzing your business and industry involves your mind, looking to yourself involves your heart. Assess your skills, motivation level, and dreams.

Exploring Your Exit Options

Once you've decided to sell, the next step is to explore your potential exit options. Your decision will determine what you should do to prepare your business for sale. The value of your business will vary widely depending on who the buyer is and their reason for acquiring you. For example:

- Financial buyers are constrained to valuing a company based on its fair market value by paying a multiple of a company's earnings. Their objective is to buy your business for as little as possible, with the idea of selling it at a profit in three to seven years.

- Strategic buyers are companies looking to buy businesses in the same or similar industry to capture synergies. Because a strategic buyer is expecting to get more than intrinsic value out of your company – usually in the form of increased sales and enhanced productivity – they are more likely to pay a premium price.

But no two companies will view your business through the same lens – either on an individual or collective basis. Value is subjective and differs from buyer to buyer. Once you understand who is most likely to buy your company and their reasons for doing so, you can probe deeper into the other factors that can affect the value of your business.

Your business can have a wide range of possible values. Nonetheless, there are a common set of value drivers that most buyers within an industry find important. Identify the type of buyer most likely to buy your business, and then focus on the value drivers most important to that type. By educating yourself about the different kinds of buyers in the marketplace, you can identify which kind is most likely to pay the highest price for your business. This is essential to knowing what your business may be worth and maximizing its value.

Exit Options

All exit options can be broadly categorized into three groups:

- **Inside:** Inside exit options include selling to your children or other family members, your employees, or to a co-owner. Inside exits require a professional who has experience dealing with family businesses, as they often involve emotional elements that must be navigated and addressed discreetly, gracefully, and without bias. Inside exit options also greatly benefit from tax planning, because if the money used to buy the company is generated from the business, it may be taxed twice. Inside exits also tend to realize a much lower value than outside exits. Due to these complexities, most business owners avoid inside exits and choose outside options, which is what most M&A advisors specialize in.

- **Involuntary:** Involuntary exits can result from death, disability, or divorce. Your plan should anticipate such occurrences, however unlikely they may seem, and include steps to avoid or mitigate potential adverse effects.

- **Outside:** Outside exit options include buyers from outside your company or family. They can be categorized into the buyer types summarized next.

Buyer Types

There are four outside buyer types: Wealthy individuals, financial buyers, strategic buyers, and industry buyers.

- **Buyer Type 1 – Individual Buyers:** The primary pool of buyers for small businesses that sell for less than $5 million are wealthy individuals rather than companies. Individual buyers have two primary goals – income and freedom. Their primary concerns are how risky the opportunity is and whether financing can be obtained for the purchase. For these individuals, the process of buying a business can be emotional. For this reason, they often stick to less risky investments and prefer to buy companies with proven track records. When selling your business to an individual, minimize the perception of risk.

- **Buyer Type 2 – Financial Buyers:** Financial buyers consist primarily of private equity firms. They value a business based mainly on its numbers without taking into account the impact of any synergies. PE firms are the largest and most common buyers of mid-sized companies. Most require a minimum EBITDA of $1 million per year. Like other companies, they must hire a management team, which reduces the cash flow of your business. They then deduct the cost of hiring a manager when calculating EBITDA. Financial buyers have two primary goals – generating a high return and developing an exit plan while retaining your management team. When selling to a financial buyer, focus on building a strong management team and increasing EBITDA.

- **Buyer Type 3 – Strategic Buyers:** Strategic, or synergistic, buyers also acquire small and medium-sized businesses. Strategic acquisitions frequently occur in developing industries, especially those dominated by venture-capital-backed companies or "winner take all" industries, such as technology platforms. There are a variety of reasons a company may seek to acquire you. Understanding these motivations will help you maximize the energy you spend improving the value of your business. Strategic buyers are often considered the holy grail of buyers and may pay a higher multiple than others if they can't easily replicate what your company has to offer. Strategic buyers have longer holding periods and have no defined exit plan. They usually intend to fully integrate your company with theirs and focus on long-term fit. When selling to a strategic buyer, focus on building value that's difficult to replicate and hire an M&A intermediary to conduct a private auction.

- **Buyer Type 4 – Industry Buyers:** Industry buyers tend to acquire direct competitors. If your business is asset-intensive with less than favorable margins, selling to an industry buyer may be your only suitable option. In some industries, selling to a financial or strategic buyer may not be a possibility. Or your business may be so specialized that only a competitor will be interested in purchasing it. Industry buyers are often seen as the buyer of last resort because they usually pay the lowest price. These buyers know the industry well and aren't normally willing to pay for goodwill if they can easily replicate what your business has to offer. Selling to industry buyers carries an additional risk – a potential leak in confidentiality. When selling to an industry buyer, hire a professional to negotiate on your behalf, build value that can't be replicated, carefully track the release of confidential information, and never act desperate.

The Planning Process

The key to planning is prioritizing the action steps you can implement. Take another sweep through this book and make a list of potential actions you can carry out to improve the value of your business. Once you've made this list, then prioritize those actions using the Morgan & Westfield Return on Value Drivers Model (RVD Model), which takes into account the following:

- **Risk:** What's the risk associated with implementing the potential value driver?

- **Return:** What's the potential impact, or return, of implementing the value driver on the value of your business?

- **Time:** How much time will the value driver take to implement?

- **Investment:** What financial investment is required to implement the value driver?

Improving the value of your business shouldn't be done in a haphazard fashion. Rather, you should prioritize the potential actions you can take, and then strategically execute a few value drivers at a time in a systematic way. Most business owners take a hodge-podge approach to value maximization as opposed to a more orderly process. The objective of the RVD Model is to provide you with a strategic, structured approach to increasing the value of your business. It helps prioritize the actions you can take based on potential returns, the risk involved in achieving those returns, and the associated cost in terms of time and money.

The purpose of applying ratings is to allow you to loosely prioritize the potential actions you can take. This helps you focus first on the highest-impact actions that are the lowest in risk and require the least amount of time and energy to implement.

Before you know it, your business will be in tip-top shape, and you'll be prepared to sell at any time, including dealing with any attractive unsolicited offers.

Valuation

Valuation is one of the most critical components of your exit strategy. The size and type of your business will determine both how your business is sold and how it's valued. When planning the sale of your company, you should consider not just how to value your business, but also the factors that will have the greatest impact on its worth.

How Size Impacts Value

The degree to which your business is considered a Main Street or middle-market operation will impact how your company is valued. The primary differences between smaller businesses and those in the middle market are who the ultimate buyer will be and their goals for purchasing a particular business. Each group of buyers has different value expectations, and the value of your business can vary tremendously depending on who is most likely to purchase it.

Small businesses are marketed on business-for-sale websites with a set price to a broad audience of buyers. Additionally, the business may require no specialized skills to operate, so a larger audience of buyers may be qualified to run the business. The value for a small business is easier to measure and predict than the value for a mid-market business.

Mid-market businesses are often sold using a targeted approach, which involves creating a list of potential acquirers and contacting them directly. If you own a mid-sized business, it's possible you may sell your business to a strategic buyer. If so, the value is more difficult to predict, and the best you can do is to establish a baseline price based on fair market value. The only way you can determine the actual value is to conduct a private auction and sell your company.

Regardless, understanding whether your business is likely to be classified as Main Street or middle market is the first step to knowing who is most likely to purchase your company and determining its value.

Normalizing Financial Statements

The process of normalizing or adjusting your financial statements involves making numerous adjustments so the true earning capacity of your business can be measured. Removing owner-specific perks, benefits, and expenses is necessary to determine your business's actual earning capacity.

Adjusting your financial statements is one of the most important steps in valuing your business. Buyers compare potential acquisitions using SDE or EBITDA. By comparing the SDE or EBITDA of one company with another, buyers can easily understand the value of your business based on your business's actual profit rather than its taxable income. This helps facilitate a more accurate comparison between companies when valuing a business.

Here are some tips for normalizing your financials:

- All adjustments should be concise and verifiable.

- The fewer the adjustments when selling your business, the cleaner your financials will look.

- The ideal scenario is to eliminate adjustments altogether at least two to three years prior to a sale.

Measuring Cash Flow

It's critical that you understand how SDE and EBITDA are calculated and which measure of cash flow is right for your business.

SDE is used to value small businesses in which the owner actively works. SDE makes sense when valuing a small owner-operated business because it's difficult to distinguish business profits from the owner's compensation in a small business. Calculating an appropriate manager's salary for a small business is also more subjective than doing so for a mid-sized company. SDE is normally utilized with businesses that have less than $1 million in SDE. The SDE calculation is mainly used by business brokers since most business brokers sell businesses that are run by an owner-operator.

EBITDA is used to value mid-sized businesses that can be run by an outside manager. In a small business, the buyer would keep the owner's salary, but in a mid-sized business, the new owner would need to pay a manager to run the business. It makes sense to use EBITDA when valuing mid-sized businesses because the majority of businesses in the middle market are purchased by other companies that must hire and pay a manager or CEO to run the business post-closing. EBITDA is used to value mid-sized businesses with an EBITDA of greater than $1 million per year and that can be run by an outside manager. If the owner currently runs the business, the owner's compensation is normalized to market levels.

Valuation Rules

Here is a recap of the eight critical valuation concepts you should understand before valuing your business:

Rule 1 – Standard of Value Determines Methods Used: A standard of value is the definition of value that's being measured and determines the best valuation method to use. Most business appraisals use fair market value (FMV) as the standard of value, but FMV has the potential to undervalue your company. The standard of value is a critical premise in any valuation and determines the specific methods used to appraise the business. Using the wrong standard of value may result in underestimating the value of your business.

Rule 2 – Size Affects Multiples: The methods used to value businesses with less than $5 million in revenue are different from those used to value middle-market businesses with more than $5 million in revenue. You must use the right methods for a business of your size.

Rule 3 – Valuations Aren't Exact: The range of possible values for a business is wider than for other investments such as real estate. When obtaining an appraisal, you're paying for a professional's opinion as to what a hypothetical buyer might pay for your business. An experienced appraiser should explain to you how wide the potential range of values is for your company and what factors will most affect that value.

Rule 4 – Comparable Data is Limited: The ideal way to value your business is to determine what similar businesses have sold for. Unfortunately, there may have been few, if any, recent sales of businesses similar to yours. Every business is unique and accurate information on comparable transactions is limited.

Rule 5 – Valuations Are Based on a Hypothetical Buyer: An appraiser is making an educated guess as to what a hypothetical buyer might pay for your business. It isn't easy to estimate the value of a business because you're guessing how a diverse group of buyers are likely to behave.

Rule 6 – You Won't Know What Your Business Is Worth Until You Sell It: No pricing formula, expert estimate, or clairvoyant can accurately provide a sales figure that's exactly "right." You won't know how much your business is really worth until the day a buyer writes you a check.

Rule 7 – Transaction Structure Impacts Price: In most transactions, some portion of the purchase price is contingent. The terms of your sale – such as the amount of the down payment, the repayment period, and the interest rate – can all affect how much a buyer may be willing to pay.

Rule 8 – Your Situation Affects Value: Not only can the transaction structure affect the value of your business, but your personal needs also have the potential to affect your business's worth. For example, if you aren't willing to stay for an extended transition period, this may close off several exit options and negatively impact the value of your company.

Valuation Methods

Pricing a business is based primarily on its profitability. Profit is the number one criteria buyers look for when buying a business, and the number one factor buyers use to value a business. There are other variables that buyers may consider, but the majority exclusively look for one thing: profit.

With that in mind, here are two primary ways to value a business:

- **Method 1 - Multiple of SDE or EBITDA:** Multiply the SDE or EBITDA of the business by a multiple. Common multiples for most small businesses are two to four times SDE. Common multiples for mid-sized businesses are three to eight times EBITDA.

- **Method 2 - Comparable Sales Approach:** Research prices of similar businesses that have sold and then adjust the value based on any differences between your company and the comparable company.

Know Your Buyer

What do buyers look for? The most important factor 99% of buyers look for is profitability. Beyond that, individual buyers and corporate buyers have different criteria. Following is a summary of what individual and corporate buyers seek when looking to acquire a business:

Individuals: If your company is valued at less than $5 million, chances are it will be sold to an individual buyer. Here is a description of their goals and criteria:

- Many individual buyers evaluate a business based on the income it can generate for them. Most individual buyers of small businesses will consider buying any business that they have the skills to operate and that provides them a level of income that meets their goals. This type of buyer is primarily looking for an income stream.

- These buyers are likely to consider businesses in a variety of industries. For example, they may be open to looking at a service business, an online business, a retail business, or a wholesale business. They often have general criteria regarding a business, such as proximity to their home, work hours required, or licensing requirements – but not specific criteria.

- Most individual buyers don't have skills that are limited to a specific industry or business. As a result, they don't usually confine themselves to particular industries.

- These buyers usually prefer non-specialized businesses. If your business is a highly specialized one that requires a rare set of skills, knowledge, or experience, the universe of potential buyers will be smaller than normal, and your company may be difficult to sell. The price of your business will often be lower as a result – especially if it's likely to be sold to an individual.

- Infrastructure isn't as important to individual buyers because most will be involved in the day-to-day operations. If your business is small enough to appeal to an individual, it may not be necessary to invest a significant amount of money in building infrastructure before selling.

- These buyers are highly numbers-driven. To build a business that's highly desired by individual buyers, you should prioritize profitability over building infrastructure until your EBITDA exceeds $1 million per year. If your business is valued at less than $5 million, it's usually more beneficial to invest in sales and marketing to increase the revenue or profitability of your business than to invest in building infrastructure. Adding infrastructure helps, but most individual buyers prefer more cash flow to more infrastructure.

- These types of buyers focus heavily on the numbers in the deal, as they're often looking for the highest return on their investment. They scour the business-for-sale portals looking for businesses selling at the lowest multiple, which is determined by dividing the asking price by your EBITDA. Your number one priority should be to maximize the SDE or EBITDA of your business.

Corporate Buyers: Corporate buyers primarily consist of direct and indirect competitors and financial buyers, or private equity firms. The following is a description of their goals and criteria:

- Direct and indirect competitors will examine the extent to which they can replicate your business. It may be possible to replicate your business by starting a similar business from scratch, acquiring another similar company, or launching a new product line comparable to what your company offers. The more difficult it is to replicate your business, the higher the multiple you'll receive. The degree to which a buyer can replicate your business depends on your industry and competitive advantage, and how difficult that advantage is to copy. While other factors may influence the price, the degree to which your business can be easily replicated is one of the most important factors buyers consider when evaluating your company.

- Corporate buyers also look for a business that's scalable or that has the potential to quickly grow. This usually involves an owner who's burned out or who hasn't built effective sales and marketing systems – but whose company has operational systems in place that allow the business to quickly scale once sales and marketing are ramped up. If you want to sell your business for the maximum amount possible, focus on building a business that's scalable from day one.

- Companies prefer businesses with strong infrastructure in place. The degree to which corporate buyers require infrastructure in your business depends on if they will be integrating your business with theirs, or if they will run your business as a stand-alone entity post-closing. Corporate buyers who will be integrating your company with theirs require less infrastructure in your company than if it will be run as a stand-alone business after the closing. Corporate buyers who will keep your business as a stand-alone entity will require significant infrastructure. Financial buyers or private equity firms expect to double or triple their investment in three to five years before selling the business again to another buyer. This is often possible only with systems and infrastructure in place, and installing these systems and infrastructure costs money. If your business lacks these systems, the buyer must invest money to build them. This capital will be deducted from the purchase price of your company when the buyer calculates potential returns and the price they can afford to pay.

- Most private equity firms require that management remain to run the business after the closing. Partners in private equity firms focus their time on purchasing companies and don't become actively involved in the management of their investments. So, either existing management must remain to operate the business, or the private equity firm must hire a management team to run the business after closing. The only exception to this rule is when the private equity firm owns a portfolio company that competes directly with yours and they plan to integrate your business with that company.

Regardless of who is most likely to buy your business, prepare a short plan that outlines the potential growth opportunities. Most buyers will ask why you're selling when you're at a supposed inflection point in your business. Your answer will either maximize or destroy your positioning. You should be in the process of executing your growth plan, and the assumptions in it should be based on current data. Prepare a short business or growth plan with simplified financial projections. Highlight the major ways you can grow your business, and include a short bulleted list for each growth opportunity. Doing this will help ensure you receive top dollar when you sell.

Start With an Assessment

If you feel overwhelmed and need help prioritizing the actions you can take, consider starting with an assessment of your business from an M&A advisor.

There's no substitute for experience. While there are hundreds of potential factors that can affect the value of your business, there are usually just a handful that can have a greater impact than all of the other factors.

For example, at Morgan & Westfield, we review all aspects of your business, including your financial data, key performance indicators (KPIs), your product or service, and competitive, unique selling point (USP). We also include detailed discussions about your personal goals, your expectations for your employees, your wishes for the future of your company, and more. We discuss your objectives, timing, and current market conditions, and assess your readiness for a sale.

An objective and thorough assessment of your business assists you in deciding if the time is right to sell, helps you maximize value, assists you in prioritizing your value drivers, and addresses any preparedness issues before going to market. Your assessment outlines important presale steps you can take to meet your goals and ensure a successful, profitable sale. It lays out your options and allows you to intelligently plan your next steps to maximize the value of your business. If a sale today won't support your personal goals, the assessment helps you decide how to close value and marketability gaps.

You can find additional information on our assessment as well as learn more about buying, selling, valuing a business, or dozens of other topics related to mergers and acquisitions, visit the Resources section of the Morgan & Westfield website at morganandwestfield.com/resources.

Strategies and Tactics

Once you've decided to sell, had your business valued, and determined the buyer most likely to buy your business, it's time to roll up your sleeves and start the planning process. Begin by reviewing the potential actions you can take. Once you've made a list of possible actions, prioritize the list using the RVD Model. Here's what those lists might look like:

Products and Services

- Reduce product concentration.

- Reduce distribution channel concentration.

Financial

- Increase revenue.

- Increase SDE or EBITDA.

- Normalize your financial statements.

- Minimize the number of adjustments you make to your financials three years prior to a sale.

- Prepare backup documentation for adjustments to financial statements.

- Increase gross margins.

- Reduce expenses.

- Increase recurring revenue.

- Reduce the cash flow cycle.

- Reduce working capital.

- Reduce capital expenditures.

- Organize your financial records.

- Hire a third party to conduct pre-sale financial due diligence.

Customers

- **Customer Base:** Establish relationships with large, established customers. Gain a mix of different types of customers. Build a diverse customer base consisting of a critical mass of customers at various adoption stages of your business. Build sales infrastructure and a team that gives you the capability to acquire larger customers.

- **Customer Contracts:** Ensure customer contracts are assignable in the event of a sale. Develop incentives to convert customers to long-term contracts, such as grandfathered pricing or free add-on modules.

- **Customer Acquisition:** Track your customer metrics in a dashboard, and work to improve them over time by building marketing strategies that can be automated and scaled.

- **Customer Sales Pipeline:** Track your sales pipeline in your CRM so buyers can project your revenue.

- **Customer Database:** Build a robust customer database that contains detailed information on your customers that allows a buyer to develop scalable, targeted campaigns.

- **Customer Metrics:** Build a centralized dashboard to track your key metrics. Prepare a backlog of projects designed to improve and track the improvement of your metrics over time to serve as the foundation for your financial projections.

- **Close Relationships:** Reduce any personal relationships you have with customers before the sale.

- **Customer Concentration:** Minimize customer concentration. Institutionalize customers that generate a significant percentage of your overall revenue and reduce your personal involvement in these relationships.

Operations

- Diversify your supplier base if you're dependent on any suppliers.

- Implement cosmetic improvements to your premises.

- Improve your online presence and online reviews. Push any bad reviews down in search results.

- Gather customer testimonials and other awards or recognitions.

- If you own the real estate, move it to a separate entity and pay your business the going market rate.

- Negotiate options to renew your lease and make sure the lease can be transferred on the current terms.

- Prepare an inventory and equipment list.

- Purge your inventory and equipment, if necessary.

- Perform an equipment inspection and repair any broken equipment.

- Consider paying off your equipment leases. Perform a calculation to determine the return on doing so.

- Perform a lien search and clear up any liens on your business.

- Check to make sure your entity is up to date.

- Document your intellectual property. Consider consulting with an attorney specializing in intellectual property law if your business has valuable IP.

- Create a written training plan for the buyer.

- Resolve any pending litigation.

Staff

- Reduce your business's dependency on you.

- Replace any co-owners or family members that won't stay after the sale.

- Pay all owners and family members a salary based on market rates.

- Seek the approval of all partners and your spouse to sell the business.

- Build out your management team.

- Ensure all employee compensation is at current market levels.

- Reduce key employee concentration or dependency on any key employees.

- Prepare an employee manual or handbook.

- Consider whether – and when – to inform your employees about the sale.

- Create a retention plan and bonus for key staff.

- Ask key employees to sign a confidentiality and non-solicitation or non-compete agreement.

Team

- Hire an M&A advisor to help identify the factors that will have the greatest impact on the value of your business.

- Retain an M&A attorney in advance to help you conduct pre-sale legal due diligence.

- Ask your accountant to conduct pre-sale financial due diligence on your business.

- Check with your insurance advisor to ensure you're carrying adequate coverage.

- Hire a commercial real estate agent to determine an appropriate market rent if you own the property.

- If your business is a franchise, check with your franchisor in advance to ensure their cooperation.

- Make sure your franchise is listed on the SBA Franchise Directory, if applicable.

- Assemble your professional advisors to perform an annual audit on your business.

Finding Buyers

- Prepare a list of potential buyers with complete contact information.

- Prepare a list of sources of potential buyers, such as industry catalogs or other publications.

- Compile a list of potential publications to market your business sale in.

Financing

If your business is valued at more than $5 million, the buyer will often arrange their own financing. If your business is valued at less than $5 million, I recommend considering your financing options in the following order:

1. **SBA Financing:** First, consider Small Business Administration (SBA) financing. SBA financing offers the most lenient terms, including the lowest down payment and the longest amortization period. If you want to increase the chances that a buyer will be able to obtain an SBA loan to purchase your business, maximize your taxable income at least two years prior to the sale. I estimate that over 95% of the loans made to purchase a small business are 7(a) SBA loans. For this reason, I recommend first exploring if your business would qualify for an SBA loan.

2. **Other Options:** If your business can't get approved for SBA financing, you have two options:

   a. **Offer Seller Financing:** Consider seller financing if SBA financing is not available or if you prefer to offer seller financing due to other reasons such as tax benefits.

   b. **Sell for All Cash:** But be prepared to reduce the purchase price.

Due Diligence

- Compile all documents that buyers typically request during due diligence.

- Ask a third-party accountant to perform pre-sale due diligence on your company.

- Ask your attorney to make sure all your legal ducks are in a row before you begin the process.

Taxes

Tax implications can significantly impact the realized value of a business to both the buyer and the seller. Consult with your tax advisor well in advance to mitigate the tax impact of the sale. Consider how a sale is going to be structured from the outset, and keep in mind that advanced planning is essential to maximize the selling price of your business.

Confidentiality

Maintaining confidentiality is a critical component of selling your business. A confidentiality agreement is one of many strategies to preserve confidentiality. A well-drafted confidentiality agreement should be paired with the strategies recommended below to ensure confidentiality is maintained throughout the sales process.

- Prepare for the sale to ensure the sale unfolds as quickly as possible, which minimizes the possibility of a leak.

- Control the narrative by deciding in advance how to handle disclosing the sale to your key stakeholders.

- Consider informing your employees about the sale – couple this with an NDA and retention bonus plan.

- Control what and when information is released to potential buyers by redacting information, releasing information in stages, developing separate strategies for different categories of information, using a data room, and using email to create a paper trail.

- Control who information is released to by thoroughly screening buyers, releasing sensitive information to neutral third parties, and using the attorney-client privilege.

- Handle any breaches immediately.

- Consider informing others involved in your business about the sale, such as your landlord and franchisor.

Final Thoughts

Preparing to sell your business is not unlike getting ready to present yourself in the job market. The idea in both endeavors is to showcase past accomplishments and make a case for the future.

For those of you entrepreneurs who, in a past life, ever had to update a resume and sweet-talk a potential suitor, you've already got a taste of what to expect. But as you know by now, the process of selling a business is much more complex than writing a convincing cover letter.

And that's where this book comes into play. The clear, practical, and actionable advice provided here is the culmination of two decades in the proverbial trenches, from where I've successfully bought and sold hundreds of companies in the real world. I trust that the guidance offered in the preceding chapters will help make the sale of your company a little less stressful and a lot more profitable.

If you have any comments about how any of the suggestions and advice here worked for you (or didn't), I'd love to hear them. You can reach me at info@morganandwestfield.com. In the meantime, good luck with your sale and with the next stage of your life.

Sincerely,

Jacob Orosz

President of Morgan & Westfield

morganandwestfield.com

Host of *M&A Talk* – The #1 Podcast on Mergers & Acquisitions

Author of:
The Art of the Exit
A Beginner's Guide to Business Valuation
The Exit Strategy Handbook
Closing the Deal
Acquired

ADDITIONAL RESOURCES

Thanks again for turning to the *The Exit Strategy Handbook* and putting your trust in me. I have written this book to help you navigate the complex process of selling your business.

More information on every aspect of selling your business can be found in the Resources section of the Morgan & Westfield website at morganandwestfield.com/resources/. Here's what's included:

- **Ask the Expert:** Links to common M&A questions and answers. Ask any question related to buying, selling, or valuing a business. Receive expert advice from industry professionals with real-world experience.

- **Downloads:** Links to forms and other useful resources for selling your business.

- **Books:** A complete list of my books on selling, valuing, or buying a business, and all other topics related to M&A.

- **Glossary:** A glossary of terms used throughout the M&A world. Don't be confused or intimidated by any terms or abbreviations in the M&A world. You'll find answers here.

- **M&A Encyclopedia:** The most exhaustive collection of M&A articles in the industry with over 800 pages of insight on every step of the M&A process. This encyclopedia includes comprehensive articles on every topic having to do with buying or selling a business.

- *M&A Talk:* The #1 podcast on mergers and acquisitions, produced by Morgan & Westfield and hosted by me. At *M&A Talk*, we bring you exclusive interviews with a wide variety of experts in private equity, business valuations, law, finance, and all topics related to M&A.

- **M&A University:** Complete courses related to buying, selling, or valuing a business. Courses are led by industry experts with decades of industry experience and are designed to give you in-depth knowledge regarding every aspect of the process of preparing your business for sale, valuing it, and closing the deal.

Morgan & Westfield Website Articles

- *Earnouts When Selling or Buying a Business: Complete Guide:* A detailed 30-page article on earnouts at morganandwestfield.com/knowledge/earnouts/.

Highly Recommended Books

- *Scaling Up* by Verne Harnish (Gazelles, Inc., 2014)

- *The New One Minute Manager* by Ken Blanchard and Spencer Johnson (Harper Collins, 2016)

- *Ready, Fire, Aim: Zero to $100 Million in No Time Flat* by Michael Masterson (Michael Masterson, 2008)

- *The Founder's Dilemmas* by Noam Wasserman (Princeton University Press, 2021)

- *Work Rules!* by Laszlo Bock (Hachette Book Group, 2015)

- *Organizational Physics* by Lex Sisney (Lulu.com, 2013)

- *High Output Management* by Andrew S. Grove (Vintage, 1995)

- *Measure What Matters* by John Doerr (Portfolio, 2018)

Further Reading

- *Who: The A Method for Hiring* by Geoff Smart and Randy Street (Ballantine Books, 2008)

- *Ownership Thinking* by Brad Hams (McGraw Hill, 2011)

- *Scrum: The Art of Doing Twice the Work in Half the Time* by Jeffrey Victor Sutherland (Currency, 2014)

- *The Breakthrough Company* by Keith R. McFarland (Currency, 2009)

- *Business Model Generation* by Alexander Osterwalder and Yves Pigneur (John Wiley and Sons, 2010)

Thank you for turning to Morgan & Westfield for your M&A information needs. You made the right choice.

"One doesn't discover new lands without consenting to lose sight, for a very long time, of the shore."

– André Gide, French Author

APPENDICES

Appendix A: Glossary

Appendix B: Due Diligence Checklist

Appendix C: Recommended Reading

Glossary

Accrual Basis: One of two primary accounting methods which recognizes income and expenses based on when they are "accrued" or when they actually occur.

Add-Backs: An adjustment made to the income or expenses in a financial statement when calculating the cash flow of a business (i.e., SDE or EBITDA).

Add-On-Acquisition: The purchase or acquisition of a smaller company which is added on to a larger platform company by a corporate buyer to complement the acquirer's business model.

Allocation of Purchase Price: The allocation of the purchase price of a business, for tax purposes, among various classes of assets which are defined by the Internal Revenue Service, such as inventory, goodwill, land, or buildings.

Asset Deal: One of three ways to structure an acquisition for legal purposes in which the buyer purchases the individual assets of the seller, as opposed to purchasing the seller's stock or merging with the seller.

Basket: The minimum dollar threshold amount that must be met before a seller becomes liable for the buyer's losses caused by the seller's breach of representations and warranties. A basket functions similarly to an insurance deductible in which the seller is not liable for breaches until the threshold amount, or deductible, is exceeded.

Bill of Sale: The document with which ownership of the assets of a business are transferred from seller to buyer – if the sale is structured as an asset sale.

C Corporation: A corporation that has been elected to be taxed as an entity separate from its shareholders in accordance with Subchapter C of the Internal Revenue Code, and may therefore be subject to double taxation if the sale is structured as an asset sale.

Cash Basis: One of two primary accounting methods which reports income when received and expenses when paid out.

Cash Flow: The amount of cash generated in a business after all expenses, inflows, and outflows of cash. This term is also loosely used to refer to SDE, EBITDA, or other measures of cash flow. You should always ask for a definition if this term is used.

Confidential Information Memorandum (CIM): A document compiled by a business broker, M&A advisor, or investment banker that describes a company as a potential acquisition target and is used to generate interest in a company from prospective buyers. A typical CIM is 20 to 30 pages long and is only released to pre-screened buyers after they have signed a non-disclosure agreement.

Depreciation: An annual tax deduction that allows for the loss of value of a tangible capital asset, such as a business vehicle or real estate improvement, due to a decline in value over a period of years. Assets can either be expensed (written off in one year), depreciated (written off over a number of years), or amortized (for intangible assets).

Double Taxation: The taxation of income twice on the earnings of a C Corporation. Income is first taxed at the corporate (entity) level and then taxed again at the individual level when dividends are paid to shareholders. Double taxation is a concern when the owner of a C Corporation sells their business and structures the sale as an asset sale. The solution to avoid double taxation is to structure the sale as a stock sale or merger.

Due Diligence: The buyer's thorough verification and investigation of a business after the seller accepts a letter of intent to determine if both parties wish to proceed with the transaction. Most due diligence periods range from 30 to 90 days, and some may be indefinite as long as the parties continue to negotiate in good faith.

Earnings Before Interest, Taxes, Depreciation, and Amortization (EBITDA): The most popular measurement of the cash flow of a middle-market company which includes earnings before interest, taxes, depreciation, and amortization.

Earnout: An agreement whereby the buyer pays part of the purchase price to the seller based on the future performance of the company or the fulfillment of some other specified event.

Entity: A separate, legal entity authorized to act separately from its owners, such as a C Corporation, S Corporation, or LLC.

Exclusivity: A provision in a term sheet or letter of intent in which the seller agrees not to solicit offers or negotiate with other potential buyers for a specific period of time.

Fair Market Value (FMV): The most common standard of value used in business appraisals. FMV is the amount at which property would change hands between a willing seller and a willing buyer when neither is acting under compulsion and when both have reasonable knowledge of the relevant facts.

Generally Accepted Accounting Principles (GAAP): The common set of principles, standards, and procedures established by the Financial Accounting Standards Board (FASB) that companies use to compile their financial statements.

Goodwill: An intangible asset associated with the acquisition of a company normally carried on the acquiring company's balance sheet. It is the portion of the purchase price allocated to the value in excess of the tangible assets acquired.

Gross Profit: The total revenue minus the cost of goods sold, or the profit a company makes after deducting the direct costs related to manufacturing and selling products and services from the total revenue.

Holdback (a.k.a. Escrow): An amount of the purchase price that is withheld from the seller, usually by a neutral third party (i.e., escrow agent) in a separate account, for a period of time after the closing to satisfy any of the seller's indemnification obligations. The amount is paid to the seller after a specified amount of time following the closing, typically 6 to 18 months, if the buyer makes no indemnification claims.

Indemnification: A provision in the purchase agreement that allows a buyer to seek recourse against the seller for losses suffered due to breaches of representations and warranties.

Intellectual Property (IP): The legally protectable intangible assets of a business, which can include patents, copyrights, trade names, domain names, trade secrets, and trademarks or service marks. Intellectual property can be registered (e.g., trademarks, patents) or unregistered (e.g., trade secrets).

Internal Rate of Return (IRR): The annual rate of growth an investment produces. The most common measure of return used by private equity firms to measure the performance of their funds (i.e., acquisitions).

Letter of Intent (LOI): A preliminary agreement that outlines the essential terms of an acquisition and signifies the parties' commitment to start due diligence and begin working toward a purchase agreement. The letter of intent is replaced by a purchase agreement prior to or at the closing.

Main Street: The segment of the business landscape made up of small "mom-and-pop" businesses such as restaurants, coffee shops, landscaping companies, auto and truck service centers, convenience stores, most franchises, and small businesses that offer services. Main Street businesses are predominantly valued using a multiple of SDE and sold by business brokers.

Merger: One of the three primary methods of structuring a transaction for legal purposes. The combination of two or more companies into one with a single entity by filing a Certificate of Merger with the secretary of state. Transactions can be structured for legal purposes as an asset sale, stock sale, or merger.

Middle Market: The segment of the business landscape consisting of mid-sized businesses, such as manufacturing firms, distribution companies, wholesalers, and large service-based companies. The middle market is further divided into the lower, middle, and upper-middle markets and is primarily served by M&A advisors and investment bankers.

Non-Compete Agreement: A contract that limits the seller or key employees from competing with the business after the closing. Most non-competition agreements range from two to five years. A non-compete agreement is legal in all states in the sale of a business, whereas non-compete agreements in an employment context are illegal in some states.

Non-Disclosure Agreement (NDA): A legal contract between the buyer and seller that outlines confidential material, knowledge, or information that both parties want to share with each other for specific purposes, but with restricted access to or by third parties. The NDA is typically signed early in the transaction, after the teaser profile is provided, but before the buyer is given access to the confidential information memorandum (CIM) or financial statements.

Non-Solicitation Agreement: An agreement signed by employees and management whereby they agree not to solicit customers or other employees (e.g., regarding job opportunities) upon the termination of their employment agreement. Non-solicitation agreements are commonly used as an alternative to non-compete agreements because they are viewed as more enforceable.

Normalize (a.k.a. Adjust, Recast): The process of adjusting, normalizing, or recasting a business's financial statements to determine the true earnings (i.e., SDE or EBITDA) of a company.

Normalized (Adjusted, Recasted) Financial Statements: Financial statements that have been adjusted to calculate a company's SDE or EBITDA.

Net Income: The amount of money earned after deducting all expenses, including overhead, employee salaries and benefits, manufacturing costs, inventory costs, distribution costs, and marketing and advertising costs from a company's gross revenue.

Platform Company: A large company that is the foundation to acquire and add smaller companies to, such as through an add-on or bolt-on acquisition, or by a financial or strategic buyer to complement the acquirer's business model.

Private Equity Firm: A company that raises money from institutional investors (i.e., limited partners) and then invests these funds into private companies. A private equity firm normally has multiple funds that each have a lifespan of 10 to 12 years. Private equity funds are often structured as a general partnership, or other similar entity, in which the private equity firm is the general partner and the investors are limited partners.

Promissory Note: A document signed by a purchaser of a business that includes a written promise to pay the balance of the purchase price over an extended period of time.

Representations and Warranties: Statements and guarantees by a buyer or seller of a business relating to the assets, liabilities, and contacts of the business that are being acquired, or the business that is making the acquisition. Breaches of representations and warranties are addressed in the indemnification section of the purchase agreement. A percentage (usually 10%) of the purchase price is normally held back (known as a holdback) in an escrow account for 6 to 18 months following the closing to fund any indemnification claims. This amount is later released to the seller if no claims are made during this time period.

Return on Value Drivers: A proprietary model developed by Morgan & Westfield in which implementable strategic actions are prioritized based on which drivers will have the biggest impact on the value of a business in the shortest period of time and which also pose the lowest risks to implement.

Roll-Up: The purchase or consolidation of smaller companies in an industry by a larger company in the same industry. The strategy is to create economies of scale and "roll-up" all the small companies into one big company to sell in the future with the hope of expanding the multiple (i.e., multiple expansion).

S Corporation: Short for "Subchapter S Corporation," a state-incorporated business that elects to receive special tax treatment. An S Corporation is restricted to 100 shareholders, shareholders must be U.S. citizens/residents, and only one class of stock is permitted to be issued, although it can have both voting and non-voting shares. Most small and mid-sized companies are structured as an LLC or S Corporation, whereas most larger companies are structured as a C Corporation.

Seller's Discretionary Earnings (SDE): The most common measure of cash flow used to value a small business; uses pre-tax net income plus the owner's compensation, interest, depreciation, amortization, and discretionary expenses, as well as adjustments for extraordinary, non-operating revenue or expenses, and non-recurring expenses or revenue.

Seller Financing: A loan which is payable (i.e., promissory note) from the buyer of a business to the seller or owner of a business, and is commonly used to acquire businesses as an alternative to third-party (i.e., bank) financing.

Stay (Retention) Bonus: A bonus given to employees, usually by the seller, to ensure they stay on board after the business is sold. A typical bonus ranges from 5% to 20% of annual base salary and is released in multiple stages (i.e., ⅓ at closing, ⅓ at 6 months, ⅓ at 12 months after the closing).

Stock Sale: One of the three primary methods of structuring a transaction for legal purposes whereby the buyer purchases the stock, or entity (a stock sale), of the seller, as opposed to purchasing the assets of the seller (an asset sale). Transactions can legally be structured as an asset sale, stock sale, or merger.

Strategic Buyer: A buyer or company that may provide similar or complementary products or services to the target and is often a competitor, supplier, or customer of the target, or one that brings other synergies to a potential acquisition.

Successor's Liability: Liability that passes from the seller of a business to the buyer of a business by operation of law without an express contractual agreement for the buyer to assume the liabilities of the seller. Successor's liability is most common in the areas of tax and environmental liabilities, and can be imposed by governmental institutions. Successor's liability is mitigated through extensive due diligence, representations and warranties, and escrowing a portion of the purchase price to fund indemnification claims.

Teaser Profile: A short summary of a business that doesn't normally reveal the company's identity. This is provided to prospective buyers before the buyer signs a non-disclosure agreement.

Term Sheet: A document that outlines the key terms of the purchase or sale of a business.

Uniform Commercial Code (UCC): A standardized set of laws and regulations for transacting business with the aim to make business activities consistent across all states, and that has been adopted to some extent in all 50 states.

Working Capital: The amount by which current assets exceed current liabilities in a business. Working capital is calculated as the value of accounts receivable, inventory, and prepaid expenses, less the value of accounts payable, short-term debt, and accrued expenses. Working capital is normally included in the purchase price of mid-sized businesses.

Due Diligence Checklist

This is a sample due diligence checklist:

Assets

- Description of any real estate owned

- Recent equipment inspections

- Equipment leases

- Equipment list

- List of all assets included in price

- List of all titled assets

- Inventory list

Financial/Tax

- Accounts payable schedule

- Accounts receivable aging schedule

- Annual personal property tax certificate

- Backup data of adjustments to financials

- Bank statements

- Breakdown of sales by customer

- Breakdown of sales by product type

- Copies of existing loan or financing agreements

- Customer or client agreements

- Documentation for add-backs to financial statements

- Federal income tax returns

- Financial budgets and projections

- Full accounting software file

- General ledger or detailed list of all transactions and expenses

- List of monthly sales since inception

- Merchant account statements

- Payroll tax reports

- Profit and loss statements

- Sales and use tax reports

- Utility bills

Insurance

- Health insurance policies

- Liability insurance policies

- Workers' compensation policies and history

Legal

- Articles of incorporation/organization

- Business license

- Certificate of Status/Good Standing from the Secretary of State

- Copies of all licenses, permits, certificates, and registrations

- Copies of all key contracts

- Corporate/LLC by-laws or operating agreements

- Corporate/LLC minutes

- Description of environmental liabilities

- Fictitious business name statement (FBNS/DBA)

- Financing agreements

- Information for copyrights

- Information for patents

- Information for trademarks and service marks

- List of liens against the business

- Other third-party agreements or contracts

- Pending lawsuits

- Phase 1 and 2 environmental studies

- Preliminary UCC search results

- Previous purchase agreement and related business documents

- Resale permit

- Seller's disclosure statement

Operations

- Advertising contracts

- Customer list

- Inventory count

- List of key competitors

- Marketing material

- Operations manual

- Preliminary equipment inspection

- Premises lease

- Summary of key lease terms

- Supplier and vendor list

- Supplier and vendor contracts

Staff

- Benefit plans

- Compensation arrangements

- Detailed schedule of payroll expenses

- Employment, agency, and independent contractor agreements

- Job descriptions

- List of outside contractors

- Other employment-related agreements

- Overview of personnel turnover

- Schedule of owners, officers, employees, independent contractors, consultants and their titles, length of service, and compensation benefits

- Summary biographies of key management

To download an editable version of this checklist or learn more about buying, selling, valuing a business, or dozens of other topics related to mergers and acquisitions, visit the Resources section of the Morgan & Westfield website at morganandwestfield.com/resources.

Recommended Reading

The Lean Startup by Eric Ries (Crown Business, 2011) and ***Running Lean*** by Ash Maurya (O'Reilly Media, 2012) These books teach you the "lean" system in business strategy as opposed to the outdated waterfall method of business planning in which each stage of the process has to be completed before moving on to the next stage. Being lean and agile in business can help you quickly accomplish many goals and speed up the process of the steps involved.

Work the System by Sam Carpenter (Greenleaf Book Group Press, Revised 3rd edition, 2019) This is a book that walks you through, step-by-step, how to document your business and prepare an operations manual for your company. This is a great resource if you have never automated, documented, and delegated processes in your business.

The E-Myth by Michael E. Gerber (Ballinger Publishing, 1988) This is a classic book that all entrepreneurs should read and many franchisors recommend. The essence of the book is that entrepreneurs spend too much time working *in* their business and too little time working *on* their business.

Scaling Up by Verne Harnish (Gazelles, Inc., 2014) This popular book, a sequel to ***Mastering the Rockefeller Habits***, teaches you the four essential processes any small business needs to install before they begin scaling their business. This book is a collection of skills, tools, and processes but installing these tools is easiest if you have a management team to help you. Implementing all the suggestions contained in this book may take you from 6 to 12 months.

Duct Tape Marketing by John Jantsch (Nelson Business, 2007) This book will help most small business owners create scalable marketing processes. Yes, you need scalable, repeatable marketing processes in your business. These are practical, easy-to-implement suggestions. Like all the suggestions contained here, though, implementing these processes entails a lot of time and help from your core management team.

Focal Point by Brian Tracy (Amazon, 2001) This book assists you in establishing a laser-like focus on critical goals in your life. Focus is paramount to entrepreneurs. Most entrepreneurs suffer from an overabundance of ideas rather than a dearth of ideas. In other words, they have a "lack of focus."

Getting Things Done by David Allen (Penguin Books, 2015) The GTD system is widely known as the most effective time management system in business. David Allen's book, in my opinion, is the best book available on time management. David teaches specific techniques you can implement in your life to improve your time management.

Your Brain at Work by David Rock (Harper Collins, 2020) I always say that energy management is more important than time management. This is the case once you possess rudimentary time management skills, such as daily planning, prioritizing, and delegating. I always run out of energy before I run out of time – you're likely the same. ***Your Brain at Work*** recognizes that energy is a limited resource, and it teaches you how to strategically use this scarce resource. You should treat energy like any other limited resource, such as time or money. Did you know that multitasking can turn a Harvard MBA into the mental equivalent of an eight-year-old? Yet, we all do this all the time. This book offers practical insights on how to earn the highest ROI on your energy investment.

How to Hire A-Players by Eric Herrenkohl (Wiley, 2010) Management starts with hiring the right people. Sourcing and interviewing are skills that can be learned. This book teaches you a step-by-step process for hiring superstars. It takes a lot of practice, and hiring is simpler if you have a management team to assist you in establishing the right systems for attracting the talent you need.

Carrots and Sticks Don't Work by Paul L. Marciano (McGraw Hill, 2010) Most small-business owners with fewer than 50 to 100 employees manage their employees using the carrot-and-stick method, which uses rewards and punishment as tools to motivate. Unfortunately, this method produces poor results in any industry in which engagement is important. This book teaches you 5 to 10 management techniques you can use to develop an engaged long-term workforce.

Made in the USA
Monee, IL
15 November 2024

70205086R00181